"In taking us straight to the heart of the text, Phil Moore has served us magnificently. We so need to get into the Scriptures and let the Scriptures get into us. These notes, coming from a preacher and a teacher, and with such submission to the Bible as the Word of God, will surely help us to do this, and I commend them warmly."

"Fresh. Solid.

– R. T. Kendall

"Phil makes the deep truths of Scripture alive and accessible. If you want to grow in your understanding of each book of the Bible, then buy these books and let them change your life!"

– PJ Smyth – GodFirst Church, Johannesburg, South Africa

"Most commentaries are dull. These are alive.
Most commentaries are for scholars. These are for **you**!"

– Canon Michael Green

"These notes are amazingly good. Lots of content and depth of research, yet packed in a **Big Breakfast** that leaves the reader well fed and full. Bible notes often say too little, yet larger commentaries can be dull – missing the wood for the trees. Phil's insights are striking, original, and fresh, going straight to the heart of the text and the reader! Substantial yet succinct, they bristle with amazing insights and life applications, compelling us to read more. Bible reading will become enriched and informed with such a scintillating guide. Teachers and preachers will find nuggets of pure gold here!"

– Greg Haslam – Westminster Chapel, London, UK

"The Bible is living and dangerous. The ones who teach it best are those who bear that in mind – and let the author do the talking. Phil has written these studies with a sharp mind and a combination of creative application and reverence."

– Joel Virgo – Leader of Newday Youth Festival

For more information about the Straight to the Heart series, please go to **www.philmoorebooks.com**.
You can also receive daily messages from Phil Moore on Twitter by following **@PhilMooreLondon**.

Psalms

60 BITE-SIZED INSIGHTS

Phil Moore

MONARCH
BOOKS

Oxford, UK & Grand Rapids, Michigan, USA

Published by Monarch Books
an imprint of
Lion Hudson plc
Wilkinson House, Jordan Hill Road,
Oxford OX2 8DR, England
Email: monarch@lionhudson.com
www.lionhudson.com/monarch

ISBN 978 0 85721 428 7
e-ISBN 978 0 85721 429 4

First edition 2013

This book is for the people of
Everyday Church, London.
Let's be the kind of church together
which is music to God's ears.

CONTENTS

BOOK III – PSALMS 73–89: SING OUT HOW YOU REALLY FEEL

BOOK IV – PSALMS 90–106: SING ABOUT GOD'S PLAN

BOOK V – PSALMS 107–150: SING YOUR RESPONSE TO GOD

About the *Straight to the Heart* Series

On his eightieth birthday, Sir Winston Churchill dismissed the compliment that he was the "lion" who had defeated Nazi Germany in World War Two. He told the Houses of Parliament that *"It was a nation and race dwelling all around the globe that had the lion's heart. I had the luck to be called upon to give the roar."*

I hope that God speaks to you very powerfully through the "roar" of the books in the *Straight to the Heart* series. I hope they help you to understand the books of the Bible and the message which the Holy Spirit inspired their authors to write. I hope that they help you to hear God's voice challenging you, and that they provide you with a springboard for further journeys into each book of Scripture for yourself.

But when you hear my "roar", I want you to know that it comes from the heart of a much bigger "lion" than me. I have been shaped by a whole host of great Christian thinkers and preachers from around the world, and I want to give due credit to at least some of them here:

Terry Virgo, David Stroud, Dave Holden, John Hosier, Adrian Holloway, Greg Haslam, Lex Loizides and all those who lead the Newfrontiers family of churches. Friends and encouragers, such as Stef Liston, Joel Virgo, Stuart Gibbs, Scott Taylor, Nick Sharp, Nick Derbridge, Phil Whittall, and Kevin and Sarah Aires. Tony Collins, Jenny Ward and Simon Cox at Monarch Books. Malcolm Kayes and all the elders of The Coign Church, Woking.

My fellow elders and church members here at Everyday Church in Southwest London. My great friend Andrew Wilson – without your friendship, encouragement and example, this series would never have happened.

I would like to thank my parents, my brother Jonathan, and my in-laws, Clive and Sue Jackson. Dad – your example birthed in my heart the passion which brought this series into being. I didn't listen to all you said when I was a child, but I couldn't ignore the way you got up at five o' clock every morning to pray, read the Bible and worship, because of your radical love for God and for his Word. I'd like to thank my children – Isaac, Noah, Esther and Ethan – for keeping me sane when publishing deadlines were looming. But most of all, I'm grateful to my incredible wife, Ruth – my friend, encourager, corrector and helper.

You all have the lion's heart, and you have all developed the lion's heart in me. I count it an enormous privilege to be the one who was chosen to sound the lion's roar.

So welcome to the *Straight to the Heart* series. My prayer is that you will let this roar grip your own heart too – for the glory of the great Lion of the Tribe of Judah, the Lord Jesus Christ!

Introduction: Music to God's Ears

Sing joyfully to the Lord, you righteous; it is fitting for the upright to praise him.

(Psalm 33:1)

God wants to grab your attention. He could hardly have made it any clearer. He made Psalms the central book of the Bible. He made it contain the Bible's middle chapter and middle verse.[1] He made it by far the longest book of the Bible, with more than twice as many chapters as the next longest book. He made it contain the longest chapter in the Bible and then, for effect, he made it home to the shortest chapter too.[2] He inspired the writers of the New Testament to quote more from Psalms than from any other book in the Old Testament – at least seventy-five times directly and many more times indirectly. So don't miss the many ways that God is shouting for your attention. He has something vitally important to teach you through the book of Psalms.

Psalms is a book which shows us how to relate to God. The fourth-century writer Athanasius observed that this book is unique because, while the rest of the Bible speaks *to* us, Psalms speaks *for* us.[3] It teaches us how to relate to God as friends, which is why no other book in human history has been as loved, valued and memorized by so many people from so many different

---

[1] The middle chapter of the Bible is Psalm 117. The middle verse is Psalm 103:1.

[2] The longest chapter of the Bible is Psalm 119. The shortest is Psalm 117.

[3] He wrote this in his *Letter to Marcellinus on the Meaning of the Psalms* in about 370 AD.

nations. The American president John Adams spoke for millions when he told Thomas Jefferson that *"The Psalms of David, in sublimity, beauty, pathos, and originality, or in one word poetry, are superior to all the odes, hymns, and songs in any language."*[4] God gave us these 150 worship songs because he wants to teach us how to pray the kind of prayers which are music to his ears.

Psalms makes it clear that God wants us to sing to him. Spiritual discussions and resolutions have their value, but they can never substitute for building a relationship with God through singing simple love songs. One of my friends discovered this when he started coming to some of the meetings at the church I lead. As a typically reserved Englishman, he was so appalled by our worship that he went home and googled *"churches without singing"*. Thankfully, he couldn't find any, because he later shared at his baptism that it was the sight of hundreds of people singing out their love for God which melted his heart and turned him into a passionate worshipper too.

The Hebrews called Psalms *tehillīm*, which means *songs of praise*. The Greeks called it *psalmoi*, which means *songs*, and it is from this that we get our own name for this collection. In case we forget that a relationship with God always involves singing, Psalms tells us that God wants us to worship him *"with stringed instruments"* and on the *"trumpet... harp and lyre... strings and pipe... with resounding cymbals"*.[5] Shortly after he triggered the greatest Christian revival Europe has ever seen, Martin Luther told his converts that *"Music is a gift and grace of God, not an invention of men. Thus it drives out the devil... I would allow no man to preach or teach God's people without a proper knowledge of the use and power of sacred song."*[6] We discover this as we read the book of Psalms.

---

[4] This quote comes from David McCullough's biography, simply entitled *John Adams* (2001).

[5] See the titles of Psalms 4, 6, 54, 55, 61, 67 and 76. See also Psalms 33:1–3, 92:1–3, 144:9 and 150:3–5.

[6] Quoted by Kenneth W. Osbeck in *"101 Hymn Stories"* (1982).

But don't imagine that Psalms is like Julie Andrews in *The Sound of Music*, shutting her eyes to reality by singing about a few of her favourite things. The psalms teach us how to relate to God in the bad times, in the dark times and in times so confusing that we want to throw in the towel on our faith altogether. The psalmists are shockingly honest with God about how they feel, because life isn't always easy. They teach us to sing the blues as well as happy songs because how we worship in the difficult times is just as much music to God's ears. The Christian writer Eugene Peterson confesses that without Psalms he would not know how to keep on worshipping at all:

> *I need a language that is large enough to maintain continuities, supple enough to express nuances across a lifetime that brackets child and adult experiences, and courageous enough to explore all the countries of sin and salvation, mercy and grace, creation and covenant, anxiety and trust, unbelief and faith that comprise the continental human condition... Where will we acquire a language that is adequate for these intensities? Where else but in the Psalms? For men and women who are called to leadership in the community of faith, apprenticeship in the Psalms is not an option; it is a mandate.*[7]

13

Psalms took almost 1,000 years to write – far longer than any other book in the Bible. Moses wrote Psalm 90 in about 1410 BC and Psalm 137 appears to have been written in about 530 BC. Some time after that, God inspired some of the worship leaders at the Temple in Jerusalem[8] to compile a collection of 150 of the best psalms from the several thousand which were then in

---

[7] Eugene Peterson in *Working the Angles: The Shape of Pastoral Integrity* (1987).

[8] 1 Chronicles 25:1–6 indicates that some these temple worship leaders were *prophets* and *seers*. They probably divided Psalms into five books in order to mirror the five books of the Jewish Torah.

circulation.[9] Some of the psalms they collated were already part of mini-collections,[10] but God inspired them to gather them into the five books which make up Psalms in order to teach us how to pray and worship.

Book I comprises **Psalms 1–41** and it focuses on the character of God in order to teach us how to **sing about who God is**. Book II comprises **Psalms 42–72** and it teaches us how to **sing when times are hard**. Book III comprises **Psalms 73–89** and it models how God wants you to **sing out how you really feel**. Book IV comprises **Psalms 90–106** and it charts the history of God's dealings with the human race so that we can learn to **sing about God's plan**. Book V comprises **Psalms 107–150** and it ends the book of Psalms with a call for you to **sing your response to God**.

It's very tempting to ignore the way that the Temple worship leaders structured Psalms and to study its contents by theme, but I am convinced that this structure is our God-given commentary on the meaning of these worship songs. Throughout this book we will therefore resist the urge to pluck a few favourite verses out of context, looking instead at each psalm or cluster of psalms as a unit which teaches us a particular lesson about how we are to worship God. As we do so, we will learn how we can get to know God deeply as our friend, as did the writers of the psalms.

Make no mistake about it: God wants to grab your attention. He wants to teach you how to grow in a relationship with him. He wants to teach you how to sing the kind of worship songs which have always been, in every generation, sweet music to God's ears.

[9] There are many psalms in Scripture which were not included in the book of Psalms: see Exodus 15:1–21, Deuteronomy 31:30–32:47, Judges 5:1–31, 1 Samuel 2:1–10 and Isaiah 38:9–20. Similarly, 1 Kings 4:32 tells us that Solomon wrote 1,005 songs, but only two of them were included as Psalms 72 and 127.

[10] We can still see the names of these mini-collections in the titles of some psalms, for example, the "songs of ascents". Psalm 72:20 must have been the end of a mini-collection, since many more psalms of David follow.

Book I – Psalms 1–41:

Sing About Who God Is

The King of Kings
(1:1–2:12)

I have installed my king on Zion, my holy mountain.

(Psalm 2:6)

If you want to understand Psalms 1 and 2, you only need four words: *anyone, Solomon, Jesus, us.* There you have it. That's the meaning of the first two psalms in just four words.

Psalm 1:1–6 is about *anyone.* It acts as a preface to the entire book of Psalms by calling each of us to make an up-front choice between righteousness and wickedness, between listening to God's Word or to the world, between living for ourselves or pursuing friendship with God. It begins by promising that *blessed* or *happy* is anyone who delights in God's Word and who studies it day and night.[1] It promises that if we plant ourselves in a place where we can deepen our relationship with God, we will drink from the non-stop stream of blessings which flows from his throne. It's significant that the first word of Psalms is *"happy"*. This book holds the key to our enjoying the deeply fulfilling friendship with God for which we were created.[2]

But this first psalm also warns us that anyone can be deceived into missing God's purpose for their life. The drift is often gradual, since 1:1 reminds us that *walking* with sinners easily becomes *standing* with sinners and eventually *sitting*

16

---

[1] The word used for *law* twice in 1:2 is *tōrāh*, which means literally *instruction* and was used to refer to the five books of Moses' *Law*. It later came to refer to the Old Testament as a whole.

[2] Note the deliberate similarity between 1:3 and Genesis 2:10–14 and Revelation 22:1–2. See also Jeremiah 17:7–8.

with sinners. It is often unnoticed, since those who turn away from God often think that they are still part of *"the assembly of the righteous"*.[3] Psalms isn't just a collection of pretty choruses; it demands that we make an active decision from the outset. It warns us that, unless we meditate on the words of this book and apply them, God will sweep us away like dust before the scorching wind. Psalm 2 was deliberately placed after Psalm 1 because the same Hebrew word *hāgāh* is used for the nations *plotting* to cast off God's rule in 2:1 as is used for the righteous *meditating* on his Word in 1:2.[4] Psalm 2:1–3 therefore tells us that many people will despise the happiness described in Psalm 1 and will choose to view God's commands as *chains* and *shackles* which restrict them from having a good time. Ancient kings and rulers or modern media and social networking unite the human race in trying to throw off the rule of God and of his Messiah.[5]

Psalm 2:4–9 is therefore about *Solomon*. Even though these two psalms are untitled, we can tell from Acts 4:25 that David wrote them after God promised him in 2 Samuel 7 that *"I will raise up your offspring to succeed you, your own flesh and blood... I will be his father, and he will be my son... Your house and your kingdom will endure forever before me; your throne will be established forever."* David wrote this psalm for Solomon's coronation to rejoice that his wise son had chosen the righteous life described in Psalm 1 and that no foreign ruler would be able

---

[3] The Hebrew words *ēdāh* and *qāhāl* are used repeatedly in Psalms to describe the *congregation* or *assembly* of Israel. The normal Greek word used to translate them is *ekklēsia*, the word which Jesus chose for the *Church*. *"The wicked"* and *"the righteous"* are referred to in the plural because true believers always gather together.

[4] Another big clue that these two psalms belong together can be found in the way that the phrase *"Blessed is anyone"* acts as bookends in 1:1 and 2:12.

[5] The word for *anointed one* in Hebrew is *messiah*. The Old Testament uses this word to describe Saul, David and Solomon as the anointed kings of Israel. See for example 1 Samuel 16:6 and 24:6.

to his resist his righteous reign.[6] *"I have installed my king on Zion, my holy mountain,"* he hears God saying. *"You are my son; today I have become your father."*[7]

If you know anything about Solomon's reign, you will grasp why Psalm 2:4–9 is also about *Jesus*. Solomon proved to be one of Israel's greatest failures, because even the best of men are only men at best. He was enticed by his pagan wives into walking, standing and sitting in their pagan temples. Within five years of his death, Israel was torn apart and an invading Egyptian army succeeded in plundering Jerusalem.[8] Solomon was not the true Messiah that God's People needed. He was simply a picture of a greater descendant of David who was yet to come.

The early Christians understood this. They prayed this psalm back to God in Acts 4:23–31 and asked him to give the nations of the earth to *"your holy servant Jesus, whom you anointed"*. John quotes from this psalm in Revelation 19:11–16 in order to tell us that Jesus rules with an iron sceptre and that he laughs at human rebellion because he is *"King of kings and Lord of lords"*. Paul quotes from this psalm in Acts 13:33 to tell us that God the Father declared to the world that Jesus is his Son by raising him from the dead.[9] We have failed to live the righteous life which is described in Psalm 1, so God sent Jesus to live it for us and to establish a Kingdom of those who want to choose afresh to pursue relationship with God.

That's why Psalm 2:10–12 is about *us*. Note the way in which the final sentence of Psalm 2 follows the same

---

[6] David made Solomon king in a hurry due to a conspiracy in 1 Kings 1, but his use of the word *gōyīm* indicates that his primary concern was the resurgence of the hostile *pagan nations* which he had conquered.

[7] David normally refers to Jerusalem as *Zion* because this was the hill in the city where he had constructed God's Tabernacle and his own royal palace. This is what made Zion God's *"holy mountain"*.

[8] 1 Kings 12:16–19; 14:25–26.

[9] Psalm 2 is quoted a massive seven times in the New Testament (Acts 4:25–26; 13:33; Hebrews 1:5; 5:5; Revelation 2:27; 12:5; 19:15). Jesus did not so much *become* God's Son as *become revealed* as God's Son.

construction as the first sentence of Psalm 1. David repeats that *blessed* or *happy* is anyone who takes refuge in God's Messiah as their Saviour because only he can equip them to live the righteous life which God requires. Note that it is also the same construction which Jesus used in his Beatitudes in Matthew 5 to tell us that *"Blessed are the poor in spirit... Blessed are those who hunger and thirst for righteousness... Blessed are the pure in heart."* Jesus came to turn us from the path of destruction and to become our refuge from God's judgment. He calls us to find true happiness by discovering the deep friendship with God for which we were originally created.[10]

So can you see why God placed these two psalms together? Can you see what God is saying through these two chapters as a whole? Both psalms lay out a choice between happiness and destruction. Both psalms call us to live fruitful lives as friends of God. They tell us that Jesus is King of kings, that he laughs at human rebellion, and that he invites us to rule as *"kings and priests"* with him.[11] In case we miss this, he quotes from Psalm 2:9 in Revelation 2:27 and promises that we have authority to extend his rule over the nations. He makes us co-heirs with him to the Father's promise in 2:8: *"Ask me, and I will make the nations your inheritance, the ends of the earth your possession."*

Anyone, Solomon, Jesus, us. Psalms 1 and 2 belong together and can be summed up in four simple words, but their message is life-changingly profound. They call us to pour out the rest of our lives in submission to God's Word and to his Messiah. They call us to make an up-front choice to take the path to true happiness. They call us to surrender our lives to Jesus, the glorious King of kings.

---

[10] The NIV translation of 2:12 can be unhelpful since Exodus 34:6 makes it clear that David is not saying God is easily angered. He is telling us that Jesus is our only refuge *when God's anger flares up even a little*.

[11] This is the way that the simplest Greek manuscripts express Revelation 5:10.

The Rejected One
(3:1–5:12)

Many are saying of me, "God will not deliver him."

(Psalm 3:2)

God likes contrasts. He made the elephant and the ant. He made the sunshine and the rain. He made the forest and the desert. And he made Psalms 3–5 come straight after Psalms 1–2.

The forty-one psalms which make up Book I are all psalms of David. In theory, this could mean that they were written *for* him rather than *by* him, but the New Testament makes it clear that he authored of over half of the 150 psalms,[1] and the Old Testament tells us that he praised the Lord on his deathbed that he had been *"the sweet psalmist of Israel"*.[2] Psalm 3 is the first of fourteen psalms with titles which tell us at what point in his life David wrote it, but note that these psalms do not appear in chronological order.[3] David wrote Psalm 3 towards the end of his life but it was placed here to form a contrast with the message of the two psalms which go before. God wants to make it clear to us from the outset that if we choose friendship with him, it means suffering alongside the Rejected One as well as reigning with the King of kings.

---

[1] For example, in Mark 12:36; Luke 20:42; Acts 1:16; 2:25, 34 and 4:25, and Romans 4:6 and 11:9. Some 73 of the titles in the Hebrew text and 83 of the titles in the Greek Septuagint identify David as the author.

[2] 2 Samuel 23:1 (King James Version). Amos 6:5 also singles this out as a key aspect of David's reign.

[3] The fourteen psalms are 3, 7, 18, 30, 34, 51, 52, 54, 56, 57, 59, 60, 63 and 142. They are not in chronological order, but arranged in a way which illustrates the unfolding message of the book of Psalms.

Note the deliberate contrast between *"I have installed my king on Zion, my holy mountain"* in 2:6 and *"A psalm of David. When he fled from his son Absalom"* in the title of Psalm 3. The Lord doesn't want us to take Psalm 1 out of context and expect the Christian life to be trouble-free, or to misunderstand Psalm 2 as a promise that God's People will never see short-term defeat along the way. He gives us Psalm 3 as a rude awakening which warns us that his Messiah's Kingdom is both now and not yet, and that believers will be persecuted for their decision to side with him. We read in 3:1–2 that the godly will be hated, defeated and taunted that their God has abandoned them altogether.[4] Just as Absalom captured Mount Zion and usurped the throne, the wicked will often look as though they have defeated the Lord.

That's why 3:2 ends with the Hebrew word *seláh*, a musical term which is used seventy-one times in Psalms and which either means *silence* or an *instrumental solo*.[5] Either way, it instructs us to stop singing and recall what we know about God's character before we dare to say a single word more. When David stops singing, he suddenly remembers the words of Genesis 15:1, where the Lord promised the downcast Abraham that *"I am your shield, your very great reward."*[6] Suddenly the tempo of Psalm 3 changes. David spends the rest of the song modelling how we are to worship God when he doesn't look like the King of kings at all. Jesus warned in Matthew 7:24–27 that those who fail to apply his words will be swept away when trials come, but David has built his house on the rock and finds strength to

---

[4] Martin Luther saw Psalm 3 as the words of Jesus from the cross, based on Matthew 27:39–43. He therefore saw Jesus as the true Rejected One and 3:5 as a prophecy about his death and resurrection.

[5] With the exception of two songs of David in Psalm 140 and 143, this musical term is only used in Books I to III. The only other place it is used in Scripture is in a psalm in Habakkuk 3.

[6] The Hebrew word *hāgāh* or *to meditate* means literally *to mutter*. Because David kept on repeating Genesis 15:1 until it was part of his thinking, he was able to draw strength from it in his hour of need.

trust that God is still enthroned on *"his holy mountain"*, despite all appearances to the contrary. He still trusts the Lord to be his defender, his glory and his joy, even in the midst of trouble.[7] After a second *selāh* at the end of 3:4, he sings out his confidence that the Lord will indeed deliver and bless him as he promised in 1:1 and 2:12.[8]

Psalm 4 is the first of fifty-five psalms which are marked *"for the chief musician"* who led worship at the Tabernacle on Mount Zion.[9] If Psalm 3 was the song of the rejected Messiah, Psalm 4 is a song for those who follow him and suffer for his name.[10] It teaches us to address the Lord as *"the God of my righteousness"* because only he can make us righteous, like the man in Psalm 1, in a world which chases after idols.[11] A *selāh* at the end of 4:2 gives us time to remember that God has set us apart for himself,[12] so we must not sin against him by getting angry that he doesn't bring our suffering to a rapid end.[13] Another *selāh* at the end of 4:4 helps us to remember that we can trust in his blood sacrifice for sin and in his promise to keep

[7] There is a play on words here in Hebrew since the word for *shield* is *māgēn*, which can also mean *king* (as in Psalm 84:9).

[8] David is so confident that he actually uses the Hebrew perfect tense of completed action to state literally in 3:7 that *"You **have** struck all my enemies on the jaw; you **have** broken the teeth of the wicked."*

[9] David appointed *chief musicians* to lead worship at the Tabernacle in 1 Chronicles 6:31–32 and 15:21, and he uses the same word to describe them in these titles. See also Habakkuk 3:19.

[10] David uses the perfect tense again to pray literally in 4:1 that *"You **have** given me relief from my distress – have mercy on me and hear my prayer!"* He makes God's faithfulness in the past the basis for his faith in the present.

[11] The NIV translation *"my righteous God"* is therefore misleading. Paul's quotation of Psalm 32:1–2 in Romans 4:6–8 makes it clear that David knew that we can only be made righteous through God's blood sacrifice.

[12] The Hebrew word *hāsīd* in 4:3 is the equivalent of the Greek word *hagios* and means *saint* or *holy one*. It is used about 25 times in Psalms to refer to those whom God has chosen for salvation.

[13] *Tremble* in 4:4 could either refer to fear or to anger. Paul follows the Septuagint interpretation when he quotes this verse in Ephesians 4:26 as a warning for us not to sin when we are angry.

us safe and prosper us.[14] *"You have filled my heart with greater joy than when their grain and new wine abound,"* David tells us to sing with faith in 4:7.[15] It is far better for us to be rejected with the Lord while we wait for his Kingdom to be revealed than to get drunk on the short-term prosperity of the wicked.

This leads into Psalm 5, another song which David marked to be sung by the worshippers at the Tabernacle. Yet again he links back to Psalms 1–2 by using the same Hebrew word *hāgāh* to remind the Lord in 5:1 that he has *meditated* on God's Word and not on how he can rebel against him.[16] He also links back to Psalm 2:6 by declaring in 5:2 that, although he is king of Israel, the Lord is the true King and true deliverance will come from him. He tells us to rejoice that God hates the wicked and will destroy them, however much they seem to prosper in the short term. He tells us to rejoice that God loves the righteous, however much they suffer in the short term, and that he invites them in 5:7 into his Tabernacle to enjoy friendship with him.[17] David therefore ends this cluster of psalms in 5:12 the same way he began them in 3:3, with confidence that the Lord shields his rejected followers in their day of trouble. Their pain and suffering cannot undo the promises in 1:1 and 2:12, since *"Surely, Lord, you bless the righteous."*[18]

---

[14] The Hebrew words which David uses in 4:5 are *zābah* and *zebāh*, which almost always refer specifically to *the slaughter of blood sacrifices*.

[15] Like most Hebrew poetry, the text of Psalms can be ambiguous and is open to different interpretations. I therefore quote throughout this book from both the 1984 and 2011 NIV translations, since they differ.

[16] Not all English translations make it clear that *hāgāh* links 5:1 back to 1:1 and 2:1, but this is very important.

[17] David tells us in 5:4–5 that God hates sinners so much that he cannot even bear to be in the same room as them, and Paul quotes 5:9 to describe the utter sinfulness of humankind in Romans 3:13. Nevertheless, God can make sinful humans so righteous that he invites them to dwell with him in his Tabernacle in 5:7.

[18] Although the title of Psalm 5 probably means that it is a song *"for flutes"*, just as Psalm 4 was a song *"for stringed instruments"*, the Hebrew can also be translated to mean a song *"concerning our inheritance"*.

So don't be mistaken into thinking that friendship with God will mean a life free from suffering. Those who follow the Rejected One will often be rejected with him. And don't make the opposite mistake of thinking that the world which has rejected God can ever resist him. The Rejected One is still the King of kings and he will do all he has promised. He will bless, he will protect and he will delight in anyone who follows him. He will not be ashamed to call those who suffer with him friends of God.

The Forgiver (6:1–7:17)

*The Lord has heard my cry for mercy; the Lord
accepts my prayer.*

(Psalm 6:9)

I was just getting ready for a New Year's Eve party when the
telephone rang. It was a man my wife and I had met on a recent
trip to the theatre. I hadn't shared the Gospel with him when
we met him but something on my business card had made
him suspect I was a Christian. *"Will God forgive anyone – truly
anyone?"* he stammered as he confessed a list of sins which had
tormented his conscience across the Christmas period. It made
me very glad that Psalm 6 follows on from Psalms 1–5.

Perhaps surprisingly, that question isn't just posed by
non-Christians. I've lost count of the number of times that I've
counselled a believer whose basic problem is that they aren't
sure whether or not God has truly forgiven them. I will never
forget the agonized words of a Christian who had aborted her
baby many years earlier and yet still choked back the tears
as she confessed, *"I can't forgive myself. I've confessed this sin
a thousand times and yet I still feel so much shame."* That also
made me very glad that Psalm 6 follows on from Psalms 1–5.
God placed these psalms in exactly the right order that we need
them.

The very first verse of Psalms reminded us that we often
choose to sin instead of following God's ways. The first two
psalms compounded this by telling us that God is angry with
our sin and has set a day when he will judge the wicked. If that
isn't scary enough, Psalms 3–5 warn us that God will *"break the*

teeth of the wicked", "destroy those who tell lies" and "banish them for their many sins". That's why Psalm 6 is the first of the seven "penitential psalms", a name which isn't used by the psalmists themselves but which is used by most commentators to describe the songs of repentance which we find in Psalms 6, 32, 38, 51, 102, 130 and 143. If you have understood what David says in the first five psalms about God's anger and judgment against sin, then you will see why we need them to be followed by this prayer of repentance.

Psalm 6:1–7 describes the intense emotion which the man from the theatre expressed down the phone line on that New Year's Eve. It confirms our worst fears about God's *anger* and his *wrath*, and it describes the *agony, anguish, groaning, weeping* and *sorrow* which mark anyone whose conscience has been awoken to their sin. Worse than that, David mentions *she'ōl* for the first time in 6:5 to alert us to the fact that our trespasses are far more serious than we imagine. This Hebrew word sometimes refers simply to the realm of the dead in general (as in 88:3), but it is also used in Psalms to refer to *hell* as a place of torment for the wicked (as in 139:8).[1] That's how David uses the word here. It was the thought of hell which made my friend so anxious.

That's why David also uses another key Hebrew word in 6:4. *Hēsēd* means *loving kindness* or *covenant mercy*, and it is used 247 times in the Old Testament – 127 of them in Psalms – as the closest Hebrew equivalent to the Greek word for *grace* in the New Testament.[2] God hasn't given us the penitential psalms to rub in the fact of our sin. He has given them to us because he wants to rub it out.

---

[1] *She'ōl* is used 16 times in Psalms and 49 times in the rest of the Old Testament. *Hades*, the Greek equivalent, is used 11 times in the New Testament. *She'ōl* means the realm of the dead in general in Genesis 37:35, Job 14:13, Ecclesiastes 9:10 and Isaiah 38:10. It means *hell* specifically in Numbers 16:30, Job 11:8 and Proverbs 23:14.

[2] *Hēsēd* gained us entry to the Tabernacle in 5:7. It is the root of the word *hāsīd*, which Psalms uses to refer to the People of God who have been saved by grace.

David wanted his chief musician to teach Israel to sing this song of repentance to the sound of an eight-stringed lyre.[3] It would teach them in 6:1–7 not to try to minimize their sin, and it would teach them in 6:8–10 to trust that *"The Lord has heard my cry for mercy; the Lord accepts my prayer."* Humility and honesty are the only currency sinners have in heaven, but David tells us that when they are combined with faith in God's blood sacrifice they are effective every time.[4]

That's why Psalm 7 comes next as a model of the confidence we should have in our complete forgiveness through the Gospel. Sadly, my friend refused to believe in God's mercy, sobbing that *"I understand what you are saying, but I just can't believe God would forgive a person like me."* I've often had to get Christians to write down their sins on a piece of paper and then burn it in front of them to convince them that what the Gospel says is true. C.J. Mahaney laments the way that Christians all too often believe that *"cultivating condemnation and wallowing in your shame is somehow pleasing to God, or that a constant, low-grade guilt will somehow promote holiness and spiritual maturity"*.[5] David gave us Psalm 6 because we need to know how to pray for God to forgive us, and he gave us Psalm 7 because we need to be confident that he has.[6]

Many people find it shocking that David is so assured in 7:8 of his righteousness before God. Cush the Benjamite was probably one of King Saul's courtiers at his palace in Gibeah of

---

[3] The word *sheminith* in the title means literally *"an instrument of eighths"*, and the title also tells us it was a stringed instrument. It was therefore either an eight-stringed lyre or one which had a string for each octave. The word also appears in the title of Psalm 12 and in 1 Chronicles 15:21.

[4] Jesus quotes from 6:8 in Matthew 7:23 to tell us that self-confident people who think they have no need to confess their sins are in fact the ones who will be surprised when he casts them into hell.

[5] C.J. Mahaney in *The Cross-Centered Life* (2002).

[6] Habakkuk 3:1 suggests that the *shiggaiōn* in the title of Psalm 7 was a type of music played on a particular instrument. Like Psalm 7, Habakkuk 3 also asks the Lord to use his bow and arrows to judge the wicked.

Benjamin, and he had evidently slandered David to his master.[7] When David responds by asking the Lord to vindicate him *"according to my righteousness"* and *"according to my integrity"*, it sounds to some readers like the very arrogance which 5:5 told us the Lord detests.[8] They fail to notice that David confesses that God knows his inner thoughts in 7:9, that God is angered by sin in 7:11, and that God will allow unconfessed sin to gestate inside him and give birth to destruction in 7:14.[9] David isn't pretending to be better than he is. He is simply modelling the way that confession of sin (6:1–7) ought to give us confidence that we have been forgiven (6:8–10). *"I will give thanks to the Lord because of **his righteousness**,"* he rejoices in 7:17. Don't be shocked by David's confidence in the Gospel. Rather, be ashamed at how lacking in confidence we often are ourselves.

I made a final appeal to the man from the theatre by reading him the words of 1 John 1:9–2:2: *"If we confess our sins, God is faithful and just and **will forgive us our sins and purify us from all unrighteousness**... If anybody does sin, we have an advocate with the Father – Jesus Christ, the Righteous One. He is the atoning sacrifice for our sins."*

That's the amazing grace which made David want to sing and shout in Psalms 6–7. It's the amazing grace which should make you want to do the same. So don't read any further until you have confessed your sin and rejoiced with confidence over the righteousness which is yours as an undeserved gift from God the Forgiver.

---

[7] 1 Samuel 10:26; 13:15; 22:6–7.

[8] The word *tōm* which is translated *integrity* here can even be translated *perfection*.

[9] Scripture often talks about sin being conceived, gestating and coming to birth (Job 15:35; Isaiah 59:4; James 1:15). David is telling us that God knows all about sinful thoughts even before we act on them.

The Creator (8:1–9)

Lord, our Lord, how majestic is your name in all the earth!

(Psalm 8:1)

You can tell a lot about the people in my family just by looking at the shoe rack by our front door. There is a pair of tiny baby shoes, some little ballet shoes and two pairs of junior football boots. There is a pair of ladies' slip-ons and an enormous pair of size-eleven wellies. You don't have to see me or my wife or our four children to guess what we are like. You can simply look at our shoes and draw some pretty accurate conclusions.

David teaches us to do the same with God in Psalm 8. God is invisible, but the vast wonders of the universe proclaim the greatness of their Creator for all to see. Like the shoes on the rack by my front door, David encourages us to view creation as revelation into the unrivalled majesty of our Creator God.[1]

"You have set your glory in the heavens," David teaches us to sing in 8:2. He had seen the power of the Middle Eastern sun to scorch plants, dry up rivers and burn human skin, but we have more reason than him to look up at the sun and worship God. We now know that the sun emits more energy every single second than human beings have produced since the dawn of history, including all of the potential energy which is stored up in all the nuclear bombs that have ever been made. We now know that the sun is so large that the energy produced at its core takes 50 million years to make its way to the surface. The amount of solar energy which reaches Earth in a year is twice as great as

---

[1] Paul also makes this point in Romans 1:20.

could be obtained from all the coal, oil, natural gas and uranium which have ever existed on the Earth. If this makes your mind boggle, you are beginning to understand Psalm 8. Creation tells us that God has a massive pair of shoes.

David continues in 8:3, *"When I consider your heavens, the work of your fingers, the moon and the stars, which you have set in place..."* Even though the shepherd-boy knew nothing of modern light pollution when he looked up at the night sky, we have far greater cause to sing this psalm than he did. NASA's best estimate is that the sun is merely one of over 200 billion stars in the Milky Way, and one of somewhere between 10 sextillion and 1 septillion stars in the observable universe. If a rocket left Earth today on a mission to reach the nearest star, Proxima Centauri, even the fastest NASA rocket would take over 100,000 years to get there, and yet, in a throwaway statement in Genesis 1:16 which is only two words long in Hebrew, the Bible simply tells us that when God made the sun and moon *"he also made the stars"*!

Enough statistics. David's point is that the skies give everyone plenty of clues that the Lord God deserves their awestruck worship. The only question is whether we will be like Sir Isaac Newton, who concluded in his Principia that *"This most beautiful System of the Sun, Planets and Comets, could only proceed from the counsel and dominion of an intelligent and powerful being,"*[2] or whether we will shut our eyes to the evidence like Professor Thomas Nagel of New York University when he candidly admitted

> *I want atheism to be true and am made uneasy by the fact that some of the most intelligent and well-informed people I know are religious believers. It isn't just that I don't believe in God and, naturally, hope that I'm right*

---

[2] Sir Isaac Newton wrote this in Book III of his seminal work, the *Principia*, in 1687.

in my belief. It's that I hope there is no God! I don't want
there to be a God; I don't want the universe to be like
that.[3]

That is the kind of comment which prompted David to write
8:2. He rejoices in the fact that the arrogant wise men of this
world can miss the obvious while little children and suckling
infants see it clearly.[4] It doesn't bother him that Israel's pagan
neighbours believe the world was created by their idols or
by no god at all. He is happy to receive God's Kingdom like a
child and to conclude that creation is like the items on God's
shoe rack, proving that he is glorious far *"above the heavens"*.
He worships the Lord who delights to hide himself from
the arrogant and to reveal himself to anyone who is humble
enough to catch a glimpse of his glory, *"because of your enemies,*
to silence the foe".[5]

David hasn't finished. If 8:1–3 speaks of God's transcendent
greatness, 8:4–8 is about his immanence and humble willingness
to dwell with humankind. He didn't just make humans a little
lower than *elōhīm* – literally than *God* himself[6] – but he also
invested our mortal race with meaning by crowning us to rule
as his viceroys over the earth. This is amazing enough, yet we
have another reason to sing this psalm even more loudly than
David. Hebrews 2:7–9 quotes these words to remind us that

---

[3] Thomas Nagel in his book *The Last Word* (1997).

[4] Hebrew women breastfed their children until they were two or three, so this
reference to *suckling infants* being able to praise the Lord assures us God that
can save our children from a very early age. The word for *praise* in 8:2 literally
means *strength*, and the reason we forget that God can save toddlers is that
we first forget the vast gulf which exists between him and even the strongest
adult.

[5] Matthew 11:25–26; Luke 10:21–24; 1 Corinthians 1:19–21. God encourages
us to pray that he will perform great acts *because of his enemies* in Exodus
32:11–13, Numbers 14:11–19, Deuteronomy 32:26–27 and Ezekiel 36:20–23.

[6] Although the most natural reading of 8:5 is *"a little lower than God"*, most
English translations follow the Septuagint translation, *"a little lower than the*
angels", because it is quoted that way in Hebrews 2:7 and 9.

Jesus *"was made lower than the angels for a little while"* and is *"now crowned with glory and honour because he suffered death, so that by the grace of God he might taste death for everyone"*. The Creator God who made the sun, stars and space was not too proud to become a human being and to wear a pair of man-sized human shoes.[7]

Our first response to this should simply be to sing about God's greatness. The facts about the universe in 8:2–8 are sandwiched between two identical exclamations of praise in 8:1 and 9. Jesus quoted from 8:2 to berate those who failed to recognize his glory and left it to children to sing his praise in Matthew 21:16. Our second response should be to sing about God's humility in becoming a human being in Jesus Christ in order to win back the authority which Adam lost over this world. That's the point which Paul makes when he quotes from this psalm in 1 Corinthians 15:27 and encourages us to rise up as servants of the Creator God to extend his Kingdom throughout the world.

Oliver Wendell Holmes, one of the best-read judges ever to sit on the US Supreme Court, concluded that *"When one thinks coldly I see no reason for attributing to man a significance different in kind from that which belongs to a baboon or to a grain of sand."*[8] That's the philosophy of our foolish culture and David calls us to reject it as completely as he rejected the pagan philosophy of his own day. He calls us to look at the enormous working boots of the Creator God and at the man-sized sandals of Jesus Christ sitting next to one another on the shoe rack. He calls us to let the sight stir us to worship the invisible God forever.

---

[7] The Septuagint tells us that *"according to gittith"* in the titles of Psalms 8, 81 and 84 means *to sing at the winepresses*, where people harvested grapes at the time of the Jewish Feast of Tabernacles. There may therefore be significance in the fact that the feast was an Old Covenant prophecy about Jesus' incarnation.

[8] He wrote this in a letter to Sir Frederick Pollock on 30th August 1929.

The God Who Can Be Known (9:1–10:18)

Those who know your name trust in you, for you,
Lord, have never forsaken those who seek you.

(Psalm 9:10)

I once took part in a game in which wives answered a series of questions about themselves before their husbands came into the room and were forced to guess their answers. It was a lot of fun for the audience to discover how clueless we husbands were, but if you are ever invited to take part in a similar game, my best advice for you is *run*. I acquitted myself relatively well, but one of my friends didn't know his wife's favourite food, her ideal date night or even the name of her best friend. When he guessed that her favourite possession was their car and it turned out to be her wedding ring, you could actually hear the audience wincing. I'm glad I didn't have to listen to the heated conversation they must have had when they got home!

Sadly, very few of us know God as well as we think we do. Sure, we know enough about him to walk with him when times are good, but we haven't studied his character intently enough to sustain us when times get harder. We haven't listened to David's call in 1:2 to meditate on Scriptures which describe God and his way of working. We are more like the people whom Jesus rebuked in Mark 12:24 by asking them, *"Are you not in error because you do not know the Scriptures or the power of God?"* David wrote Psalms 9–10 to remind us that the Lord is the God

Who Can Be Known. We need to study his character if we want to flourish instead of flounder when life throws difficulties at us.

David emphasizes this even by the way in which he structures these two psalms. We can tell that they were originally one psalm because they form an acrostic poem together: 9:1 begins with the first letter of the Hebrew alphabet, 9:3 begins with the second letter, 9:5 begins with the third letter and so on, right up until the twenty-second letter in 10:17.[1] They were split into two when Psalms was compiled so that worshippers could choose to sing the general prayer of Psalm 9, the specific prayer of Psalm 10 or both together.[2] Hebrew poems rarely rhymed (if you know anything about the complexities of Hebrew word endings, it's easy to see why!), so writers found ways to make their poems beautiful by making patterns with their words. Acrostics were seen as some of the most beautiful poems of them all, but they were rare because they were so difficult to write (have a go yourself at writing an acrostic poem about God's character, beginning each line with *G-O-D-A-L-M-I-G-H-T-Y*). David painstakingly wrote Psalms 9 and 10 as an acrostic poem in order to show us that our prayer life deserves our mind's fullest attention.[3]

David demonstrates this in 9:1–2 by starting out by worshipping God for his *wonderful deeds* and for his *name*. I find it very easy to forget both of those things when I'm under pressure, so I am challenged by David's statement that such worship requires me to focus on the Lord *"with all my heart"*. I have learned to keep a journal of answered prayers and spiritual milestones because I find it easy to forget what God has done for

---

[1] This is also why, unlike almost all the other psalms in Book I, Psalm 10 has no title. The Greek Septuagint treats these as one psalm, keeping the total number to 150 by dividing up a later psalm instead.

[2] There are 22 letters in the Hebrew alphabet but only 36 verses in these two psalms because not all the letters feature as precisely as in other acrostics such as Psalms 25, 34, 37, 111, 112 and 119 or Proverbs 31:10–31.

[3] The title implies that he also set it to a catchy well-known tune in order to make it especially memorable.

me. I have also learned to read devotional books which explore the character of God because I need help to get to know the different aspects of his name. David tells us that nothing less than such devoted attention will deepen our friendship with the God Who Can Be Known.

David demonstrates this further when he describes his own experience through various crises in 9:9–10. He tells the Lord that he knows he is only a refuge for *"those who seek you"* and for *"those who know your name"*. Not knowing enough about your wife can get you embarrassed in a game, but not knowing enough about the Lord can spell disaster. David tells us this again in 20:1 and 7 when he urges us to *"trust in the **name** of the Lord our God"* and *"the **name** of the God of Jacob"* to protect us. We will read something similar in 91:14, when the Lord comes to the aid of the one about whom he can say, *"Because he loves me, I will rescue him; I will protect him, for he acknowledges my name."* Spiritual laziness and passivity isn't just a twenty-first-century problem, so David warns us that we need to get to know the Lord during the good times if we want to flourish in our faith during the bad times which are inevitably coming. He teaches us the same thing which he taught his young son Solomon: *"The name of the Lord is a fortified tower; the righteous run to it and are safe."*[4]

David gives us an example of this when he shares about his own trials in 9:11–20. He begins with a statement that God is *"the Lord, enthroned in Zion"* – the true King of Israel who reigns from his Tabernacle in Jerusalem.[5] He follows this up with a statement that *"the Lord is known by his acts of justice"* and that we can trust the Lord to be the one *"who avenges blood"*. In times of suffering we tend to forget that God is on the throne, that he

---

[4] Solomon writes this in Proverbs 18:10, probably inspired by the way he saw his father seek the Lord.

[5] Since David's royal palace was also on Mount Zion, 9:11 links with 10:16 to state that the Lord is the true King of Israel and that his Tabernacle is the true royal palace of Israel.

dwells in us through the Holy Spirit, and that he fights on our behalf. That's why 9:16 and 20 tell us to take a *selāh* to consider God's character, and why 9:16 tells the chief musician to play a long instrumental solo while we meditate on God's name.[6]

It's also why Psalm 10 forms the second half of the acrostic poem, since it demonstrates how David applied this general lesson during a specific personal crisis. When the Lord seemed far-away (10:1), David still trusted he would save him if he fell back on what he knew about God's character and his way of working. He cried out to the Lord about his enemy's sinful refusal to make room in his thoughts for God (10:4), to seek the Lord (10:4), to read Scripture (10:5), or to remember that the Lord sees our every action and will judge us for being too busy or too distracted or too plain rebellious to pour out our energy on getting to know him (10:11 and 13).[7]

So don't you be too busy or too distracted to respond to the lesson of these two psalms by studying the character and marvellous deeds of the God who calls you to be his friend. Those who cry out for experiences of God but fail to feast their minds on him will find themselves plagued by doubts and suffering when trouble comes. But those who study God's character will find that they have built reservoirs of faith from which they can drink deeply in the future. They will find that they have become strong and resilient followers of the God Who Can Be Known.

---

[6] The word *higgāiōn* in 9:16 comes from the word *hāgāh* and means *meditation* (see also 19:14). The same word is used in 92:3 to refer to *strumming which aids meditation*.

[7] This is why Paul quotes from 10:7 in Romans 3:14 as part of his famous statement that nobody seeks God.

The Culture-Changer
(11:1–15:5)

When the foundations are being destroyed, what can the righteous do?

(Psalm 11:3)

The sociologist Peter Berger argues that Western culture has undergone a seismic shift in the past fifty years. Church attendances have plummeted, Christian influence has evaporated and our culture has become hostile towards its Judeo-Christian foundations. Faith has become privatized (it's fine in churches and mosques but not in parliaments or marketplaces). Faith has become pluralized (every belief is equally valid except for the belief that this isn't true). Faith has become compartmentalized (it's fine on Sunday mornings and at bedtime prayers but not at school or at work or anywhere else that we spend the bulk of our waking hours). Even in America, where church decline has so far not been as rapid as in Europe, Peter Berger believes this culture change has taken place at break-neck speed. He argues that *"If India is the most religious country on our planet, and Sweden is the least religious, America is a land of Indians ruled by Swedes."*[1]

If you are a thoughtful Christian, this can't have escaped your notice, so it's comforting that David saw a similar seismic shift take place in his own national culture. He spent the first half of his psalm-writing days as an outlaw who was forced to watch King Saul dismantle the godly foundations Samuel had laid for Israel and replace them with wicked foundations of his own. He

---

[1] Peter Berger is quoted by Huston Smith in *Why Religion Matters* (2001).

cried out in 11:3, *"When the foundations are being destroyed, what can the righteous do?"*[2] He is uniquely positioned to teach us how to respond to this culture change because he then spent the second half of his psalm-writing days rebuilding Israel's godly foundations, and it led to a great national revival. The five short prayers which have been clustered together as Psalms 11–15 are a call for us to cooperate with God the Culture-Changer.

Psalm 11 warns us not to panic or give up in despair. David's friends might urge him to *"Flee like a bird to your mountain,"* but he isn't frightened by the thought that wicked people want to kill off the righteous and forge a new culture which hates the Lord.[3] He has practised what he preached in Psalms 9–10 and he therefore knows God's character well enough to remember that the Lord is still on the throne of heaven and still reigning over the earth from his Tabernacle on Mount Zion.[4] God laughed in 2:4 at the rulers who plotted against him, and he laughs at them again in 11:2 as they gather up their arrows. He has fiery coals, burning sulphur and scorching wind in his arsenal which can easily overcome their puny little missiles.

Psalm 12 warns us not to forget the promises in God's Word. Israel might be full of liars and deceivers – mouthy people who despise righteousness and who honour what is vile – but that doesn't make David doubt that everything God says is true. When the godly lose all influence (12:1) and those who seize power deny that they have any Lord at all (12:4), God promises to rise up from his throne and sweep them away. David promises us that *"the words of the Lord are flawless, like silver purified in a crucible, like gold refined seven times."*

---

[2] It is not clear whether these are David's words or those of his friends. Either way, he knows how we feel.

[3] He uses a perfect tense in 11:1 to say literally that *"In the Lord I **have taken** refuge."*

[4] The word translated *temple* in 11:4 and elsewhere in Psalms was also used for God's *Tabernacle* (1 Samuel 1:9; 3:3). The Temple was not completed until 958 BC, twelve years after David died.

Psalm 13 warns us that we may need to wait a little while for God to get up and revive our culture, and it tells us how we should pray while we wait. David shows us it is good to tell the Lord that we feel abandoned and confused, so long as we follow the path he lays out for us towards deeper faith in God. Two verses of lament lead into two verses of prayer,[5] which lead in turn into two verses of faith-filled praise. David remembers that God *"has been good to me"* in the past and uses that fact to bolster his faith that further grace and salvation must be just around the corner.[6]

Psalm 14 tells us what to do when our culture rejects belief in God entirely.[7] David calls atheists fools in 14:1 and asks with astonishment in 14:4, *"Do all these evildoers know nothing?"* A good example of this was when Richard Dawkins, the author of *The God Delusion*, gave an interview in which he sought to discredit the idea of faith in God. When the interviewer asked him to give the full title of Charles Darwin's *On the Origin of Species*, he struggled to remember the name of the sacred text of atheism and exclaimed with unwitting irony *"On the Origin of Species... erm... with... oh God, oh God, what was it?!"*[8] David tells us that people do not become atheists through careful consideration of the facts, but by refusing to accept in their hearts what the facts all around them shout out is true.[9] If the

---

[5] 1 Samuel 14:27 and 29 shows us that *"give light to my eyes"* in 13:3 means *"restore my strength to me"*.

[6] The word used for God's *unfailing love* in 13:5 is *hēsēd*, which means his *covenant grace and mercy*.

[7] This is such a big issue that Psalm 53 repeats Psalm 14 entirely, marking it as a psalm of instruction. The word it uses for a *psalm of instruction* is *maskīl*, the very word which is used in 14:2 for *one who understands*.

[8] Richard Dawkins made this slip-up during an interview on the *Today* programme on BBC Radio 4 on 14th February 2012. Afterwards some of his former friends labelled him an *"embarrassment to atheism"*.

[9] Paul quotes from 14:2–3 in Romans 3:11–12 and tells us that most people are happy to consent to this folly.

root of atheism is folly, then 14:1 and 5 tell us that its fruit is corruption, depravity and terror.

Psalm 14:5–7 begins to tell us how we can fight back and deliver our nation from destruction through friendship with God the Culture-Changer. Verse 2 told us literally that the wicked have turned against the Lord *"all together"*, so 14:5 mirrors this by telling us that our fight back must begin with Christian unity, since *"God is present in the company of the righteous."* That's why the titles of these four psalms instruct the chief musician to teach God's People to sing them all together. It is also why David prays in 14:7 that salvation will *"come out of Zion when the Lord restores his people"*. David's hope lay in the congregation of believers who gathered to worship the Lord at his Tabernacle. In modern terms, he tells us that the way to turn our culture back to the Lord is to build churches which demonstrate a way of life which is so different that it converts an entire nation.[10]

Psalm 15 is therefore a description of the kind of church that has this power to change a nation. David tells us that the lifestyle of a worshipper at the Tabernacle on Mount Zion should be the exact opposite of the lying, self-assertive, grasping culture which is spawned by an atheistic worldview.[11] He tells us not to compartmentalize our Christian lives and to allow God to shape our character in every area. He tells us to resist the march of secularism by speaking up for God at school, at work, in the arts, in the media and in government. He tells us to stand up to militant pluralism by proclaiming that the Lord is the only true Saviour. When we do so, he promises that we will see our nations won to Christ. That's what happens when people defy their culture because they have become friends with God the Culture-Changer.

---

[10] This should be obvious since Jesus didn't create a strategy document but a community of believers. Yet many Christians sadly aid their nation's spiritual decline by giving up on the Church.

[11] The same Hebrew word which is used for *falling* in 13:4 is deliberately used for not being *shaken* in 15:5.

The Messiah (16:1–11)

You will not abandon me to the grave, nor will you let your Holy One see decay.

(Psalm 16:10)

If you have heard the song "Knockin' on Heaven's Door" performed by Bob Dylan, Eric Clapton, Guns N' Roses, Avril Lavigne and Babyface, you will know that the five versions sound very different. It's the same lyrics and pretty much the same tune, but they are very different songs. The same is true of Psalm 16. It's a psalm which is sung in three distinct versions.

David is the original writer and he sings it first, as a follow-on from Psalms 11–15. The temple worship leaders who compiled the book of Psalms placed this song here because 16:1 links back to 11:1 and 14:6 when David tells the Lord he is his *refuge*,[1] and 16:8 links back to 15:5 when he adds that as a result he *"will not be shaken"*. The wording of 16:3 links back to 14:5 when David tells us that his delight is in the *"holy people who are in the land"*, and 16:4 links back to Psalms 11–15 in general, as David promises not to worship the idols of his backslidden nation. God alone can satisfy him, so he will praise him all day and meditate on his Word all night.[2] He will be the loving friend of God that Psalms teaches us to be.

The last three verses of David's song give one of the

---

[1] This is a Hebrew perfect tense, so David is not so much saying that he *takes refuge* in the Lord as that *he **has taken** refuge* in him. Taking refuge in God is a one-off decision which we then draw on daily thereafter.

[2] 16:7 is a "synonymous parallelism" in Hebrew which likens *God guiding us* to *our inner being instructing us*. When God fills us with the Holy Spirit, he guides us through a sense of inner peace in our hearts.

clearest Old Testament prophecies about what happens beyond the grave. He proclaims that God will not abandon his body to *she'ōl*, which we saw in 6:5 is a Hebrew word which can either mean *the realm of the dead* in general, or *hell* in particular. David is confident that he is a *hāsīd* – one of God's *holy ones* who have been saved by his *hēsēd*, or *covenant mercy* – and that death will therefore never put an end to the friendship he has been granted with God. He knows that the Lord will not abandon his soul to hell or his body to decay, so he praises God that *"you make known to me the path of life"* beyond the grave and *"fill me with joy in your presence, with eternal pleasures"* in heaven for evermore. David's song is so glorious that we might have thought that nobody else would ever dare to make a cover version of it.

But somebody did. In fact, they sang it far better than David. We saw earlier that when the Old Testament refers to David as God's *anointed one* it uses the Hebrew word *messiah*,[3] and so the second version of Psalm 16 was sung about 1,000 years later by the true Messiah. David had labelled this psalm as a *miktām* in the title,[4] which means either that he had *engraved* it somewhere special or that it was a song which contained *hidden treasures*.[5] Jesus of Nazareth drew out these hidden treasures when he sang it, telling the Father that he would drink the cup of suffering at Calvary because his delight in the Father was such a sweet cup and portion that it more than offset the bitter taste of crucifixion. Although the link between 16:5 and Matthew 26:39–42 is not explicit, Jonah quotes from 16:4 while in the belly of the fish in Jonah 2:4 and Jesus tells us in Matthew

[3] For example, in 1 Samuel 16:6; 2 Samuel 19:21; 22:51; 23:1; Psalms 18:50; 20:6; 28:8.

[4] We can tell from ancient manuscripts and from the way that David addresses Psalms 39 and 62 to his contemporary, Jeduthun, that most of these titles are as old as the psalms themselves.

[5] This word only occurs elsewhere in the Bible in the titles of Psalms 56–60. The Septuagint assumes it comes from the verb *kātham* or *to engrave*, but it also looks similar to the Hebrew word for *hidden*.

12:39–41 that this was a picture of his own death, burial and resurrection.

There is a much more explicit link between the promise of resurrection in 16:9–11 and what happened in Matthew 28. Peter quoted these verses in Acts 2:25–32 on the Day of Pentecost and applied them to Jesus, and Paul applied them in the same way in Acts 13:35–38 at the start of his missionary journeys.[6] Because Jesus took refuge in the Father (16:1) for the sake of saving a holy People (16:3), the Father saw his innocence (16:4) and raised him from the dead (16:10). He declared him to be the true *hāsīd* – the true *Holy One* – and he brought him back to heaven to reign at his right hand forever (16:11).[7]

It's amazing to say it, but the third person who gets to sing this psalm is you and me. Jesus told us in Revelation 2:27 that we can sing Psalm 2 as our own song, even though it was written for the Messiah, and the same is true of Psalm 16. God is waiting to hear our cover version. Unlike many of the other psalms in Book I, this one hasn't been marked for congregational singing because God wants to hear us sing it as a solo song which expresses our personal faith in what Jesus' death and resurrection have achieved for us. He wants us to take refuge in the Gospel, to tell him that he alone can satisfy us and to pledge ourselves to playing our role in the Church as part of his holy People. He wants us to sing out our confidence that he will not abandon our soul to hell or our body to the grave. He wants to hear our own cover version of the final verse of Psalm 16, where we celebrate our faith that heaven is real and fully satisfying for evermore.

Last month I visited Bill, a 74-year-old man in the church I lead, who was dying. He had suffered from worsening dementia

---

[6] Note that Peter says David was a prophet who was aware when he wrote Psalm 16 that he was writing a song for the Messiah to sing centuries later.

[7] Because of the ambiguous meaning of the Hebrew word *she'ōl*, we cannot use this verse to argue that Jesus descended to hell between his death and resurrection. In fact, Luke 23:43 suggests he didn't.

for six years and was unconscious when I reached him at his deathbed. I knew from earlier visits that the one thing which still made him lucid and animated was hearing somebody pray or read Scripture to him, so I read him Psalm 16. When I came to verses 9–11, he started groaning with recognition. These verses broke through his dementia and struck a chord with the faith he had sung about for over fifty years. A few hours later he died.

Preaching at Bill's funeral was easy. The family were crying and so was I, but the grief was ours and not his. None of us had any doubt about what Bill was enjoying now that his soul had left his fragile body. I shared with the congregation how he had made his last excited noises when he heard the words of the messianic promise at the end of Psalm 16. I told them that his groaning was some of the sweetest music that I had ever heard. It was his own cover version of the song he had been given to sing through the death and resurrection of Jesus the Messiah.

So sing. Sing your own cover version of Psalm 16. Jesus hands you the words of this psalm and invites you to meditate on its marvellous words. He is waiting to hear you sing it back to him as a worship song of your own.

The Promise-Keeper
(17:1–19:14)

The word of the Lord is flawless. He is a shield for all who take refuge in him.

(Psalm 18:30)

Have you ever wondered what kinds of prayers are prayed by people who bring revival to their nation? Then all you need to do is read the writings of Martin Luther's close friend Philip Melanchthon: *"I have often gone to him unawares, and found him dissolved in tears and prayers for the Church of Christ. He devoted a certain portion of almost every day to reading the Psalms of David, with which he mingled his own supplications with sighs and tears."*[1] Luther's housemate Veit Dietrich also observed that

Not a day passes in which he does not spend in prayer at least three hours, such as are most precious for study. On one occasion I chanced to hear him pray. Good Lord, what a spirit, what faith spoke out of his words! He prayed with such reverence that one could see he was speaking with God, and with such faith and such confidence as is shown by one who is speaking with his father and friend... He spoke so familiarly, so earnestly, and reverently with God, and in his prayer insisted on the promises in the Psalms, as one who was certain that everything he prayed for would be done.[2]

---

[1] Melanchthon is quoted by John Stoughton in his book *The Homes and Haunts of Luther* (1875).

[2] He wrote this in a letter to Melanchthon on 30th June 1530.

It really shouldn't surprise us that those who have spearheaded great advance for Jesus' Kingdom have usually been people who prayed through the promises in the Psalms. The New Testament tells us that this is how we should pray when it describes the early Christians calling on God to fulfil the promises of Psalm 2 in Acts 4:24–31. Athanasius grasped this when he taught fourth-century believers that,

> *No matter what you seek, whether it be repentance and confession, or help in trouble and temptation or under persecution; whether you have been set free from plots and snares or, on the contrary, are sad for any reason; whether, seeing yourself progressing and your enemy cast down, you want to praise and thank and bless the Lord; each of these things the Divine Psalms show you how to do, and in every case the words you want are written down for you, and you can say them as your own.*[3]

This explains why Psalms 17–19 are clustered together. They teach us to pray God's promises back to him because he is the Promise-Keeper.

Psalm 17 is the first of the psalms to be marked explicitly in its title as a prayer. David tells the Lord in 17:4 that he has learned to follow him by meditating on *"what your lips have commanded"*, and he demonstrates this by praying Scripture promises back to God throughout the psalm and most obviously in 17:8. He uses a very strange turn of phrase when he asks the Lord to protect him *"as the apple of your eye"*. It means the pupil of the eye, one of the most delicate and precious parts of the human body, and it is the phrase which the Lord used when he promised in the psalm which is recorded in Deuteronomy 32:10 to protect his People *"as the apple of his eye"*. David uses another unusual metaphor when he asks the Lord to *"hide me in*

---

[3] He wrote this in about 370 AD in his *Letter to Marcellinus on the Meaning of the Psalms*.

the shadow of your wings", but if we read into the next verse we discover that this is an allusion to Deuteronomy 32:11, where the Lord promises to protect his People *"like an eagle... that spreads its wings"*.[4] Don't miss the fact that David is modelling for us how to bring the promises of Psalms back to God in prayer. Psalms isn't just a great book of worship songs. It is also our manual for prayer.[5]

This leads into Psalm 18, which is perhaps the most curious psalm of them all. It is simply a repetition of a psalm which the temple worship leaders knew was already preserved in Scripture as 2 Samuel 22,[6] so it begs the question why they chose to repeat it with only minor changes instead of including one of the many psalms which never made it into the Bible. The answer is that they wanted to help us see that our prayers should be based on the psalms we find in Scripture. The Lord is the Promise-Keeper, and his Word is full of promises to stoke the fire of our prayers.

Psalm 18 is particularly crammed with great promises about the power of God's Word. It likens his voice to thunder in verse 13 and tells us it can part the oceans in verse 15. It reminds us that *"the Lord's word is flawless"* and totally reliable in verse 30,[7] helping us to pray.[8]

Psalm 19 celebrates God's world in verses 1–6 and God's Word in verses 7–14. It inspired the German philosopher

---

[4] There is yet another link back to Deuteronomy 32:15 when 17:10 tells us that the wicked are literally *enclosed in their own fat*.

[5] There is also a link back to 16:9–11 when 17:14–15 tells us that God stores up judgment for the wicked after death, but that he raises the righteous from the dead to vindicate them and grant them access to his presence.

[6] I love Psalm 18 but I will not comment on it in great detail here because I have already done so in *Straight to the Heart of 1&2 Samuel*.

[7] Verse 30 links back to 12:6 when it tells us literally that God's Word is *smelted* or *refined* like a precious metal.

[8] Paul quotes from 18:49 in Romans 15:9 to explain how *"the promises made to the patriarchs"* have been fulfilled through the Messiah coming to Israel and sending his People as missionaries to the nations.

Immanuel Kant to confess freely that *"Two things fill the mind with ever new and increasing wonder and awe, the more often and more seriously one reflects on them: the starry heavens above me and the moral law within me."*[9] David wants us to understand that God's promises aren't simply restricted to Scripture.[10] We can also glean non-stop promises about his character by looking at the wonders of creation. Paul quotes from 19:4 in Romans 10:18 to argue that everyone has heard the promises of God because creation shouts what he is like to all the earth. David turns our attention back to Scripture in verses 7–11, referring to God's Word as his *law* or *instruction*, as his *testimony* or *witness*, as his *precepts*, as his *commands*, as his *fear*, and as his *verdicts* or *rulings*. He tells us to see Scripture as *perfect, reliable, right, radiant, pure, never-past-its-sell-by-date, certain, righteous, more precious than gold* and *sweeter than honey*. He reminds us that God's promises carry with them *great reward.* If we fail to bring them back to God in prayer, we are even stupider than a man who flushes bank notes down the toilet.

That's why this cluster of three psalms ends with David asking the Lord to make the *"words of my mouth"* and the *"meditation of my heart"* pleasing to him. The root word here is *hāgāh*, the word which was used back in 1:2 to urge us to *meditate* on God's Word day and night if we want to prosper and be fruitful. That's what David did, what the early Christians did, what Athanasius did and what Martin Luther did, as they all used the promises in Psalms as the fuel which helped them to pray world-changing prayers. Martin Luther explained his faith in God the Promise-Keeper in very simple terms:

---

[9] Kant wrote this at the start of the conclusion to his *Critique of Practical Reason* (1788).

[10] Some Christians feel uncomfortable with this statement, but Scripture itself tells believers to learn about God's character by looking at the world which he has made (Matthew 6:26–28; Luke 12:24–27; 21:29).

When Jesus Christ utters a word, He opens His mouth so wide that it embraces all heaven and earth, even though that word be but in a whisper. The word of the Emperor is powerful, but that of Jesus Christ governs the universe.[11]

---

[11] This is point 230 in Martin Luther's *Table Talk*, published in 1566.

The Victor (20:1–21:13)

Now this I know: The Lord gives victory to his anointed. He answers him from his heavenly sanctuary with the victorious power of his right hand.

(Psalm 20:6)

If you have ever been to a football match, you will know that what matters isn't what fans sing at the beginning of the game but at the end. I recently went to see my favourite football team play, and I chanted with the other fans that *"West Ham United are the world's greatest football team."* Ninety minutes later, we left the ground having lost 2–0 to a team which was languishing at the bottom of the division. Needless to say, none of us were singing that song on the way home.

This appears to be why the worship leaders who compiled Psalms put these two songs immediately after David's call for us to pray to God the Promise-Keeper. Psalm 20 is traditionally viewed as the marching anthem which the Israelite army sang before a battle, and Psalm 21 is traditionally viewed as their marching anthem on the way home after winning. We can see this in the symmetry between the two psalms. Israel's troops bless their king before battle by praying in 20:4–5, *"May he give you the desire of your heart... May the Lord grant all your requests"*, and they bless the Lord on their way home by singing in 21:2, *"You have granted him his heart's desire and have not withheld the request of his lips."*[1] David has just told us to trust the Lord to keep his promises, so now he backs this up with his

---

[1] The word for *you* in 20:1–5 is singular in Hebrew. David marked this as a psalm for his troops to sing about their messianic king.

own personal example. His army often sang these two psalms because the Lord is the all-powerful Victor who cannot be thwarted by any foe who stands in his way.

David tells us firstly to expect victory from God because it is *part of his name*. There is an episode of *The Simpsons* in which Homer changes his name to "Max Power" and discovers that that his new name immediately catapults him to greatness.[2] He is promoted, meets Bill Clinton and is hailed as a major celebrity. It's just a cartoon, but it carries an important message. Everything changes when we understand God's name is "Victory". In 20:1 the soldiers sing, *"May the name of the God of Jacob protect you."* In 20:5 they equate *the name of our God* with *victory* as much as they equate their *shouting for joy* with *lifting up banners.*[3] In 20:7 they state this even more explicitly: *"Some trust in chariots and some in horses, but we trust in the name of the Lord our God."*

David tells us secondly to expect victory from God because it is *part of the Gospel*. He instructs his soldiers in 20:2–3 to base their prayer for victory on the *sacrifices* and *burnt offerings* which took place at the Tabernacle on Mount Zion, so it's important that we understand that no burnt offerings were ever offered at David's Tabernacle except on the day when it was opened. David dressed as a priest to offer those one-off sacrifices personally, instead of letting a priest from Aaron's family do so, because he was prophesying that the Messiah would be a better high priest in the order of Melchizedek.[4] That's why he puts a *selāh* at the end of 20:3, even though it comes right in the middle of a section, because he wants his troops to take some time to meditate on the Gospel as their source of victory. It's also why he asks them

51

---

[2] *The Simpsons*, Season 10, Episode 13: "Homer to the Max".

[3] They do this by using a particular feature of Hebrew poetry known as a "synonymous parallelism", in which the two lines of a verse both state the same concept in a complementary fashion.

[4] 1 Chronicles 16:1–2; Psalm 110:4; Hebrews 7:11, 27. We will look at this in more detail later in the chapter "Melchizedek".

to call him God's *anointed one* or *messiah* in 20:6, and why the word he uses for *victory* in 20:6 is *yeshū'āh*, the Hebrew name which would later be given to *Jesus*.[5]

David tells us thirdly to expect victory from God because it is *part of his character*. The Lord didn't blow with his mouth in 18:15 to part the Red Sea because his biggest challenge was how to restrict his power enough to avoid destroying the Israelites on the shore! The breath of his nostrils was enough to perform one of the greatest miracles of the Old Testament. In view of this, David tells his troops in 20:6 to sing about *God's right hand* and *victorious power* as one and the same thing. It didn't matter if the opposing army had horses and chariots – the superweapon of the ancient world – it wouldn't be able to defeat them because victory is an eternal and unchanging aspect of God's character.[6]

David's soldiers therefore had the chance to sing Psalm 21 very often. We read in 2 Samuel 5 and 8 that David led them to victory over the Jebusites, Philistines, Moabites, Arameans, Edomites, Ammonites and Amalekites. We read twice that *"The Lord gave David victory wherever he went."*[7] Imagine a football team which won every match and every trophy every week of every year. That's how it is for those who are friends with God the Victor. We have a lot to sing about.[8]

David tells his troops in 21:1-6 to sing about the victories God has already given them. He tells them to rejoice that their

---

[5] Jesus' name is normally written in Hebrew as *Yeshū'ā*, without the final *"h"*, but don't let that make you miss what David is prophesying here. The name *Jesus* can mean either *The Lord Saves* or *The Lord is Victorious*.

[6] An example of the Lord destroying a massive army of charioteers can be found in Judges 4:1–16.

[7] 2 Samuel 8:6, 14. Once again the word for *gave victory* means literally *saved*, and it is the root of the Hebrew name for Jesus. To speak about Jesus losing is a complete contradiction in terms.

[8] Verse 1 tells us literally that David *rejoices* in God's strength and *spins around with joy* at his victories. Christians who aren't genuinely excited about the Gospel probably haven't understood it.

king now wears the crowns of his former enemies, just like David in 2 Samuel 12:30 when he snatched the crown from the head of the Ammonite king and put it on his own head on the battlefield, and just like Jesus in Revelation 19:12 when he rides out wearing the crowns of his defeated enemies. David doesn't tell them to rejoice in the enemies they have slaughtered but in the fact that victory proves their Messiah has power to grant them eternal life, eternal blessings and eternal access to God's presence. Nor does David tell us to celebrate the fact that we ourselves are winners. Psalm 21 focuses on the fact that our Messiah is the Victor and that we get to participate in his victory.

This explains why David tells them in 21:7–13 to sing about God's future victories. Winston Churchill reminded one of his generals during World War Two that *"It is at the moment when the victor is most exhausted that the greatest forfeit can be exacted from the vanquished."*[9] Jesus never tires, so we must never tire of praying for further victories either. Since the Lord had promised David that his *zera'* or *offspring* would be the Messiah and conquer every nation of the world, he tells his troops not to be too easily satisfied with each little victory. He tells them to pray in 21:10 that the Lord will completely destroy the *zera'* or *offspring* of his enemies before his conquering Messiah.

"You ask, What is our policy?" Winston Churchill thundered when he became prime minister in one of the darkest moments of the war. *"You ask, What is our aim? I answer in one word: Victory – victory at all costs, victory in spite of all terror; victory, however long and hard the road may be."*[10]

So let's sing these marching songs tirelessly by faith that we are marching in the army of God the Victor.

---

[9] He wrote this in a letter to General Wavell after a victory in North Africa on 13th December 1940.

[10] He said this in a speech to the British House of Commons on 13th May 1940.

The Blood-Drenched Shepherd (22:1–23:6)

The Lord is my shepherd, I lack nothing.

BOOK I: SING ABOUT WHO GOD IS

Psalms 22 and 23 are among the best loved and most quoted psalms in the Bible. They are also two of the most misunderstood. The problem – as is so often the case when people cherry-pick verses from Psalms without stopping to think about their context – is that these two worship songs were placed together for a reason. We can't fully understand either of them without the other.

Without Psalm 22, we will misapply Psalm 23. It is the most famous psalm in the Bible and a favourite at funerals, but are its words really true for many of those who claim it as their own? Should unbelievers truly fear nothing in the valley of the shadow of death? Can they truly expect God to refresh their soul and let them dwell in the house of the Lord forever? The previous psalms suggest the opposite, promising terror and torment and judgment for anyone who has refused to surrender their life to God. Psalm 23 isn't a description of what any of us ought to expect from God. It is a song which Jesus the sinless Messiah alone deserves to sing.

At the same time, without Psalm 23, we will also misapply Psalm 22. How can the King of kings in Psalm 2 and the Victor in Psalms 20–21 possibly become the defeated and suffering prisoner who is executed in Psalm 22? It doesn't make sense if we divorce it from the psalm which follows it, so it is easy to see why the Jewish leaders ignored the message of Psalm 22 when Jesus the Messiah finally came. They had no room in their theology for a Messiah who looked weak and could be nailed to a cross by a squad of Roman soldiers. That's why we need to treat these two psalms as a pair in which each one provides the answers to the questions posed by the other.

Some Greek manuscripts of Matthew 27:35 tell us that David was a *prophet* who wrote Psalm 22 about the future crucifixion of God's Messiah.[1] It's important that we recognize that David wrote this song for somebody else to sing.[2] He was never pierced through his hands and feet (22:16), and to the best of our knowledge nobody ever cast lots to divide his clothing (22:18). Jesus treated this psalm as one which had been written for him to sing when he quoted its first verse as a prayer from the cross in Matthew 27:46: *"My God, my God, why have you forsaken me?"*[3] The truth is that all of us are like the lost sheep in Luke 15:1-7. The only reason we can sing Psalm 23 is that Jesus became the lost sheep in our place so that we might be found.

Jesus' enemies fulfilled 22:3-8 when they mocked him as he died. They unwittingly quoted from these verses in Matthew 27:39-43 when they sneered that *"He trusts in God. Let God rescue him now if he wants him."* They also fulfilled 22:12-18 when they surrounded him like beasts of prey,[4] dislocated his joints through crucifixion and refused to quench his terrible

---

[1] These words are not included in many modern translations, but they are included in the King James Version and Young's Literal Translation.

[2] He set it to a popular secular tune and labelled it for congregational singing because he wanted Israel to sing it while they waited for their Messiah. Only four psalms are quoted more often in the New Testament.

[3] He actually quoted from the Aramaic translation of 22:1. Matthew 27:45 also implies that 22:2 was fulfilled when day was turned to night as Jesus died.

[4] *Bashan* was home to the most fertile fields in Israel, so its bulls grew very fat (Deuteronomy 32:14; Amos 4:1). David likens Jesus' crucifiers to the very strongest bulls and lions.

thirst.[5] John 19:23–24 tells us that the soldiers fulfilled 22:18 when they cast lots for his clothing, and John 19:34 may describe the fulfilment of 22:14. David wrote this psalm for Jesus to sing from the cross at the Passover of 30 AD so that we would be able to sing the shepherd psalm which follows. John 1:29 describes Jesus as *"the Lamb of God, who takes away the sin of the world"*, and 1 Corinthians 5:7 describes him as *"Christ, our Passover lamb"*. We can only sing about the Lord being our shepherd because he first became the sheep which was slaughtered in our place.

Psalm 22:19–31 describes the Messiah's resurrection and ascension. Hebrews 2:12 quotes from 22:22 and tells us that this is what Jesus proclaims now that he has been raised from the dead and glorified. Only because of Jesus' sacrifice can he now build a mighty Church from *"all the families of the nations"* and from what were *"future generations"* when David wrote this psalm.[6] No wonder Jesus turned 22:31 into his victory cry as he died in John 19:30. The Greek word *tetelestai* means *"It is finished!"* but we could also translate it roughly as *"He has done it!"*

Only now are we ready to read Psalm 23 and apply it to ourselves. It makes no sense if we divorce it from Jesus' statement in John 10:11 that *"I am the good shepherd. The good shepherd lays down his life for the sheep."* We can only lie down in green pastures because Jesus lay down *"in the dust of death"* in 22:15. We can only find rest and refreshment for our souls because, in 22:2, Jesus found no rest when he bore the punishment which we deserve. We can only eat and drink from green pastures and quiet waters because he bore our thirst in

---

[5] John 19:28–29 tells us that they tormented Jesus by giving him wine vinegar which would actually make a thirsty man even thirstier. It tells us that they did this *"so that Scripture would be fulfilled"*.

[6] There is a deliberate contrast in Hebrew between *the assembly of the wicked* in 22:16 and the *great assembly* of the righteous in 22:22 and 25. The Greek word used by the Septuagint in 22:22 and 25 is *ekklēsia*, or *Church*.

22:15, and because 22:26 tells us that we get to eat and drink what we don't deserve because of what he has done. We can only fear no evil in the valley of the shadow of death because Jesus has passed that way before us and defeated death before we get there. We can only dwell in the house of the Lord forever because in 22:1 Jesus was abandoned by the Father. We can only sing Psalm 23 at all because Jesus has become our Blood-Drenched Shepherd.[7]

So enjoy Psalm 23, but enjoy it for the right reasons and in all its fullness. Through the Gospel you will have many trials (23:4), but you will lack nothing as Jesus leads you through them (23:1).[8] Through the Gospel you will make many enemies, but David promises that God will vindicate you, anoint you with the oil of his Holy Spirit, and bless you until you can be blessed no more (23:5).[9] Through the Gospel you will be pursued and persecuted, but David promises that God's goodness and covenant mercy will pursue you even harder, both in this life and for evermore (23:6).[10]

What a Saviour. What a Shepherd. And, as the temple worship leaders wanted to show us when they placed these two songs together, what a Blood-Drenched Shepherd.

---

[7] David was a shepherd-boy who risked his life to save his sheep (1 Samuel 17:34–35; Psalm 78:70–71), so he describes the Lord this way here and in 28:9. The rest of Scripture also does so in Psalms 79:13 and 80:1, Isaiah 40:11, Jeremiah 23:3–4, Ezekiel 34:11–31, John 10:11–27, Hebrews 13:20, 1 Peter 2:25 and 5:4, and Revelation 7:17.

[8] Verse 3 reminds us that our hope for God to guide us lies in his *name*, just like our hope of victory in 20:7.

[9] Although the Hebrew text talks about our cup overflowing, the Septuagint translates it as *"your cup makes me drunk like the best wine"*.

[10] David uses the same word for God's *hēsēd* following us in 23:6 as is normally used for people *pursuing* and *persecuting* God's People throughout the Old Testament.

The Indweller (24:1–28:9)

Lord, I love the house where you live, the place where your glory dwells.

(Psalm 26:8)

Everything changes when a great dignitary comes to town. My house is in the same part of London where the Pope lives whenever he is in the UK and, when he last visited, my normally quiet neighbourhood was totally transformed by the fact that he was there. If you want to understand Psalms 24–28, you have to realize that something similar happened to a hill in Jerusalem in about 1000 BC.

David loved God's Tabernacle. The Ark of the Covenant had long been forgotten and neglected, but as a shepherd-boy he often looked up at the lights of Kiriath Jearim and swore to bring it back from its obscurity there to its rightful place at the heart of Israel. Since the town lay just across the fields from Bethlehem, where David grazed his father's sheep, Psalm 132 tells us he vowed that once he became king, *"I will allow no sleep to my eyes or slumber to my eyelids, till I find a place for the Lord, a dwelling for the Mighty One of Jacob."*[1] He reaffirmed this vow in 1 Samuel 17:54 after killing Goliath, when he took the giant's head to enemy-occupied Jerusalem as a statement to the Jebusites that their city was his next target, and when he took

---

[1] *Ephrathah* was the ancient name for Bethlehem, and the word translated *Jaar* in most English Bibles was a variant of Kiriath *Jearim*, only eight miles away from Bethlehem. The Ark had been left there in 1 Samuel 7:1–2.

the giant's sword to what was left of Moses' Tabernacle at the nearby town of Nob.[2]

Sure enough, as soon as he became king, David captured Jerusalem and brought the Ark up to his new capital city. We will see later in Psalm 110 that David understood this was to be the site for a new worship centre because it had been the ancient home of the priest-king Melchizedek, whose life had pointed to the future ministry of the Messiah. That's why David didn't bring the Ark back to Moses' Tabernacle, but built a new tent for it on Mount Zion. He offered blood sacrifices as the new priest-king of Israel on the day the new Tabernacle was opened, but then commanded that no more blood be shed there in order to prophesy about the once-for-all sacrifice which would be offered by the Messiah. This new tent had no inner room and was freely accessible to any believer because the Messiah's sacrifice would bring God's presence to us all.[3] David wanted Israel to know that the time was coming when they could all know the Lord personally as God the Indweller.[4]

That's quite a lot of background, but you need it if you want to understand the cluster of five psalms which follow on from Psalms 22–23. They pick up on the double reference to the *assembly* of God's People in 22:22 and 25, and on the invitation to *"dwell in the house of the Lord forever"* in 23:6. These five psalms all focus on the importance of David's Tabernacle and they end in the same place as they started by talking about the Lord as our shepherd in 28:9. They are a description of the intimacy with God which is ours through the sacrifice of the

---

[2] Some English translations misunderstand this verse to mean that he put Goliath's sword *in his own tent*, but David was too young to have his own tent and 1 Samuel 21:8–9 clarifies that it should read *in God's tent*.

[3] This pointed to New Testament verses such as Matthew 27:51 and Hebrews 10:19–25.

[4] David's Tabernacle is explained in more detail in *Straight to the Heart of 1&2 Samuel*.

Blood-Drenched Shepherd. God the Indweller has moved into town and nothing will ever be the same again.

Psalm 24 proclaims that the Lord is King of all the earth (24:1 corresponds to 22:28).[5] It refers to him five times as *"the King of glory"* and declares that he is so great that even the mighty gates of Jerusalem are too puny to receive him (24:7–9). Even though David doesn't date the psalm in its title, it looks as though he wrote it for the day on which he finally brought the Ark of the Covenant to his new Tabernacle on Mount Zion. *"Who may ascend the mountain of the Lord? Who may stand in his holy place?"* he asks in 24:3. This psalm acts as a theme tune to 1 Chronicles 15–16.[6]

Psalm 25 is an acrostic poem with one verse for every letter of the Hebrew alphabet.[7] Since David looks back to *"the sins of my youth"*, he clearly wrote it during one of the crises which marked his older years, but it was placed here to carry on this same theme of God the Indweller.[8] It is a psalm in which David seeks guidance from the Lord (25:4–5) and expects the Lord to speak to him (25:8) because he is humble (25:9), obedient (25:10), and afraid of him (25:12). This builds up to a crescendo in which David declares that the Lord loves to share his *sōd* or *secret thoughts* with those who fear him (25:14). The Tabernacle was more than just a dwelling place for God on earth. It was a communication centre where he promised to share his thoughts with anyone who came to see him.

In Psalm 26, David tells the Lord that he hates *"the*

---

[5] Paul quotes from 24:1 in 1 Corinthians 10:26 to argue that everything belongs to the Lord. We are not to be scared of the non-Christian world, since it already belongs to the God who is our friend.

[6] The awestruck question David asks in 24:3 was probably provoked by his first and fatal attempt to bring up the Ark to Jerusalem in 1 Chronicles 15.

[7] No verse begins with the letter *waw*, so the 22nd verse begins with a repeated letter.

[8] There is a deliberate link in Hebrew between worshippers at the Tabernacle not *lifting up their souls [in trust] to* an idol in 24:4 and David's promise to *lift up his soul [in trust] to* God in 25:1.

assembly of evildoers" and loves *"the house where you live, the place where your glory dwells".* He has already told us in 22:3 that the Lord *inhabits the praises of Israel,*[9] so he now adds in 26:12 that all true believers will want to be in the place where he is worshipped too. There is no such thing as a believer who doesn't want to share his life with the rest of God's People. True believers will always say gladly, *"In the great congregation I will praise the Lord."*[10]

David models this himself in Psalm 27 by longing to hide himself away in the Lord's *dwelling place* and *sacred tent* (27:5). *"One thing I ask from the Lord, this only do I seek: that I may dwell in the house of the Lord all the days of my life, to gaze upon the beauty of the Lord."*[11] This psalm should stir our hearts to want to offer our own sacrifices of praise in the house of the Lord (27:6).[12] We are heirs to the Gospel about which these psalms prophesy, so we must not hunger any less than David for intimate fellowship with God.

Psalm 28 completes this cluster of five psalms, and it finds David away from Jerusalem but still lifting up his hands from afar *"towards your Most Holy Place".*[13] He is desperate to commune with the Lord and for God to come down from his Tabernacle to carry him to safety like a shepherd. This brings us back to where we started and to the first mention of God's

---

[9] This is one literal translation of 22:3. Another is that he is *enthroned on the praises of Israel*.

[10] When David pleads with God not to judge him like a *man of blood* in 26:9, he uses the same phrase as his accuser Shimei uses in 2 Samuel 16:7. This may mean he wrote this psalm while on the run from Absalom.

[11] 27:10 links back to 22:1. God will always answer this kind of prayer because Jesus was abandoned in our place. Even if our own parents abandon us, God the Father will always welcome us in.

[12] David speaks literally about *the sacrifices of loud joy* in 27:6. No blood sacrifices were offered at his new Tabernacle after the first day because the Gospel simply calls us to bring sacrifices of praise (51:17 and 141:2).

[13] David uses the unusual word *debir* to describe God's *Most Holy Place* in 28:2. It comes from the Hebrew verb *to speak* and reminds us that if we seek God's face, we are sure to hear his voice.

dwelling place at the end of Psalm 23. These five psalms span the different seasons of David's life but they all show the same enduring passion to spend time in the presence of the Lord.

As you read these psalms, Jesus the Blood-Drenched Shepherd invites you to devote your life to pursuing the intimate friendship with God about which David's Tabernacle prophesied. He urges you to *"Seek his face!"* in 27:8, and to ask God the Indweller to come and turn you into a new Tabernacle for his Holy Spirit. If you will let him, he promises that neither you nor your neighbourhood will ever be the same again.

The God Who Speaks
(29:1–30:12)

The voice of the Lord twists the oaks and strips the forests bare. And in his temple all cry, "Glory!"

(Psalm 29:9)

The safety pin was a very simple idea but it is still ranked among the top fifty inventions of all time.[1] It might have made its American inventor, Walter Hunt, a millionaire several times over after he patented his design in 1849. Unfortunately for him, he sold the patent in order to settle a debt of a mere fifteen dollars with a friend. He could have become one of the richest men of the nineteenth century, but instead he threw away his golden opportunity because he simply didn't realize its value.

63

The temple worship leaders who compiled Psalms were concerned that you might be like Walter Hunt when it comes to David's promises about God the Indweller. That's why they follow up with two psalms which explain the power which is unleashed when the Lord decides to make his home among us. We need to read these verses slowly because it's very easy to forget that the Lord is the God Who Speaks and that his voice is the most powerful sound in the entire universe.

David addresses the first of these two psalms to *the sons of God* in 29:1. Most English translations assume that this means *angels* or *heavenly beings*, but he may be addressing us and reminding us that through the Messiah we can become

---

[1] It is listed among the Top 30 by Rob Shaw in his book *Great Inventors and Inventions* (2003).

children of God.[2] In just eleven verses he calls God *Yahweh* or *the Lord* fourteen times and refers to *"the voice of the Lord"* a massive seven times.[3] He tells us that the Lord's voice is strong enough to control the oceans (29:3), the mighty forests (29:5), the mountains (29:6),[4] the lightning bolts (29:7), the hostile deserts (29:8)[5] and the animals (29:9).[6] It doesn't matter what floodwaters may stand in our way today (29:10), since the Lord is enthroned among his People and it only takes one word from the mouth of the King to change everything.

The word translated *temple* in 29:9 is also used in Scripture to refer to any *tabernacle* which is here to stay.[7] David therefore tells those who know God the Indweller to exclaim *"Glory!"* and recalibrate their view of what it means to be invited to be friends with the God Who Speaks. At the very least, it should inspire us to spend more time reading the Bible and meditating on what it says than we currently do. It should make us want to carve out large chunks of time in our diaries to still our busy hearts so that we can hear what the Lord wants to say to us each day.[8]

But it should also do more than that. It should build our faith that the words we speak as a result of waiting in God's

---

[2] The Greek Septuagint translates it literally as *sons of God*, and it may be a prophecy of what would later be explained in John 1:12–13, Romans 8:14–25, Galatians 3:26, Philippians 2:15 and 1 John 3:1–2.

[3] Revelation 10:3–4 may link back to this when it refers to *the voice of the seven thunders*.

[4] Deuteronomy 3:9 tells us that *Sirion* was the Sidonian name for *Mount Hermon*.

[5] The reference to *the Desert of Kadesh* is important because that was where Moses sinned in Numbers 20:1–13 by using force instead of simply speaking a faith-filled command in God's name.

[6] Although a few English translations understand 29:9 to talk about *oaks twisting*, a more accurate translation is that God's voice causes *the deer to give birth*.

[7] For example, in 1 Samuel 1:9 and 3:3, in 2 Samuel 22:7, and throughout Psalms.

[8] David warned us in 27:14 that we need to *wait in expectation* if we want to hear the voice of the Lord.

presence carry irresistible power. This psalm tells us to expect to see breakthrough all around us if we simply preach and prophesy and pray and proclaim God's Word to people. If the Lord's voice causes the deer to give birth, it will also cause people to be born again when we share the Gospel with them. If it shakes the arid deserts, it will also bring revival to the spiritual wastelands all around us. We don't have to summon up power when we proclaim the Word of God. David tells us that if we simply speak out the Word of God, we will find that mighty power is its default factory setting.

The title of Psalm 30 tells us that David wrote it for the dedication of his new Tabernacle on Mount Zion.[9] It therefore tells us how we should respond to God the Indweller now that we have a proper understanding of what it means to know that he is the God Who Speaks. He tells us to use our own voices to cry out to the Lord for help and for healing (30:2), and for mercy and for help (30:8–10). God is after a friendship in which we speak to one another and in which our voices unleash the power of his mighty voice as he responds to our prayers with a mighty echo which dwarfs our own voices. He tells us to use our voices to exalt the Lord (30:1), to sing praises to the Lord (30:4), to express our faith in the Lord (30:6), to reason with the Lord (30:9) and to express our uninhibited delight in the Lord (30:11–12). The God Who Speaks is looking for followers who will speak back to him, because our weak voices unleash the power of his mighty voice so that we can speak with voices as powerful as his own.

Think about it. God made Adam so that he could talk with him in the cool of the day and gave him authority to speak names over all the animals.[10] God spoke to Abraham while he was still

---

[9] It tells us that the psalm is a *"song for the dedication of the house"*, and David would only ever refer to one dwelling place as **the** house. This ties in with his talk of the Lord establishing Zion as his *mountain* in 30:7. The reference to his dancing in 30:12 also ties in with 2 Samuel 6:14–23.

[10] Genesis 2:19–20; 3:8–9.

worshipping idols in Mesopotamia and gave him power to shape the course of world history through his prayers.[11] He spoke to Moses at the burning bush and commissioned him to deliver Israel from slavery by speaking to Pharaoh in his name.[12] He promised a bunch of Galilean fishermen and tax collectors that he would speak to them and give them such great power that when they proclaimed the Gospel to the nations they would surrender to the Messiah as King. *"What I tell you in the dark, speak in the daylight; what is whispered in your ear, proclaim from the roofs,"* Jesus simply instructed his disciples in Matthew 10:27. He still gives this same commission to us today as a new generation of ambassadors for the God Who Speaks. The great eighteenth-century revivalist George Whitefield took this verse seriously and described it as the secret to his preaching which led tens of thousands of listeners to salvation:

66

> *Had we a thousand hands and tongues, there is employment enough for them all: people are everywhere ready to perish for lack of knowledge... Oh, let us stir up that gift of God, and with all boldness preach him to others. Freely we have received, freely let us give; what Christ tells us by his Spirit in our closets, that let us proclaim on the house top. He who sends will protect us. All the devils in hell shall not hurt us, till we have finished our testimony.*[13]

---

[11] Genesis 12:1–3; 18:16–33. God wouldn't even heal a Philistine king in 20:7 without first requiring Abraham to unleash his power through prayer.

[12] Exodus 3:4; 4:10–12; 6:28–7:2.

[13] He wrote this in a letter to a friend on 10th November 1739.

What to Sing on Sundays (31:1–33:22)

For the director of music... A teaching psalm.

(Psalms 31 and 32, titles)

Some people just can't get enough of fly-on-the-wall documentaries. The TV schedule seems to be full of programmes in which camera crews follow round police officers and customs officials and doctors and business leaders to see how they spend their day. No matter how much we read about their professions, there is no substitute for being able to watch them as they go about their work. That's why I'm so grateful that we have Psalms 31–33. They are a fly-on-the-wall view of the worship which was sung at David's Tabernacle.

67

The New Testament teaches us relatively little about the way that churches should structure their worship today. Arthur Patzia writes that *"The challenge of writing about worship in the early Church is not unlike the work of a detective gathering pieces of evidence to solve a crime or a person attempting to assemble a complicated jigsaw puzzle."*[1] People who like rock music argue that worship should be loud. People who like classical music argue it should be reflective. People who like techno argue it should be a non-stop party. People who like poetry or art argue that there should be more room for experimenting with new ways of worship. All agree – at least in theory – that in the end it should be God who gets to decide the kind of worship that he wants us to bring, but in the end his tastes sound suspiciously

---

[1] Arthur Patzia in *The Emergence of the Church* (2001).

like their own. Psalm 31 is marked for the chief musician to use in the Tabernacle, and Psalm 32 is marked as a *maskīl*, which means a *psalm of instruction* or a *teaching psalm*.[2] These three psalms are intended to give us a fly-on-the-wall view of the kind of worship which is music to God's ears.

Psalm 31 is a cry of anguish and a prayer for deliverance. It tells us that the Lord doesn't want our Sunday worship to be a time of happy-clappy pretending that we are doing better than we actually are. This is important because many worship leaders feel under pressure to deliver an upbeat, feel-good time of worship to their congregations every Sunday. David warns us that a good time of worship as far as God is concerned is simply one in which we express to him together whatever is on our hearts. Jesus loved this psalm so much that he used a quotation from 31:5 as his last words on the cross in Luke 23:46 before he died.[3] If this is the kind of worship which is music to God's ears, we need to rethink our song choice and even to write new kinds of song. A church which never sings songs of lament and confusion and desperation is not like the congregation which David gathered at the Tabernacle on Mount Zion.[4]

But Psalm 31 also teaches us that songs of anguish mustn't end the same way that they begin. David confesses in 31:10 that some of his troubles have been caused by his own sin.[5] He hands his life over to the Lord in 31:5 and 15 with a confession

---

[2] This is the first of 13 *teaching psalms*. The others are 42, 44–45, 52–55, 74, 78, 88–89 and 142. Unusually for Book I, Psalm 33 has no title. Since 32:11 leads well into 33:1, it may be that they were originally one psalm.

[3] The rest of the psalm therefore also points to Jesus. He was rejected like David in 31:11–12, and the only other place in the Bible which uses the same Hebrew word as 31:13 for *conspiring* is the messianic Psalm 2:2.

[4] The word used for God's *dwelling place* in 31:20 is the same word that is used in Amos 9:11 and Acts 15:16 to describe God's desire to rebuild *David's fallen tent* through the Church.

[5] The Hebrew word *'āwōn* means *iniquity* or *guilt*, but some English translators are so surprised that frank confession of sin should form part of this worship song that they mistranslate it as *poverty* or *affliction*.

that the Lord has the right to choose at any time whether he lives, prospers, suffers or dies. He ends in 31:19–24 with trust that the Lord has goodness and mercy in store for us just around the corner. He does what Paul instructs us to do in Ephesians 5:19 by telling us to turn to one another in 31:23 and stir one another to keep on loving and trusting in the Lord. Matt and Beth Redman wrote this kind of worship song after suffering a miscarriage:

> *Blessed be Your name on the road marked with suffering,*
> *Though there's pain in the offering, Blessed be Your*
>   *name.*
> *You give and take away, You give and take away,*
> *My heart will choose to say, Lord, blessed be Your*
>   *name.*[6]

Psalm 32 tells us that confession of sin should also be a feature in our corporate times of worship. This is the second of the seven penitential psalms and it reminds us we are often better at singing that we are forgiven than we are at singing for forgiveness. David marks this as a teaching psalm because our worship gatherings are God's prime-time opportunity to teach the community of believers how to pray. This psalm warns us that there are many different types of sin (32:1–2),[7] that failure to confess them is spiritual suicide (32:3–5), that God's offer of forgiveness will not last forever (32:6) and that those who are forgiven must live differently as a result (32:8–10),[8] full

---

[6] Extract taken from the song "Blessed Be Your Name" by Matt & Beth Redman. Copyright © 2002 Thankyou Music. They tell their story in a book of the same name (2005).

[7] David uses four different words for sin in 32:1–2. *Pesha'* means *transgression* or doing what we shouldn't; *hatā'āh* means *sin* or not doing what we should; *'āwōn* means *iniquity* or twisting what is good; *remīyāh* means *deceit* in order to cover up the other three.

[8] The word for *you* in 32:8–10 is singular in Hebrew, so this must be the Lord addressing the forgiven worshipper and warning that true repentance is proved

of praise towards the God who has forgiven them (32:11). Paul quotes from 32:1–2 in Romans 4:6–8 as a sign that confession of sin should still feature highly in our worship songs.

Psalm 33 is an exuberant song of celebration which reminds us that our worship should engage our minds, our emotions and our bodies. David calls us literally in 33:1–3 to *shout for joy*, to *praise*, to *throw out worship*, to *make music*, to *sing* and to *play skilfully* on musical instruments. Having warned us that our corporate worship times must not be a non-stop noisy celebration, he now challenges us that they must not be anything less than this at times either. There are times to weep and times to confess, but there are also times to raise the roof with our uninhibited praise. He even calls in 33:3 for space to be made for spontaneous new songs to be sung. David's Tabernacle was known as a place of great joy, and so must our churches be today.[9]

But Psalm 33:4–22 reminds us that worship leaders need to do more than simply exhort people to look a bit happier. The bulk of this psalm contains a list of reasons which help stir us to worship as we should. David reminds us that we should rejoice in the Lord because of his Word (33:4), because of his character (33:4–5), because of his works (33:6–9), because of his sovereign power (33:10–11) and because of his great purposes (33:12–19).

Louie Giglio warns that,

> *Songs alone don't change people. It's the truth that sets us free... If we're not careful, we can quickly inhale the feelings and emotion we experience in corporate worship, only to go away with little lasting and substantive change in our souls. In other words, we are prone to joyfully utter the words of praise, while continually dodging the*

---

by our subsequent actions (Luke 3:8; Acts 26:20).

[9] 1 Chronicles 15:16, 28–29; Psalm 27:6.

sword of the Spirit. As a result, our worship becomes a counterfeit shell while our hidden heart fails to embrace His truth for our lives.[10]

David teaches us that effervescent worship must always be grounded in the Word of God if it is to effect a lasting change in our lives.

So there we have it. A fly-on-the-wall view of what kind of worship took place in David's Tabernacle on Mount Zion. As we sing songs of anguish, confession and Scripture-based celebration, we make our worship services sweet music to God's ears.

---

[10] He writes this in a collection of essays by various worship leaders edited by Matt Redman and entitled *Inside-Out Worship* (2005).

Testimony (34:1–22)

This poor man called, and the Lord heard him; he saved him out of all his troubles.

(Psalm 34:6)

The only things that seem to be on TV more than fly-on-the-wall documentaries are reality TV shows. Whether it's *Who Do You Think You Are?* which explores someone's past, or *Big Brother* which records every moment of their present, or *The Voice* which promises to open up an exciting future for them, it's easy to get addicted. Nothing seems to grab our attention faster and for longer than somebody's life story. That's why Psalm 34 records another thing which used to take place in David's Tabernacle on Mount Zion. The Lord loved to hear worshippers taking the time to share about their own life story.

This is the fourth psalm so far which David has dated in its title. He tells us that he sang this song for the first time when he foolishly fled into Philistine territory while on the run from King Saul. He was mad not to trust the Lord to keep him safe in his desert hiding place in Judah, and he was even madder to cross the border into Philistia still carrying their defeated champion Goliath's massive sword. He wrote Psalm 56 when the Philistine king summoned him to the palace and he wrote Psalm 34 when the Lord got him away from the palace alive.[1] Rather than putting the two songs together, the editors of Psalms put this

---

[1] 1 Samuel 21:10–15 calls the Philistine king *Achish* which means *I Will Terrify*. David calls him by his royal name *Abimelek* since that means *My Father Is King* and therefore fits better with his testimony. Genesis 20:2, 21:32 and 26:1 suggest that *Abimelek* was a Philistine royal title, like *Caesar* or *Pharaoh* in Rome and Egypt.

one here as a further lesson in what kind of worship took place in God's tent on Mount Zion. They want to teach us how to share our personal testimonies in a way which is music to God's ears.

First, David teaches us to take time to write down our testimony. Psalm 34 is an acrostic poem in which twenty-two verses each begin with successive letters of the Hebrew alphabet.[2] Such poems are incredibly difficult to write, so it reminds us that a poorly crafted testimony does not bring the maximum glory to God. If God is as great as Psalms says he is, how we share about his work in our lives deserves our most careful preparation. When 1 Peter 3:15 tells us to *"Always be prepared to give an answer to everyone who asks you to give the reason for the hope that you have,"* it does so because it genuinely expects us to prepare.[3] David doesn't mark this song for congregational singing because each one of us needs to write down a song of our own.[4]

Second, David remembers not to go into excessive detail. We all find the intricacies of our own spiritual journey fascinating, but David is too focused on the effect his testimony will have on others to act like a longwinded raconteur. He doesn't mention his trip to Nob to get Goliath's sword, his arrival in Gath or any of the details of his temporary imprisonment. It is clear from 34:1–3 that he doesn't want anything to detract from his testimony bringing glory to the Lord and stirring his listeners to exalt God's name with him.[5] His focus in 34:2 is on helping *"the afflicted"* to come to faith, and so must ours be.

---

[2] The Hebrew letter *waw* is actually missing, so the final line begins with a repeated letter.

[3] Peter also quotes from 34:8 in 1 Peter 2:3 and from 34:12–16 in 1 Peter 3:10–12.

[4] John 19:36 tells us that 34:20 was part of the song which Jesus sang on the cross, since not one of his bones was broken during the crucifixion.

[5] In 34:3, David literally tells those who hear him to *magnify* the Lord with him (see also 35:27; 40:16; 69:30; 70:4; 138:2). A magnifying glass doesn't make objects bigger; it just makes them *appear bigger*. David is determined to give his hearers a bigger view of God through his testimony.

Third, David places the focus on God and not on himself. If I were David, honestly, I would be rather proud of myself for getting away from the king's palace safely. He had used his best acting skills to pretend to be a madman and had pulled his role off so convincingly that King Abimelek had him deported back to Israel. I would have tried to claim an Oscar or at the very least have boasted about my stage success to my friends back home, but David doesn't. He states what happened briefly in the title so that we can locate this song in his life story, but he doesn't mention his own clever ruse at all in the twenty-two verses of the psalm. *"This poor man called, and the Lord heard him; he saved him out of all his troubles,"* he simply explains. We tend to focus too much on ourselves when we share our testimonies, so David models for us that we need to put God in his rightful place on centre-stage. That is the kind of testimony which creates faith in the hearts of those who listen and which is music to God's ears.

Fourth, David doesn't underestimate the power of his personal story. Many people complain that they don't have much of a testimony to share at all, particularly if they were saved at a very young age. If you feel that way, note that David was probably saved even younger than you were and that by the time he wrote this psalm in his twenties he was probably as squeaky-clean as anyone in Israel. If we are not careful, our reticence to share our testimony betrays a view that we didn't need saving as much as other people. David, in contrast, freely confesses that he was nothing but a *"poor man"* in need of a Saviour. It doesn't matter that you weren't a drug dealer, gang leader, prostitute or pimp before you started following Jesus. You were a sinner who deserved hell but who was delivered by the unwarranted grace of God, and you shouldn't hesitate to say so.

Fifth, David is very clear that he is telling his testimony for a reason. He wants to glorify God and he wants to stir his listeners to glorify God with him. Don't miss the way he constantly makes appeals to his listeners throughout his story. He addresses *"the afflicted"* and asks them to join him in worship (34:2–3), then he asks the *"holy people"* in the Tabernacle to *"taste and see that the Lord is good"* for themselves (34:8–10). He addresses the children and tells them that his testimony reveals the secret to a long and happy life (34:11–16),[6] then he turns to *"the broken-hearted"* and the *"crushed in spirit"* to promise them that *"no one who takes refuge in God will be condemned"* (34:17–22).[7] In all of this, David is ruthlessly focused on moving his audience to faith and towards experiencing God for themselves.[8] A chance to share our testimony isn't five fame-filled minutes on a platform but a chance to use our past experiences to transform the lives of others.

So if you are a worship leader or a church leader, make room for testimonies in your times of worship. Give people opportunities to glorify the Lord by testifying to what he has done in their lives.

And if you are a worshipper, make time to prepare your testimony before the chance comes to share it. Plan it, shorten it, focus it on God, and make sure it calls those who hear it to take action. Put God centre-stage in your story, where he belongs, and you will discover what the Lord promises about our battle against the Devil in Revelation 12:11:

> *They triumphed over him by the blood of the Lamb and by the word of their testimony.*

---

[6] David was only in his twenties when he wrote this, so he appears to be addressing actual children rather than simply using the word as an old man addressing a younger audience.

[7] David didn't know it when he wrote this psalm, but the Lord who delivered him from Gath would later deliver Gath into his hands in 1 Chronicles 18:1 and let him *blot out his enemies' names* as promised in 34:16.

[8] Verse 8 goes together with John 7:17. Faith only comes when we step out to taste and see if God is there.

The Avenger (35:1–28)

Contend, Lord, with those who contend with me;
fight against those who fight against me.

(Psalm 35:1)

A few weeks ago, I went to a Diamond Jubilee garden party with the Queen. She stood there politely next to the food for the entire afternoon and even let my children have their photo taken with her. Then it started raining and she got soggy because we forgot to bring her inside. She was the same height as the Queen and she looked like the Queen, but she was only a two-dimensional life-sized cardboard cut-out of the Queen.

Many Christians worship a two-dimensional cardboard cut-out of the Lord. They haven't read enough of the Bible to know him as he really is, and they get offended when their false god starts to wilt under the changing weathers of this world. That's why we need to move on from the series of psalms which teach us what kind of worship songs are music to God's ears, to focus once more on the character of the Lord. We need to make sure we are singing about who God really is.

Psalm 35 is what is known as an "imprecatory psalm" – a psalm which calls down curses on the psalmist's enemies. We saw a hint of this in Psalm 5, but this is the first out-and-out imprecatory psalm so far. People who worship a two-dimensional cardboard cut-out of God get very offended because they aren't used to seeing God as the Avenger. If these words don't offend them, they will be offended when Psalm 137 tells God's enemies that, *"Happy is the one who seizes your infants and dashes them against the rocks."*[1] We mustn't forget that where Scripture offends us the most is the place where we have the most yet to learn about the character of God.

Psalm 35 reminds us that *God takes sin very seriously*. We don't know when David wrote this song, but we can tell that he was ill (35:13) and that those he thought were his friends used this as their moment to attack him in his weakness. They were so unfair towards him that Jesus quoted from 35:19 on the night of his betrayal in John 15:25 to tell his disciples that, just like David, his enemies *"hate me without reason"*. Jesus' quotation from this psalm helps us not to fall into the trap of thinking that God's character has changed between the Old Testament and the New. I remember sharing with a work colleague about a man who had inadvertently been killed when his wife tried to commit suicide because she discovered he was having an affair, and my colleague retorted that, *"That's a bit Old Testament, isn't it?!"*[2] Psalms like this one remind us that God takes sin exceedingly seriously – whether in the Old Testament or in the New, in Acts 8:18–20, in 1 Corinthians 16:22, in Galatians 1:9, or almost anywhere in Revelation.[3]

Psalm 35 reminds us that *God is a warrior*. We are so used to worship songs which sound like a girl band singing about how great their latest boyfriend is that we tend to forget Moses sang in Exodus 15:3 that *"the Lord is a man of war"* and that Jesus rides out in Revelation 19 *"dressed in a robe dipped in blood"* and holding *"a sharp sword with which to strike down the nations".* The people who are cursed in the imprecatory psalms are never

---

[1] When ancient armies sacked a city, they threw babies down from the walls so that they would not grow up to avenge their city (Isaiah 13:16; Hosea 10:14; 13:16). The Jews in Babylon are simply praying that God will be their Avenger and repay the wicked men who murdered their much-loved children.

[2] The Lord talks repeatedly in Psalms about the wicked falling into their own traps which they have laid (7:15–16; 9:15–16; 35:7–8; 37:14–15; 57:6; 141:10). He also does so in Proverbs 1:18, 26:27 and 28:10.

3 Psalm 7:11 told us literally that *God is a righteous judge and God is indignant every day*. 9:12 called God literally *the seeker of blood*.

simply personal enemies of the psalmists. They are only ever people who have rejected God's authority and his commands in order to set themselves up in defiance of his claim to be Lord of all the earth. Frankly, if we have a problem with God judging those who blaspheme his name, it demonstrates that our hearts are still fighting on the wrong side of the battlefield. It isn't a mark of virtue for us to be offended by the violent language of these psalms. It is proof of our indulgent attitude towards rebellion against the Lord.

Psalm 35 reminds us that *we are not to take revenge ourselves*. Note that carefully, because the common complaint against the imprecatory psalms is that they don't sound very forgiving. They don't sound very much like Jesus praying on the cross in Luke 23:34, *"Father, forgive them, for they do not know what they are doing,"* or like Stephen praying as he was stoned to death in Acts 7:60, *"Lord, do not hold this sin against them."* Actually, it is only a three-dimensional understanding of forgiveness which can help us to forgive like Jesus or Stephen. How can the man whose daughter was raped forgive her rapist? By pretending it doesn't matter? No! By leaving the task of retribution with the avenging God in an imprecatory prayer. By praying to the one who promises us in Deuteronomy 32:35–36 that *"It is mine to avenge; I will repay... Their day of disaster is near... The Lord will vindicate his people."* Paul quotes from those verses in Romans 12 and tells us that the key to forgiving evil is to *"Leave room for God's wrath."* We can only truly forgive when we recognize that God is our Avenger.

Psalm 35 reminds us that *this is how humble people pray*. David tells us in 35:10 that these prayers are for people who recognize that they are *"poor and needy"* and wicked people are *"too strong for them"*. He tells us in 35:13–14 that these are the kind of prayers which are offered by people who fast and put on sackcloth to ask the Lord to put an end to the suffering which persists in the world and which can only be rectified through prayer. When we pick up the critic's pen to complain that the God who inspired this psalm is too harsh and vindictive for our twenty-first-century tastes, we simply prove that we are proud like David's enemies. Instead, we need to pick up the student's pen and to start taking notes on the character of the real God in all his glory.

Psalm 35 promises us that *our prayers for justice will be answered*. If David wrote this psalm when he was betrayed by his son Absalom and his close friend Ahithophel, as seems likely, we need to remember that both men died horribly in 2 Samuel 17–18. David mourned for them both, but he recognized that the Lord's salvation is three-dimensional. He reminds us of this by using the word *salvation* to describe the destruction of his enemies in 35:3 and 9, by using the word which is normally translated *justice* to mean *vindication* in 35:23–24, and by using the same word in 35:27–28 for both God's *righteousness* and his *vindication*.[4] We need to be very careful what we wish for whenever we criticize the imprecatory psalms. God is our Avenger and the psalmists expect us to welcome that as very good news.[5]

So when we pray as Jesus instructed us in Matthew 6:10, *"Let your kingdom come, your will be done, on earth as it is in heaven,"* let's be aware of what we are praying for. We are asking him to be God in all his three-dimensional glory. We are simply asking him to do what it takes to enforce justice on the earth and to bring his salvation to the world.

---

[4] The verb used in 35:28 is *hāgāh*, so David isn't so much promising he will *proclaim* God's righteousness as *meditate* on it. We need to meditate on God's character until the imprecatory psalms cease to offend us.

[5] Although it is not used in this psalm, the Hebrew word *gō'ēl* also means both *Redeemer* and *Avenger*. A three-dimensional view of God's character understands that these are two aspects of the same message of salvation.

The Judge (36:1–37:40)

The Lord laughs at the wicked, for he knows their day is coming.

The temple worship leaders thought that you might still have a problem with the language which is used in the imprecatory psalms. That's why they followed up Psalm 35 with two psalms which talk about God's judgment on the wicked. The first line in these two psalms is David's statement that *"I have a message from God in my heart concerning the sinfulness of the wicked."*[1] It tells us that there isn't any wriggle room for us to gloss over the message of the imprecatory psalms. Psalms 36–37 contain a God-given message for anyone who wants to truly know the Lord. They are part and parcel of what it means for us to sing about who God really is.

Almost all the titles of the psalms in Book I tell us that they are psalms of David, but the title of Psalm 36 is peculiar in that it tells us it is a psalm *"of David the servant of the Lord"*. No other title describes him in this way except for Psalm 18, and it is meant to remind us that there is a great conflict raging on earth between those who submit to God's Word and those who don't. This song returns to the two contrasting camps of the righteous and the wicked which David described at the very start of the book in Psalm 1. God will judge between the

---

[1] The Hebrew word *ne'um* in 36:1 means *to speak as a prophet*. It is only ever used elsewhere in the Old Testament to describe either God or one of his anointed prophets prophesying.

righteous and the wicked, and he warns us that our reaction to that last imprecatory psalm indicates which side we are on.

Psalm 36:1–4 describes the character of the wicked. They are unafraid of God (36:1)[2] and convinced of their own innocence (36:2), yet they speak forth lies and act with folly (36:3) because they do not hate sin as much as David did in Psalm 35. Their tolerance is not a virtue.

Psalm 36:5–9 contrasts this with the character of the Lord. His covenant mercy and his faithfulness are so great that they fill the entire earth and start to stack up all the way to the sky. His righteousness (remember, this is the same word which David used in the previous psalm for God's vindication) is so great that it rivals Mount Everest, and his justice (another word which David used in the previous psalm for vindication) is so vast that it rivals the deepest trenches in the Pacific Ocean. We must not dare to question God's love and mercy because of the violent language in some of the psalms. His character should be our refuge (36:7), our nutrition (36:8)[3] and our life (36:9). It should never be the source of our embarrassment. David marked this psalm for congregational singing because he wants us to pray the words of 36:10–12 as we side with the Lord against the wicked.

We are not told whether David wrote Psalm 37 at the same time as this, but the temple worship leaders clearly placed them together for a reason. It is easy to see why Psalms is grouped as one of the five books of wisdom literature in the Old Testament, because this second song deals with the thorny question of why God hasn't yet judged between the righteous and the wicked.[4]

---

[2] Paul quotes this verse in Romans 3:18 to describe the utter sinfulness of humankind.

[3] The word David uses for *delights* in 36:8 is *Eden*. This river links back to Genesis 2:10–14 and Psalm 1:3, and forward to Psalm 46:4, Ezekiel 47:1–12, John 7:37–39 and Revelation 22:1–2.

[4] Our Bibles place the five books of Old Testament wisdom literature together – Job, Psalms, Proverbs, Ecclesiastes and Song of Songs.

David wrote it in his old age shortly before he died (37:25)[5] and he crafted it ornately as another acrostic poem.[6] This psalm is the second longest in Book I so there is nothing trite or simplistic about his answer. He has crafted it to teach us how to live in a world where the wicked often seem to prosper in the short run.

Psalm 37 reinforces the message of Psalm 35 that it is very good news for us that the Lord is God the Judge. *"Do not fret because of those who are evil or be envious of those who do wrong,"* it begins. We mustn't despair when we see the wicked succeeding (37:7), getting wealthy (37:16) and flourishing in the lap of luxury (37:35), because *"like the grass they will soon wither, like green plants they will soon die away"*. Our imprecatory prayers for justice will soon be answered and those who live as if God is a weak and indulgent uncle will suddenly meet him as he really is, as God the Judge.

David tells us that it hasn't escaped the Lord's notice that the wicked sin (37:1) and scheme (37:7) and plot (37:12) and fight (37:14) and swindle (37:21) and murder (37:32). He has logged every single one of their evil deeds and has appointed a day when he will judge them and destroy them. They may laugh at the idea of a God of judgment and prefer to create their own two-dimensional cardboard cut-out of the Lord, but David tells us that *"the Lord laughs at the wicked, for he knows their day is coming"* (37:13). They may flourish like grass but the Lord is dusting off his lawnmower to cut them down.

That's why it is so important that we understand that destruction is part of the message of salvation, that vengeance is part of redemption, and that vindication is part of justice. Without this three-dimensional grasp of God's character, we

---

[5] Experience is a poor teacher of theology without God's Word, but David reminds us in 37:25–26 and 37:35–36 that if our theology does not work out in experience, we may have misunderstood God's Word!

[6] There are 40 verses but only 22 letters in the Hebrew alphabet because our verse divisions do not fully follow the structure of the acrostic poem.

will fret and worry and complain, and we will end up sinning by maligning God's character because we are actually worshipping an idol. Because the real God is the Judge, we can expect our own actions to be logged in the annals of heaven too. He will ensure that we receive the desires of our heart (37:3–4),[7] the reward of our faith (37:5–6), the fruit of our humility (37:11), a return on our generosity (37:25–26) and the blessing which comes from our meditation on his Word (37:30–31).[8] David isn't saying that we can earn these things which come through trusting in him, delighting in him, committing ourselves to him and taking refuge in him. He is simply saying that these will come to anyone who receives the Gospel and breaks ranks with the wicked to become part of God's holy People.

David therefore urges us repeatedly in this psalm to *be still* and to *wait* for the day when God's judgment comes. No sportsman worth his salt starts to panic when he sees the half-time score, and no friend of God must panic as they wait for God's final whistle to be blown. 37:28 tells us literally that *"the Lord loves justice; he will not abandon his holy ones"*.[9] David tells us to worship the Lord because he is the God of Justice. He is the three-dimensional Saviour that the human race is longing for.

---

[7] One of the recurring themes in this psalm is that of the *Promised Land* in 37:3, 9, 11, 22, 27, 29 and 34. Jesus quotes from 37:11 in Matthew 5:5 and tells us that the Old Testament promise of a small strip of land for Israel has been upgraded in Christ to encompass the whole earth. See also Romans 4:13.

[8] Like Proverbs, these verses of wisdom are not saying that we will never see hunger or failure or disaster. That would contradict 2 Corinthians 11:23–28. They are simply stating a general principle of what will happen in this life. If it doesn't, we can expect an even greater vindication in the age to come.

[9] This verse follows the structure of a Hebrew "synthetic parallelism" and tells us that it would be unjust, and therefore unthinkable, for the Lord to abandon any believer by not avenging and vindicating them.

The Healer (38:1–41:13)

I said, "Have mercy on me, Lord; heal me, for I have sinned against you."

(Psalm 41:4)

God likes healing people. A lot. The fact that this is even debated in Christian circles is simply a sign of how much we need to learn to worship God as he really is. The temple worship leaders who compiled Psalms were determined not to end Book I without stating this unchanging aspect of God's character. Psalms 38–41 are all united by a common theme that the Lord is God the Healer.

Jesus heals people on just about every page of the gospels. The apostles follow suit in Acts. But God had already healed enough people by the time of David for him to have grounds to tell Israel to worship him as their Healer. He had healed every Israelite when Moses led them out of Egypt so that they could make the long journey across the desert.[1] He had revealed himself to them as *Yahweh Rophek* or *The Lord Who Heals You* as soon as they arrived on the far side of the Red Sea. He had healed them when they were struck by a plague of venomous snakes in the desert. He had healed Job of a terrible skin disease. He had healed David's own great-grandmother Ruth.[2] So it shouldn't

---

[1] Exodus does not tell us about this healing miracle but the book of Psalms does. The Septuagint translates the Hebrew of 105:37 as *"amongst their tribes not one of them was sick"*.

[2] Exodus 15:26; Numbers 21:4–9; Ruth 4:13. The Lord *"enabled her to conceive"* because she had been infertile for ten years while married to her first husband.

surprise us that the four final psalms of Book I were intended to teach Israel to worship God for his promises to heal them.

The title of Psalm 38 marks it as a *reminder psalm*. Most English translators assume that it is God who needs reminding, so they translate it as a *petition*, but it could just as easily mean that we are the ones who need reminding that God is the Healer. David tells us in 38:1–4 that he is very ill because he has sinned, which makes this the third penitential psalm so far. He isn't saying that sickness is always caused by sin, but he is showing us that healing is a part of our salvation and that it is good for confession to accompany healing prayer.[3] David describes his physical and emotional sickness in graphic terms in 38:5–14, then confesses his sins and cries out to God the Healer in 38:15–22.

David may have written Psalm 39 at the same time, because we find him still sick and still confessing his sin. We should draw comfort from the fact that he not only marks this song for congregational singing but also dedicates it to Jeduthun, who was one of the main worship leaders at the Tabernacle.[4] If David was not embarrassed to have prayed for healing but not yet been healed, then nor should we be. When Jesus prayed for a blind man to be healed and only saw partial healing, he didn't get discouraged but simply prayed a second time until he was fully healed.[5] When David prayed for healing and saw no miracle, he didn't get discouraged but simply prayed a second prayer.

---

[3] Jesus specifically tells us that sick people are not necessarily guiltier than anyone else (John 9:2–3), but the New Testament also tells us that sin and sickness can sometimes go hand in hand (John 5:14; 1 Corinthians 11:29–32; James 5:15–16).

[4] *Jeduthun* simply means *The Praise Man*, and we will see later on in Psalm 89 that this was probably a nickname for Ethan. He led a division of worshippers at the Tabernacle (1 Chronicles 6:31–48).

[5] Mark 8:22–26. His command to the man not to go back into the village hints that the healing took longer to come because the people of Bethsaida lacked faith (Matthew 11:21). This may well be our problem too.

David confesses in 39:1–6 that his period of sickness has given him time to meditate on the fragility of human life compared to God. We must not forget that the Lord can use the time we spend waiting for healing to great effect, weaning us off the delights of this passing age and onto him alone. David confesses his sin and pleads a second time for healing in 39:7–12.[6]

This second prayer was clearly answered. He appears to have written Psalm 40 shortly afterwards and, even if he didn't, the temple worship leaders put it here to teach us what we can expect to happen when we pray to God for healing.[7] David rejoices in 40:1–5 that the Lord has lifted him *"out of the slimy pit, out of the mud and mire"*. If we are in any doubt that this refers to the sickness he prayed about in Psalms 38–39, he clarifies this by referring in 40:5 to the *miraculous deeds* which the Lord performed to deliver him.[8] Here we can read about some of the benefits which are ours when the Lord heals us. David has a *"new song"* to sing about the Lord as God the Healer (40:3). He has a new understanding about the coming Messiah, whose body would be broken so that ours can be healed (40:6–8).[9] He has a fresh testimony of God's goodness to share at the Tabernacle (40:9–10). He also has fresh faith to ask the Lord to perform more miracles in his life, based on what he has just seen (40:11–17). The words for *saving acts* and *righteousness* in

---

[6] A two-dimensional view of God assumes that, when he looks at us, all we will ever receive is blessing. David knew enough about God the Judge and about his own sin to pray that God would look away from him in 39:13.

[7] They also repeat 40:13–17 as the separate Psalm 70, for us to use when we are not praying about healing.

[8] The Hebrew verb *pālā'* is the same word which Gideon uses in Judges 6:13 to ask when the Lord is going to renew his *miraculous deeds* for those who follow him. We need to pray a similar prayer about healing.

[9] Hebrews 10:5–7 quotes from 40:6–8 and says it was a prophecy about Jesus. Although the Hebrew text is a bit ambiguous, the New Testament endorses the Septuagint and tells us David grasped that the Messiah would sacrifice his *body* so that our bodies could be healed. Matthew 8:16–17 teaches something very similar.

40:9–10 are almost the same in Hebrew. David has learned that healing is part of our salvation, and it simply whets his appetite for more.

Psalm 41 appears to date from when David was on the run from Absalom, since Jesus quoted 41:9 to describe his own similar experience of betrayal at the hands of Judas Iscariot in John 13:18.[10] Once again, David promises that God sustains the sick and heals them so they can get up from their bed of illness (41:3). Once again, he links prayer for healing with frank confession of sin (41:4), and once again he talks openly about how easy it is to grow discouraged while we wait to be healed (41:7–9). I honestly don't know why God heals some people quickly and yet with other people it takes a lot more time. Last week two of my close friends prayed for one another: one of them was instantly healed of a back condition and it has not returned, yet the other one was not healed of a serious ear condition. Even while I have been writing this chapter, he has been texting me and we have been arranging to meet up again on Sunday to pray some more. Why was one of my friends healed while the other one wasn't? I simply don't know. All I know is that David tells me to keep on praying to God the Healer, and warns me not to play into the enemy's hands by giving up on faith for healing (41:10–12).

We have reached the end of Book I of Psalms, but we have only just started to apply its call to sing about who God is. David ends with a doxology, a concluding verse of praise, in 41:13.[11] Let's also take time to stop and worship before we move on to Book II, and let's keep praying big prayers to God the Healer.

We have learned to sing about who God really is. When we do so, it is music to God's ears.

---

[10] David's close friend Ahithophel betrayed him by siding with Absalom and became a prophetic picture of Judas Iscariot. Like Judas in Matthew 27:1–10, he hanged himself in 2 Samuel 17:23.

[11] Each of the five books of Psalms ends with a doxology: 41:13, 72:18–20, 89:52, 106:48 and 150:1–6.

Book II – Psalms 42–72:

Sing When Times Are Hard

When God Feels Distant
(42:1–43:5)

I say to God my Rock, "Why have you forgotten me?"

(Psalm 42:9)

I once tried to have a relationship with a girl who lived 800 miles away in Eastern Europe. It didn't last very long. No matter how great a holiday romance feels when you are together, it can rarely bear the strain of a long-distance separation. Book II of Psalms is the bleakest of the five books because it mainly contains songs which help us to sing when times are hard. They are songs which we need to sing when God feels as distant as a summer holiday romance in midwinter.

90   The first two psalms of Book II are similar yet very different from the first two psalms of Book I. They are similar because, like Psalms 1 and 2, they appear to have originally been one psalm.[1] The two five-verse stanzas in 42:1–5 and 42:6–11 both end with the same refrain: *"Why, my soul, are you downcast? Why so disturbed within me? Put your hope in God, for I will yet praise him, my Saviour and my God."*[2] Psalm 43 consists of a third five-verse stanza which ends with exactly the same refrain. The temple worship leaders who compiled the book of Psalms must have divided the song in two in order to give people the choice

---

[1] That is why Psalm 43 is one of only two psalms in Book II which doesn't have a title. A few Hebrew manuscripts have Psalm 42 and 43 as one psalm, but not the most reliable ones.

[2] Yes, I know that 42:6–11 is technically a six-verse stanza. Some of the structure of the psalm was evidently lost on the person who divided up the Old Testament text into verses in 1448 AD.

of singing the stanzas separately or stitching them both back together.

The most obvious difference between these two psalms and those in Book I is that all the psalms in Book I were written by David, whereas Book II begins with eight psalms by the Sons of Korah.[3] We are told in 1 Chronicles 6:33–38 that a man named Heman was the chief worship leader in the Kohathite choir, which was one of the three main Levite choirs at the Tabernacle on Mount Zion, and that the Sons of Korah formed part of his choir. These psalms were not written by David but they have the same look and feel because he had trained the Sons of Korah to lead worship in his Tabernacle.

The other big difference between the psalms in Book II and the psalms in Book I is much less obvious but it's crucial. It is one of the biggest features of this second book and it is part of its call to sing about God even when times are hard. Israel called God *Yahweh* or *the Lord* in order to express their special relationship with him. This second book is known as "the Elohistic Psalter" because it rarely uses the name *Yahweh* and opts instead to use the more general name *Elōhīm* or *God*. Book I uses the name Yahweh over 250 times and Elōhīm fewer than 50 times, whereas Book II uses Yahweh fewer than 50 times and Elōhīm almost 250 times. We can tell that this isn't just coincidence because when 68:1 quotes from Numbers 10:35 it deliberately changes the name Yahweh to Elōhīm. We can also tell this because Psalm 53 is a repeat of Psalm 14 but the four references to Yahweh are all changed to Elōhīm too. This is meant to serve as a constant verbal reminder that this second book tells us how to sing when times are hard and God feels distant.

Enough background. Now on to the actual psalms. Psalm

---

[3] Psalms 42–49 probably formed a mini-collection already, long before the temple musicians compiled the definitive book of Psalms in around 300 BC. They simply took four psalms by the Sons of Korah out to include them in Book III and then split the remaining seven psalms into eight.

42 is a *maskīl* or *teaching psalm*. Its first five-verse stanza in 42:1–5 instructs us that if we ever feel that God is distant, we are not alone. The Sons of Korah say that they are as desperate for the presence of the Lord as a deer dying of thirst in the desert is desperate for water. They long to be back at the Tabernacle where they used to shout for joy and worship with the congregation of believers. For some reason they cannot get there, and their cries are meant to show us what to do when God feels a million miles away.[4] These first verses tell us to gather with other believers. We need to get to church early to find fellowship with other Christians. We need to find a small group of Christian friends with whom we can study the Bible, worship, chat and pray. When God feels distant, church gatherings are part of the way of he helps us to sing as we make the journey back to our former intimacy with him.

The second five-verse stanza in 42:6–11 turns the first metaphor on its head. The Sons of Korah no longer feel as though they are dying of thirst in the desert; they feel as though they are drowning under waterfalls and crashing waves of disappointment, which they describe as deep waters calling to deep waters. They even start to think that God must have forgotten all about them. Some readers assume that the Sons of Korah were cut off from the Temple when King Jeroboam closed off the border between the northern and southern kingdoms fifty years after the death of David. Others assume that they were cut off from the Temple when the Arameans invaded Israel and took captives into exile a hundred and seventy years after the death of David.[5] Personally, I find it far more likely that they wrote this song in the heyday of David's Tabernacle when they were temporarily away from Jerusalem, and that the reference to *Mount Hermon* is simply a metaphor. I live in

---

[4] Our mouth speaks out of the overflow of our hearts (Luke 6:45), and what the Sons of Korah pour out of their souls in 42:4 is a passionate expression of their continued desire for the Lord.

[5] 1 Kings 12:28; 2 Kings 12:17–18.

England but I have known many times when God has felt as far-away from me as Australia. The Sons of Korah marked this psalm for congregational singing because we can all feel like that sometimes.

The third five-verse stanza in 43:1–5 suggests that this song may have been written while the Sons of Korah were fleeing from Absalom with David. They cry out for vindication against their wicked enemies and their unfaithful nation, and they long to be brought back *"to your holy mountain, to the place where you dwell"*. Perhaps this is why the Lord sometimes lets us go through periods when he feels distant. I am never so excited to spend time with my wife and children as when I have been away for a few days with work. I am never so likely to call God *"my joy and my delight"* or to long to worship him as when I have felt the absence of his presence for a short while.

It's quite normal to have times when we feel that God is distant. It's helpful to prepare ourselves for such periods by singing about them together when we worship. It's also normal to find that our love for God is renewed by the experience when we sense his presence once again. Take it from the Sons of Korah: If we keep singing when times are hard, then it is music to God's ears.

When God Seems to Fail
(44:1–26)

You made us retreat before the enemy, and our
adversaries have plundered us.

(Psalm 44:10)

I can't even begin to imagine what it must have felt like for the disciples when Jesus died. Thomas was so disillusioned that he refused to believe in the resurrection. His friends were so disorientated that they locked their doors and hid in case the Jewish leaders came looking for them. Luke tells us they were miserable.[1] It's easy to see why.

The Sons of Korah clearly felt the same way. We don't know when they wrote Psalm 44 – they may have done so under one of the later kings, but their statement that Israel has not been unfaithful to God's covenant and has not committed idolatry (44:17 and 44:20–21) suggests they may have written it during one of the temporary setbacks which marked the end of David's reign. What we know for sure is that they felt as though the Lord had failed them. Their hopes had been dashed, their faith was in tatters, and they responded in the only way that they knew how. They wrote a psalm of praise to God.

I find it very challenging that the Lord chose to include this song in the book of Psalms instead of a happier, more upbeat song written by one of their contemporaries who put a brave face on the problem and convinced himself that things were fine. God chose to include this song because the

---

[1] John 20:19, 24–25; Luke 24:17.

Sons of Korah had actually got the right perspective. Israel *had* been defeated. God's promises *hadn't* been fulfilled. And the Lord was looking for people who weren't afraid to say so. Dan Allender observes that:

> *Christians seldom sing in the minor key. We fear the sombre; we seem to hold sorrow in low esteem. We seem predisposed to fear lament as a quick slide into doubt and despair; failing to see that doubt and despair are the dark soil that is necessary to grow confidence and joy... To sing a lament against God in worship reveals far, far greater trust than to sing a jingle about how happy we are and how much we trust him... Lament cuts through insincerity, strips pretence, and reveals the raw nerve of trust that angrily approaches the throne of grace and then kneels in awed, robust wonder.*[2]

The Sons of Korah tell the Lord that they believe he kept his promises powerfully in the past (44:1–8). Then they tell him straight that in the present it looks as if he has rejected them, abandoned them, scattered them, disgraced them, put them to shame and sold them over to their enemies (44:9–16). The Sons of Korah marked this as a *maskīl* or *teaching psalm* for congregational worship because we all need to pray this kind of honest prayer from time to time. In my country, the United Kingdom, in the past fifty years the percentage of people in their twenties who attend church regularly has nosedived from well over 50 per cent to only 3 per cent.[3] About a third of churches have no children and over half have no teenagers.[4] Whatever way we look at that, it's an absolute disaster. God doesn't want

---

[2] Dr Dan Allender is a leading Christian psychologist. He wrote this in "The Hidden Hope in Lament", published in the *Mars Hill Review* (Vol. 1, 1994).

[3] These figures compare 1955 and 2005. See the report by the UK Evangelical Alliance entitled *The 18–30 Mission: The Missing Generation?* (2005).

[4] This data is taken from the English Church Census in 2005. 44:1 underlines the scale of this disaster by telling us that the health of the Church requires parents to pass their faith down to the next generation.

us to bury our heads in the sand and to sing chirpy choruses about better days to come. He wants us to sing psalms of lament like the Sons of Korah.

Some of our disasters are more personal. Many of us know terrible suffering in our lives. Psalm 37 promised us peace and prosperity, but many of us are tired of having to pretend that we are doing better than we are. Our business ventures fail. We get sick and aren't healed. Horrible things happen to our loved ones. Some of them die. Is it any wonder that there are so many confused, disillusioned Christians when we very rarely sing psalms of lament when we gather together? Isn't it obvious why God wanted Psalm 44 to be sung regularly by the worshippers at his Temple? Dan Allender continues:

> *How much of the current counselling frenzy is due to an absence of opportunity to confess our hurt, anger and confusion to God in the presence of others of like mind? In many ways, one role of counselling is to legitimise pain and struggle and focus the questions of the heart towards God. How much better it would be if in concert with others we passionately cried out to God with the energy that is often expressed only in the privacy of the counselling office.*

Psalm 44 is an angry psalm. It blames God for our disasters – *"you made us retreat"* (44:10) – and it even accuses him of not being the good shepherd that we sang about in Psalm 23. The Sons of Korah liken him in 44:11 to a lazy shepherd who lets wolves eat his sheep while he is not looking. Worse, they liken him in 44:12 to a dim-witted shepherd who sends his sheep off to the abattoir and forgets to ask the butcher for any money in return. Far from feeling embarrassed by their anger, the New Testament tells us that this is how we ought to pray in times of trouble too, since Paul quotes from 44:22

in Romans 8:36 as a promise that when we go through hard times we can pray prayers such as this to lay hold of Jesus' unfailing love. Not all anger towards God is good, but it can open up a dialogue which moves our hearts away from our confusion and towards God's solution.

That is exactly what happens to the Sons of Korah as they write their song. They began by confessing that God is the true King of Israel and that they can do nothing without him, and they return to this realization in 44:17–26. They protest that they haven't worshipped idols or stopped believing in God's covenant with Israel (44:17–21). They haven't forgotten that the Lord's name is still the Blood-Drenched Shepherd and the Victor and the Healer (44:20). They recognize that they are suffering because they are caught in the crossfire of a great cosmic battle. They tell the Lord it is *"for your sake"* that they are suffering. The Devil rages against God's People because he knows he cannot lay a finger on God himself.[5] They call the Lord to *wake up* and to *stop forgetting* them for a moment longer. The final word of the psalm is *hēsēd* or *covenant mercy*.[6] Because God hasn't changed and nor has his Gospel, they end their song assured that all will be well.

I don't know when you last had a chance to sing a song of lament with other believers in church on Sunday. If you lead worship, you may need to reconsider the breadth of worship themes you use as you lead God's People. If you are a church leader, this kind of singing should certainly characterize many of your prayer meetings. Our churches can often be places where positive messages paste a wafer-thin veneer over the silent despair and confused cries and angry prayers which are just waiting to be sung. There is no need for us to be afraid of

---

[5] Revelation 12:13–17. The Devil can't touch Jesus so he attacks those Jesus loves instead.

[6] Like many of the psalms in Book II, this song does not use the name *Yahweh* at all, but the Sons of Korah do not doubt God's continued covenant with Israel despite the fact that he seems very far-away.

expressing the anger and emotion which runs throughout Psalm 44. When we dare to speak it out honestly, we will discover that it is music to God's ears.

A Few Days (45:1–17)

Listen, daughter, and pay careful attention: Forget
your people and your father's house.

(Psalm 45:10)

If you ever think you have it hard in life, spare a thought for Jacob. His uncle made him work for seven years without being paid in order to marry his beautiful cousin Rachel. When the seven years were up, his uncle tricked him and made him work for seven more years, still unpaid. At the end of fourteen years, his uncle offered him a salary for shepherding his flocks for him, but then attempted to diddle him out of his wages for the next six years. How did Jacob feel about his twenty years of suffering at the hands of his uncle to win the hand of Rachel? We read in Genesis 29:20 that *"they seemed like only a few days to him because of his love for her"*.

The Sons of Korah mainly wrote psalms which lamented their suffering. That's why most of their songs are placed at the start of Book II, although four of them appear separately as prayers of longing in Book III. The final editors of Psalms decided to make their happy wedding psalm a half-time break for us in the middle of this mini-collection of their psalms of lament in Book II.[1] They aren't changing the subject. They are showing us how we can draw strength, like Jacob, when times are hard by remembering that we are in a romance which makes our present difficulties feel like only a few days.

The king in Psalm 45 is probably Solomon. The title tells

---

[1] It seems from 45:1 that only one of the Sons of Korah actually wrote it, but it became part of their joint collection.

us it was a wedding song and it was probably used for one of Solomon's early marriages to a beautiful foreign princess.[2] Since Solomon was known as the *messiah* and was a prophetic picture of the Messiah who was to come, the New Testament quotes from 45:6–7 in Hebrews 1:8–9 and applies the words directly to Jesus as the heavenly Bridegroom.[3] It picks up on the words of this psalm in John 3:29, Ephesians 5:32, and Revelation 19:7–8 and 21:9, in order to teach us that the Church is Jesus' beautiful Bride and that he laboured for her like Jacob.[4] He became a human being, endured torture and mocking, then died on the cross *"for the joy that was set before him"*.[5] We mustn't see this wedding song as out of place in a book which tells us to sing when times are hard. It is labelled as a *maskīl* or *teaching psalm* because it teaches us how we can keep on singing through the tears.

Psalm 45:1–9 focuses entirely on the character of the King. That's the first thing which we need to learn. If we keep our eyes focused on Jesus while the storms rage around us then, like Peter, we will walk on water and be able to smile and sing in the eye of the storm. If we shift our eyes away from Jesus and onto the wind and the waves then, like Peter, we will start to drown.[6] These verses remind us that Jesus speaks words which are anointed with grace (45:2),[7] that he is a mighty hero (45:3),

[2] The title says literally that it is a *love song*. This is translated *wedding song* because of the content of the Psalm, but it stresses that this is no arranged marriage. Jesus is madly in love with us.

[3] Hebrews 1:8–9 makes much of the fact that 45:6–7 addresses the King as *God [the Son]* and promises that *God [the Father]* has set him high over every other name.

[4] The Old Testament prophets repeatedly describe God's relationship with Israel as that of a husband and wife. Isaiah 54:4–8 promises that he will bring back his estranged wife for a glorious new wedding day.

[5] Hebrews 12:2. The writer tells us to consider Jesus' trials *"so that you will not grow weary and lose heart"*.

[6] Matthew 14:23–31. Jesus was not amazed that Peter walked on water when he looked at him, but that he should ever sink by looking at the storm.

[7] Luke 4:22; John 6:68; 7:46.

and that his reign is marked by splendour, majesty, victory, truth, humility, justice and miracles (45:4–5). Things may not always appear this way during our days of trial on the earth, but our wedding day is coming and our Bridegroom couldn't look more handsome. He will reign forever (45:6), he will loathe wickedness (45:7)[8] and he is full of the Holy Spirit (45:7).[9] He is easily worth a few days of trouble while we wait.

The apostle Paul may have suffered more for the sake of the Gospel than anyone else ever has, but it was a vision of this Bridegroom which enabled him to exclaim in 2 Corinthians 4:16–18 that *"We do not lose heart... For our light and momentary troubles are achieving for us an eternal glory that far outweighs them all. So we fix our eyes not on what is seen, but on what is unseen, since what is seen is temporary, but what is unseen is eternal."*

Psalm 45:10–15 focuses on the Bride who has been chosen by this great King. Although Psalms is very clear that we start out as filthy sinners, the Bride is clothed by God's grace in the finest gold (45:9)[10] and in finely embroidered garments interwoven with gold (45:13–14). She captivates the King with her beauty (45:11), and we read literally that she is *glorious on the inside* as well as on the outside (45:13).[11] Even though the Church consists of commoners who were filthy when God saved them, her Bridegroom views her as a princess (45:13) and the

---

[8] 45:7 continues the teaching about God the Avenger and God the Judge. It is precisely because Jesus refuses to tolerate wickedness that the Father has given him the name which is above every other name.

[9] Note that the writer's name for the Holy Spirit is *"the oil of joy"*. We can rejoice in the midst of hard times because our Bridegroom fills us with the Holy Spirit to give us inner joy (46:4 and Galatians 5:22).

[10] *Ophir* was a region in the south of the Arabian Peninsula near Sheba which was famous for mining the finest gold on the market (Job 22:24; 28:16; 1 Kings 9:28; 10:11; Isaiah 13:12; 1 Chronicles 29:4).

[11] Some translators assume that *within* means that she is beautiful as she gets ready for her wedding day in her bedroom, but we should probably understand it to mean that God's work of grace is never superficial.

Sons of Korah tell her to *"Forget your people and your father's house"* (45:10). Her wedding guests include royal princesses and wealthy merchants (45:9 and 12), because her few days of being a single commoner are over and a whole new married life has just begun. When Kate Middleton arrived at the altar of Westminster Abbey to marry Prince William in April 2011, over a billion people around the world could read his lips as he encouraged her that, *"You look beautiful!"* But that's nothing compared to what the whole world will see when our few days of suffering end and we finally meet Jesus the Bridegroom on our great wedding day.

Psalm 45:16–17 switches our attention back onto the Bridegroom as we end.[12] It promises that, through the Church, Jesus will extend his Kingdom throughout the world and will draw to himself the praise of every nation.[13]

Only this view of what God is achieving through our life struggles can keep us singing throughout the hard times and make them feel like only a few days. The nineteenth-century hymn writer Fanny J. Crosby was blinded as a baby through a foolish medical blunder, but she refused to complain about her misfortune and wrote hymn after hymn of praise to God. She wrote a song while she was still a child which read: *"Oh, what a happy soul am I, although I cannot see. I am resolved that in this world contented I will be. How many blessings I enjoy that other people don't. To weep and sigh because I'm blind, I cannot and I won't."*

How did Fanny J. Crosby keep such a perspective and keep writing songs of praise to the Lord in the hard times? She revealed that her secret was the thought of this great wedding day which was coming, and which made her life of suffering feel

---

[12] The Hebrew for *you* in 45:10–15 was feminine but in 45:16–17 it is masculine.

[13] The word for *land* in 45:16 can also be translated the *earth*. Jesus' quotation from 37:11 in Matthew 5:5 shows us that we should understand this verse to carry this latter meaning.

like only a few days. She used to tell those who questioned her that *"The good thing about being blind is that the very first face I'll see will be the face of Jesus."*[14]

---

[14] These quotations come from *Fanny Crosby's Story of Ninety-Four Years, as told to S. Trevena Jackson* (1915).

Reasons to Be Cheerful
(46:1–49:20)

There is a river whose streams make glad the city of God, the holy place where the Most High dwells.

(Psalm 46:4)

One of the former pupils of the school I went to as a child was Ian Dury, who achieved fame as the lead singer of The Blockheads. If you know anything about 1970s music, you will remember his number-one single "Hit Me with Your Rhythm Stick" and his number-three follow-up single "Reasons to Be Cheerful". By the time he remixed and re-released those two songs in 1985, the big new British music sensation was Morrissey, lead singer of The Smiths. Even today, he is still famous for being miserable and depressing in pretty much all of his songs, so one interviewer asked him what lyrics he would have chosen for "Reasons to Be Cheerful" had he written it. He paused for a moment and replied without smiling: *"I think it would have been an instrumental... No, it would **definitely** have been an instrumental."*[1]

Many readers of Psalms assume that the Sons of Korah were a bit like Morrissey. They read the agonized lyrics of their psalms and assume that they were very dour people, like the man who wrote such classics as "Heaven Knows I'm Miserable Now" and "Last Night I Dreamed that Somebody Loved Me". But they weren't. They weren't at all. Their psalms of lament are full of reasons to be cheerful. Psalms 46–49 are their last songs in Book II and, amidst the grief and sorrow, they tell us some

---

[1] Morrissey famously gave this answer in an interview with the British pop music newspaper *"Record Mirror"* in August 1985.

wonderful truths about the Lord which can keep us smiling through the tears.

In Psalm 46 they tell us to be cheerful because *the Lord is our refuge*. This is the psalm which inspired Martin Luther in the midst of turmoil to write his most famous hymn. He was hated by the Pope as too reformed, by radical Protestants as too conservative, by the German noblemen as too revolutionary, and by the German peasants as too supportive of their masters, so he found solace in the words of this psalm in 1529 and wrote the hymn "A Mighty Fortress Is Our God". Although the Sons of Korah tell us in the title that Psalm 46 should be sung by a choir of young girls, its message could hardly be manlier.[2] It tells us that when God feels far-away he is still "ever-present" (46:1),[3] and just about to turn our night into glorious day (46:5). We can be as cheerful as Martin Luther under pressure because of this psalm's repeated promise that the Lord is our fortress or refuge (46:7 and 11).

Psalm 46:4 tells us to be cheerful because *the Lord fills us with his Holy Spirit.* Jerusalem was a very unusual city because it had no natural water supply and was therefore very vulnerable to capture. Babylon had the Euphrates, Damascus had the Barada and Nineveh had the Tigris, but all that Jerusalem had was the Gihon spring outside its city walls. David had managed to capture the city by sending his men up a water shaft, and his riverless new capital city remained a major military headache for Israel.[4] That's the background to the Sons of Korah singing, *"There is a river whose streams make glad the city of God."* They explain that Jerusalem's extremity is in fact God's opportunity.

[2] The Hebrew word *alāmōth* in the title means *virgin girls*. David had instructed Heman and the other leaders of the temple musicians to recruit this choir of young girls in 1 Chronicles 15:20.

[3] The Hebrew means literally *very found*. God promises that we will always find him in our hour of need.

[4] 2 Samuel 5:8. King Hezekiah later tried to solve the problem by building a special secure tunnel from the Gihon spring to a pool inside the city (2 Kings 20:20; 2 Chronicles 32:30).

God gave Israel a weak capital city in order to keep them focused on their own frailty without the divine power of his Holy Spirit.[5] He does the same for us through our trials.

Psalm 46:10 tells us to be cheerful because *the Lord is God and we are not*. The fourth-century bishop Hilary of Poitiers argued that most of our troubles and worrying are the result of our *"blasphemous anxiety to do God's work for him"*.[6] The Sons of Korah agree and tell us everything changes when we are quiet enough to reflect that God is very good at being God, and we are not. These experts at singing songs of lament don't pull their punches in reminding us that many of our trials are self-inflicted.

Psalm 47 tells us to be cheerful because *the Lord is King of all the nations*. They may not all confess it yet, but this psalm is very clear that he claims every single people group as his own. He was *the Lord Almighty* in 46:7 and he is *the Lord Most High* and *the Great King* in 47:2.[7] When we suffer for the sake of his Kingdom, we can draw great cheer from the fact that we are suffering as part of the eventual winning team.[8] God ascended Mount Zion to rule from his Tabernacle and Jesus ascended to heaven to rule over every tribe and nation (47:5).

Psalm 48 tells us to be cheerful because *the Lord is with us*. It is a song in praise of Jerusalem, and specifically Mount Zion as home to David's Tabernacle. The Sons of Korah aren't bothered that it is over fifty metres shorter than the nearby Mount of

---

[5] This is one of the main verses which Jesus refers to in John 7:37–39 when he says that *"as Scripture has said, rivers of living water will flow from within them"*. It also links to Ezekiel 47:1–12 and Revelation 22:1–2.

[6] Hilary of Poitiers wrote this in about 360 AD in his treatise *On the Trinity* (4.6).

[7] The Assyrian kings called themselves *"the Great King"* (2 Kings 18:19) so, depending on when this psalm was written, this name may be very significant. It would be like declaring in ancient Egypt that the Lord is Pharaoh, or in modern North Korea that the Lord is the Supreme Leader. See also 48:2.

[8] Verse 7 tells us to sing a *maskil* or *psalm of instruction*. The more we understand, the easier our trials become.

Olives and almost a thousand metres shorter than Mount Zaphon.[9] To them, it is the highest mountain in the world, because the Lord offsets its natural deficiencies by his presence which makes it his *"holy mountain"*. We should be challenged to love the Church as much as they clearly love Mount Zion. The structure of the psalm pivots on a central promise that *"As we have heard, so we have seen."* We can trust the Lord to dwell in our naturally unimpressive churches during times of trial and to transform them into *"the joy of the whole earth"*.

Psalm 49 tells us to be cheerful because *the Lord is our Redeemer*. When money problems get us down, we must remember that no amount of money can ever purchase what the Lord has given us for free. The vast riches of the wealthy cannot pay the ransom price for the redemption of their souls (49:7–8), yet the Lord has paid the ransom price which has redeemed us from hell (49:15).[10] Don't let financial setbacks depress you, because the Lord can use them to shift your trust away from money and onto the only currency which will be accepted by the bank of heaven.[11]

So there we have it. The Sons of Korah are not at all like the despondent Morrissey. Because the Lord is our refuge, because he fills us with his Holy Spirit, because he is God, because he is King of all the nations, because he is with us, and because he is our Redeemer, we have countless reasons to be cheerful and to sing when times are hard.

---

[9] Mount Zaphon was a high mountain which the Canaanites believed was home to Baal and their other gods.

[10] The Hebrew word used three times in 49:14–15 is *she'ōl*, which in the Psalms often means *hell*.

[11] Luke 16:19–31; 18:24–25. The problem isn't wealth itself. 49:20 tells us it is wealth without understanding.

What God Needs from You
(50:1–51:19)

I have no need of a bull from your stall or of goats
from your pens, for every animal of the forest is mine,
and the cattle on a thousand hills.

(Psalm 50:9–10)

One of my friends sent me a birthday card which asked, *"What do you give to the man who has everything?"* If any of your friends are as tight-fisted as mine, you know the answer. On the inside it simply read, *"Nothing."*

Asaph asks a similar question in Psalm 50. What does the all-sufficient God want his worshippers to give him? Asaph was well placed to answer this question because he was one of the most impressive worshippers in his generation. He was a Levite, descended from Levi's eldest son Gershon, and David had chosen him to lead one of the three worship choirs at the new Tabernacle on Mount Zion.[1] He was such a brilliant worship leader that nobody contributed more to the book of Psalms than he did except for David himself. The Old Testament refers to this emerging collection of songs as *"the words of David and of Asaph the seer"*, and the New Testament holds him in such high regard that it simply refers to him as *"the prophet"*.[2] There is no doubt about it, if God needed anything from anyone, it would be from a spiritual giant such as Asaph. That's why Psalm 50 has been

108

---

[1] 1 Chronicles 6:31, 39; 16:1–7, 37.
[2] 2 Chronicles 29:30; Matthew 13:35.

separated from Asaph's other eleven psalms in Book III.[3] It prepares us for David's prayer in Psalm 51.

Unlike most of the psalms in Book II, this one isn't marked for congregational singing. Asaph wanted his choir to sing it to the worshippers who came to the Tabernacle to teach them what kind of worship God is looking for. It warned them in 50:1–6 that they had come into the throne room of the *Lord of all the earth*, and that he was *the Mighty One*, the *Righteous One* and *the Judge*. He isn't like Tom Cruise in the movie *Jerry Maguire*, desperately looking for somebody who will complete him.[4] If we think he needs anything from us, we had better turn tail before we discover that judgment begins with the People of God.[5] If we think he needs our sacrifices, we are like the wicked people in 50:16–23 who receive a stark warning: *"You thought I was altogether like you. But I will rebuke you and accuse you to your face."*

Asaph warns us in 50:7–15 that what looks like sincere worship can easily become idolatry. The Israelites were right to bring blood sacrifices to the Lord but they were wrong to think that they could use them to curry favour with God, as the pagans did with their idols. *"I have no need of a bull from your stall or of goats from your pens,"* the Lord reminds them. *"If I were hungry I would not tell you, for the world is mine, and all that is in it."* This is the message which Paul took to Athens when he warned that God *"is not served by human hands, as if he needed anything"*,[6] and it is the message which God preaches to us today. He is so very rich that he tells us in 50:14 and 23 that he needs absolutely

109

---

[3] The rest of Asaph's collection of songs can be found in Psalms 73–83. It is significant that the editors of Psalms decided to place this one alongside Psalm 51 instead.

[4] *Jerry Maguire* (TriStar Pictures, 1996). One of the repeated romantic lines in the film is *"You complete me."*

[5] It is likely that Peter had Psalm 50:1–6 in mind when he wrote 1 Peter 4:17.

[6] Acts 17:25. David taught something similar in Psalm 40:6.

nothing from us except for *thanksgiving* for what he has done without us.[7]

John Piper puts it this way:

> *God cannot be served in any way that implies we are meeting His needs... Any servant who tries to get off the divine dole and strike up a manly partnership with his Heavenly Master is in revolt against the Creator. God does not barter. He gives* **mercy** *to servants who will have it, and the wages of death to those who won't. Good service is always and fundamentally receiving mercy, not rendering assistance.*[8]

As soon as we start to read Psalm 51, it becomes obvious why the editors of Psalms detached Asaph's song from the rest of his collection and put it here. This is David's most famous penitential prayer, and he wrote it after committing adultery with the wife of a close friend, getting her pregnant and then murdering his friend to cover up the affair. When the prophet Nathan confronted him with his sin in 2 Samuel 12, David faced the biggest crisis of his whole life. He shows us how to sing when times are hard by putting Asaph's teaching into practice. He doesn't try to give God anything to forgive him.

Don't miss how remarkable that is. When the Greek hero Hercules committed a terrible sin, he performed twelve labours to win back the gods' favour. When the Jews asked Jesus for help in Luke 7:4–5, they tried to buy his favour by pointing out that *"This man deserves to have you do this, because he loves our nation and has built our synagogue."* David had done more good deeds than Hercules and he had built the Tabernacle, but he refuses to try to give God anything in return for forgiveness. He recognizes that the Lord isn't like a lifeless idol in a man-made

---

[7] God uses the normal Hebrew word for blood sacrifice in both verses to ask for *"sacrifices of thanksgiving"*.

[8] John Piper in *Brothers, We Are Not Professionals* (2003).

shrine.[9] What do you give to the God who has everything? *"My sacrifice, O God, is a broken spirit; a broken and contrite heart you, God, will not despise."*[10]

When Nathan confronted David with his sin, he lay for seven days and seven nights on the floor. 51:1–12 reflects what he prayed, refusing to minimize his sin or to pretend that he had acted out of character.[11] He simply confesses that he has been a sinner from birth and that his only hope is for the Lord to be the Giver, granting him a mercy and cleansing which he does not deserve.[12] In due course he will share the Gospel (51:13), worship (51:14–15) and build up the People of God (51:18–19), but he will not do so as a way of trying to curry the Lord's favour. The true God is simply far too great to need our human handouts.

So don't try to give God anything in return for his help when you sin. Don't be like Hercules or like the Jews who convinced themselves that they could buy their way back into God's favour. Be like David and confess that you can give God precisely nothing. Nothing but thanks that he has already paid the price so that you can be forgiven.[13] Nothing but a request that he give

111

---

[9] David was smart enough to know that all of his labours had only been possible through God's Spirit and that they had made him *more*, not less, indebted to the Lord. We are meant to see 51:11 as a deliberate link back to 1 Samuel 16:14. David is saying that, but for the Lord's grace, he would be just like Saul.

[10] The same Hebrew word is used in 2 Samuel 12:9–10 for David *despising* God by sinning as is used in Psalm 51:17 for God not *despising* a broken spirit.

[11] Uriah and Bathsheba were also sinners, which is why David says in 51:4 that he has sinned against the Lord rather than against them. Paul quotes from 51:4 in Romans 3:4.

[12] The Hebrew word *māhāh* in 51:1 and 9 means literally to *wipe away* or *to erase*. God does not so much *blot out* our sin by covering it up as *erase* it by bearing it away from us through Jesus.

[13] David deliberately uses words from Moses' Law when he talks about *hyssop* (Leviticus 14:4–6; Numbers 19:6, 18) and *bloodguilt* (Numbers 35:31–33), because the Law was good. The blood sacrifices in Moses' Law pointed

you his Holy Spirit to make you righteous through his grace.[14] Nothing but a broken spirit which confesses we have nothing to offer him other than a fresh chance to be revealed as the great Giver.

---

to Jesus, but the Israelites had taken those pictures of grace and turned them into religious works.

[14] 51:11 contains the first use of the phrase *"Holy Spirit"* in the whole Bible. It occurs nowhere else in the Old Testament except for Isaiah 63. We receive the Holy Spirit as a free gift because we are sinful and need him.

Four Betrayals (52:1–55:23)

Arrogant foes are attacking me; ruthless people are
trying to kill me – people without regard for God.

(Psalm 54:3)

"Judge me by the enemies I have made," President Franklin D. Roosevelt told the American people.[1] David goes one step further. He wants us to judge him not merely by the enemies that he made, but also by the way in which he treated them. These four psalms don't just belong together because each of them is marked as a *maskīl* of David – a *teaching psalm* or a *psalm of instruction*[2] – but because David wrote each of them when one of his close friends betrayed him. Book II teaches us how to sing when times are hard, and there are few things harder to bear than the pain of betrayal.

David wrote Psalm 52 when he was betrayed by Doeg the Edomite in 1 Samuel 21–22. Doeg was there when David made a secret visit to Moses' Tabernacle while on the run from King Saul, and he informed Saul before volunteering to lead the royal troops to massacre the priests and their families. Psalm 53 repeats Psalm 14 almost word for word except that 53:5 replaces 14:5–6 and informs us that David's betrayer failed in his plans because he took fright for no reason. This links with 2 Samuel 17:1–23 to suggest that David wrote a new version of

---

[1] He said this in his "Portland Speech" on 21st September 1932.

[2] We have already seen this Hebrew musical term in Psalms 32, 42 and 44–45. We will see it again in the titles of Psalms 74, 78, 88–89 and 142. The word *maskīl* is also used in 53:2 to mean *one who understands*.

Psalm 14 to cope with how he felt while exiled from Jerusalem during Absalom's rebellion.[3]

David wrote Psalm 54 on one of the two occasions that he was betrayed by the Ziphites while on the run from Saul, in 1 Samuel 23:19 and 26:1. As fellow tribesmen of Judah, they should have been his staunchest allies instead of his betrayers. Psalm 55 gives us no date in the title, but its language is so similar to that of 41:9 that it is likely David wrote it when he was betrayed by his close friend Ahithophel during Absalom's rebellion. These four psalms deal with four betrayals. They teach us how to keep on singing through the tears when we are deeply disappointed by our own friends.

First, David teaches us to *be honest*. He can see that Doeg's reputation as a *"mighty hero"* means nothing and that his lust for money makes him *"a disgrace in the eyes of God"*.[4] He can see that Absalom and the atheists who surround him are *"fools"* who *"know nothing"*. But he is very open with the Lord when he can't see things as they really are, and he doesn't pretend that he can. Ahithophel makes him so distraught in 55:1–8 that his body trembles and is overwhelmed by such horror that he feels envious of the doves which have wings to flee far-away from all their troubles.[5] David shows us that faith does not mean putting on a brave face and pretending that betrayal hasn't hurt us.

Second, David teaches us to *see the bigger picture*. He doesn't deny that Doeg is prospering through his wickedness; he simply speaks out in 52:1 what his temporary promotion has

---

[3] We can also date Psalm 53 to Absalom's rebellion by the way that David asks God to *ride forth from Zion* and *restore the fortunes of his people*. The title tells us that he reworked Psalm 14 into a *mahalath* or *song of affliction* (see also Psalm 88), which shows us that David prayed his own psalms back to God. So should we.

[4] 52:7 ties in with 1 Samuel 22:7. Doeg's motive for betraying David and the priest Ahimelek was that Saul had promised wealth and promotion to anyone who helped him.

[5] He uses a vivid Hebrew metaphor in 55:4 to say literally that *"my heart is in labour pains within me"*.

made him *"in the eyes of God"*.[6] He doesn't pretend that Absalom and his courtiers have not exiled him from Jerusalem; he simply reminds himself in 53:2 that *"God looks down from heaven on all mankind."* Small vision magnifies betrayal and leads to bitter earthbound thoughts, whereas a big vision of God's plan puts betrayal in its proper context. Only a God-sized vision will give us the strength we need to forgive.[7]

Third, David teaches us to *leave vengeance with God.* At no point in any of these four psalms does David try to fool himself that people's sin towards him doesn't really matter. On the contrary, we find some of his imprecatory language very shocking because we have grown too accustomed to mouthing spiritual platitudes in prayer.[8] *"Let evil recoil on those who slander me; in your faithfulness destroy them,"* he prays in 54:5. *"Lord, confuse the wicked, confound their words,"* he adds in 55:9–11. If we are offended by his prayers for vengeance, it simply shows how much we need these psalms of instruction. The Lord answered his prayer in 54:5 by letting the Ziphites suffer several more years of Philistine raids, and he answered David's prayer in 55:9–11 by confounding Ahithophel's advice so that he despaired and took his own life in 2 Samuel 17. Forgiving betrayal does not mean pretending that traitors have

---

[6] Since Doeg was Saul's chief shepherd (1 Samuel 21:7), he serves as an Old Testament picture of the antichrist, the *man of lawlessness* whom the Lord will destroy in a moment (2 Thessalonians 2:1–8). The NIV follows the Septuagint reading of 52:1, but most English translations follow the Hebrew text which reads *"Why do you boast of evil, you mighty hero? [Only] the goodness of the Lord lasts forever."*

[7] There is a strong clue in 55:23 as to how David was able to forgive Absalom's supporter Shimei in 2 Samuel 16:5–14. Shimei accused him of being a *"man of blood"* but David uses the same Hebrew phrase to say that in God's sight Absalom's supporters are the true *"men of blood"*.

[8] Since David asks for his enemies to go down to *she'ōl* alive, he cannot possibly be talking about *the grave*. He must be asking the Lord to damn his enemies to hell. We find this kind of praying very distasteful but the New Testament appears not to. See Acts 8:18–20, 1 Corinthians 16:22 and Galatians 1:9.

not wronged us. It simply means refusing to retaliate because we trust the Lord to avenge us instead.

Fourth, David teaches us that *forgiveness may take time*. Like the monster in a cheap horror movie, just when you think you've killed it, unforgiveness often rears its ugly head and strikes again. Note David's mood swings throughout Psalm 55, the longest and most detailed of these four prayers. He expresses his pain in 55:1–8 and hands it over to the Lord in 55:9–11, but then a fresh sense of betrayal overwhelms him in 55:12–14 as he remembers how he and Ahithophel once worshipped together at the Tabernacle. Like many victims of divorce, he finds that each happy memory sparks a new feeling of pain, and yet another one overwhelms him again in 55:20–21. David teaches us to be honest with God and to walk out forgiveness as an ongoing process. It is important that we are honest about this and that we recognize forgiveness may take time.[9]

Fifth, David teaches us to *find our comfort in God's name*. He ends Psalm 52 with confidence that the Lord's good name will finally vindicate him, and he teaches us in 54:1 and 6 that God's name is our only hope of deliverance in the midst of betrayal. He reminds himself that God is his Saviour (54:1), his Helper (54:4), his Avenger (54:5) and his Deliverer (54:7).[10] He keeps reminding himself of this morning, noon and night whenever a fresh wave of hurt washes over him (55:17), and he draws comfort from the fact that the Lord's name does not change with each fresh wave (55:19). David does not hope to understand why God has allowed these four betrayals. He simply ends this group of four psalms with a childlike statement that *"As for me, I trust in you."*

---

[9] David talks literally in 55:17 about *communing in uproar* with God. This captures the way that forgiveness is a process which we need to walk out over time in honesty with the Lord.

[10] Most English translations treat 55:18 as a reference to God *rescuing* David, but the Hebrew word literally means *to redeem*. David understood that God would pay the price for his redemption.

We will all face times of betrayal and disappointment. That's why these four psalms are marked for all of us to sing. If we are honest with God, if we see the bigger picture, if we leave vengeance to God, if we accept that it takes time to forgive, and if we take comfort in God's name, he will deliver us from our betrayers. David promises us in 55:22: *"Throw your burden onto the Lord and he will sustain you."*

Heat + Pressure = Jewels
(56:1–60:12)

When I am afraid, I put my trust in you.

(Psalm 56:3)

Precious jewels are created out of hardship. We all know it, but it's very easy to forget it. Carbon remains mere coal until it is subjected to the tremendous pressure and high temperatures which turn it into a brilliant diamond. Oyster shells are worthless until a piece of irritating grit intrudes and the oyster turns it into a shiny pearl. In the same way, our character can remain unlovely until trouble and hardship refine it into a precious jewel. If we can remember that heat and pressure create jewels, we will be able to keep on singing whenever times are hard.

Despite the sin which he confessed in Psalm 51, David was one of the godliest men of Israel. The New Testament tells us that the Lord *"found David son of Jesse a man after my own heart"* and that David successfully *"served God's purpose in his own generation"*.[1] We therefore need to pay careful attention to what he teaches us in Psalms 56–60. Other than Psalm 16, these are the only five psalms which are marked as *miktāms*, a word which means they contain *hidden treasures*.[2] Charles Spurgeon saw the word *miktām* as a chain which linked these five songs together as "the psalms of the Golden Secret", and they are certainly songs that teach us the secret of godly character. In each psalm David finds himself under terrible pressure and

---

[1] Acts 13:22, 36.

[2] *Miktām* could come from the Hebrew verb to *engrave*, but it could also come from the word for *hidden*.

shows us how these great trials refined his heart to make his character very precious to the Lord.[3]

David wrote Psalm 56 while imprisoned by King Achish in 1 Samuel 21.[4] You will remember from Psalm 34 that David should never even have gone to the Philistine city of Gath, but you may not remember what 1 Samuel 21:12 tells us happened to him when he got there. When he heard the Philistines whispering that this was their perfect opportunity to kill Israel's most successful general, *"David took these words to heart and was very much afraid of Achish king of Gath."* This explains the curious phrase which David uses three times in Psalm 56, when he talks about *"the Lord, whose word I praise"*. He doesn't just praise God *for* his Word, he actually praises God's Word itself, because his trial taught him to turn a deaf ear to gossip and a listening ear to whatever God says.[5] It didn't matter that Achish's name meant *I Will Terrify*; God's Word became so real to David in his darkest hour that he was able to boast twice that *"In God I trust and am not afraid. What can mere mortals do to me?"*[6]

David wrote Psalm 57 while he was hiding in a cave from King Saul. He did this at least twice, in 1 Samuel 22:1 and 24:3.[7]

[3] Psalm 57:7–11 and 60:5–12 appear together later on as Psalm 108. This reminds us that there is nothing random about the format of Psalms. These five *miktāms* have been placed here together for a reason.

[4] He set it to a well-known secular tune known as *"A Dove on Distant Oaks"*. We can't know for sure whether this is linked in any way to his wish to fly faraway like a dove in 55:6–8.

[5] Although *God's word* refers primarily to Scripture, it also refers to God's just record of our past actions (56:8) and to the prophecies he gives us for our future (2 Samuel 5:2). David uses perfect tenses in 56:4, 9 and 11 to tell us literally that *"I have trusted in God, I will not be afraid... This I have known: God is for me."*

[6] *Achish* had a second legitimate meaning, which was *Only a Man*. David may be thinking of this in 56:11.

[7] Like Goliath's sword which was now in David's hand, Saul's hostility backfired (57:6). An army of followers flocked to David's cave and he learned how to organize and lead them into battle like a king.

It marked a new low point in his life after being anointed king, and we can see that this trial taught him the value of heartfelt worship. Despite feeling that his enemies were as powerful as desert lions (57:4) and that he was as weak and helpless as a baby bird (57:1), his repeated chorus in this psalm describes his passion for the Lord to be exalted in every nation of the earth. Even though his trials feel like blackest night, he is convinced that if he worships God for who he is (57:2–3 and 10)[8] and for what he has done (57:6), his worship will actually turn his dark night into dawn (57:7–8).[9] David would come to the throne in a blaze of glory and lead Israel into worship, but first he had to gain this character in the darkness of a cave.

Psalm 58 is set to the same secular tune as two of the other *miktāms*, but it is the only *miktām* of the five which does not tell us in the title when David wrote it. Since it complains about a ruler's injustice, we can tell that it was written while he was on the run from Saul and that he also learned a third aspect of godly character through his trials. He sees his unjust enemies as venomous cobras and fierce lions, but this simply makes him even more passionate to see God's righteousness come upon the earth. In 2 Samuel 8:15 we are told that later on he *"reigned over all Israel, doing what was just and right for all his people,"* but first he had to learn to love God's justice in the heat and pressure of life as an outlaw in the desert of Judah.[10]

---

[8] He refers to the Lord literally in 57:2 as *God Who Fulfils His Purpose for Me*. This alone gave him faith to pass up the chance to kill Saul in 1 Samuel 24, or to lead Israel in conquest of what was left of the Promised Land.

[9] Don't be confused that David talks to his own soul and commands it to worship in 57:7–8. This is what he means by *"my heart is steadfast"*, disciplining his heart to worship, regardless of his moods. A great example of the power of worship to transform a situation can be found in Acts 16:22–26.

[10] When we take offence at David's imprecatory prayer in 58:6–8, we simply show how much we need trials like David's to develop a similar passion in us to see God's justice and righteousness fill the earth. 58:11 reminds us that we actually pray this way ourselves whenever we ask God to put an end to suffering.

David wrote Psalm 59 while Saul's soldiers were surrounding his house at night in order to kill him (1 Samuel 19:11–18).[11] If you have ever wondered how David managed to dislodge the final Canaanites from Israel where all his predecessors had failed, here is your answer. Four times David tells us that he relies on the Lord to be his fortress and deliverer (59:2, 9, 16, 17). He uses the same Hebrew word to tell us that it doesn't matter that his enemies are *watching* him keenly (title) because he is busy *watching* the Lord (59:9)![12] He learned to laugh at Israel's foreign neighbours and to conquer them when he was subjected to this heavy pressure by Saul's henchmen.[13]

The title of Psalm 60 talks about David's military victories, but its content describes a time when Israel was actually defeated. It appears that while David was away defeating the Arameans, Israel was invaded by the opportunistic Edomites.[14] David was appalled that the Lord had not defended his back door, but this trial gave him even greater faith and expectation that every single one of Israel's enemies was bound to fall.[15] Sure enough, the Lord developed a precious jewel of faith in David's heart through this setback and it enabled him and his general Joab to crush the Edomite army in a decisive battle.[16]

---

[11] This explains David's reference to his enemies coming "at evening" in 59:6 and 14.

[12] 59:17 is also the same as 59:9 except that David changes one letter to teach us that if we decide to *watch* the Lord (*sāmar*), we will be stirred to *sing* to the Lord (*zāmar*) as well.

[13] David uses exactly the same words to describe the Lord *laughing* and *scoffing* at Saul's soldiers in 59:8 as he used for him *laughing* and *scoffing* at the nations in 2:4.

[14] Edom was very mountainous terrain (60:9, Obadiah 3–4), but David is convinced the Lord can turn its high mountains into a mere shoe rack (60:8).

[15] David's reference to the Lord raising a military *banner* may link back to the banner which he raised against the Amalekites in Exodus 17:15–16. It also points to Jesus raising up a victory banner over the nations in Isaiah 11:10 and John 12:32.

[16] Reading 2 Samuel 8:13 and 1 Chronicles 18:12 helps us to understand the title of Psalm 60. David's general Joab killed 12,000 Edomites in battle while his

Short-term trials are always worth it if they create in us long-term character.

The British evangelist Smith Wigglesworth taught his converts that *"Great faith is a product of great fights. Great testimonies are the outcome of great tests. Great triumphs can only come after great trials."*[17] That's why David gave us these five *miktāms* to show us that heat and pressure create jewels. It's why he marked one of them *"for teaching"*, and why he marked all five of them for congregational singing. He wants to help us sing when times are hard by reminding us that pressure and heat are what God uses to develop in our hearts the jewel of Christian character.

---

lieutenant Abishai killed 6,000 more in the rout which followed.

[17] Quote taken from Jack Hywel-Davies' biography, *Baptised by Fire: The Story of Smith Wigglesworth* (1987).

Stripped (61:1–64:10)

My whole being longs for you, in a dry and parched land where there is no water.

(Psalm 63:1)

My young children love to play the game "pass the parcel". They get excited when the music stops and another layer of wrapping paper is stripped away. They know that each layer which is stripped away gets them closer to what really matters, to the prize which is hidden underneath the wrapping paper.

The worship leaders who compiled Psalms want us to understand that with life it's just the same. In Shakespeare's play, Richard III is consumed with lust to sit on the English throne, but when his mounting troubles strip away his ambition he cries out, *"A horse! A horse! My kingdom for a horse!"*[1] The worship leaders who compiled Psalms put these four psalms of David together because they want us to grasp that, in the same way, our own troubles strip away our petty desires and make us long for that which lasts forever. They teach us to sing when times are hard by showing us that our hardships are just like pass the parcel.

In Psalm 61, David's troubles strip away everything in his heart until all he is left with is *a passion for God's presence.* Although the title does not tell us when he wrote it, the words of the psalm make it clear that he penned these words while on the run from his son Absalom's rebellion. He refers to himself as *"the king"* (61:6), longs to return to the Lord's Tabernacle (61:4) and dreams of being back in his palace on Mount Zion (61:7). He had always loved God's presence, but this psalm shows us that troubles often make such

---

[1] *Richard III* (Act 5, Scene 4), written in about 1591.

passions stronger. He has not been forced to flee even fifty miles away from Mount Zion, but he feels that *"from the ends of the earth I call to you"*. He longs to be back on his throne in his palace on Mount Zion, but above all he longs to be back in God's presence in the Tabernacle[2] – *"I long to dwell in your tent forever... Then I will ever sing in praise of your name."*[3] David was able to sing in the midst of hardship because he grasped that troubles strip away from our hearts what doesn't really matter and leave us with an even greater passion for God's presence.

In Psalm 62, David's troubles strip away everything until all he is left with is *a passion for God's character*.[4] He was a great prophet, a great theologian and a great teacher, but his trials strip him back to reliance on just two basic facts which trump everything else: *"One thing God has spoken, two things I have heard: that you, O God, are strong, and that you, O Lord, are loving."* David's courtiers are going over to Absalom's side one by one,[5] but these two facts enable him to trust that *"Lowborn men are but a breath, the highborn are but a lie; if weighed on a balance, they are nothing; together they are only a breath."*[6] Because God is all-powerful and all-loving, David is able to *"find rest"* in God alone.[7]

---

[2] There is a play on words in 61:7 in Hebrew, since the verb *yāshab* can mean either *to dwell* in God's presence or *to sit* on a throne. David saw his palace and the Tabernacle as part of one complex on Mount Zion.

[3] The metaphor of hiding under God's birdlike wings in 61:4 was first used by David's great-grandfather Boaz in Ruth 2:12, and it is repeated in Psalms 17:8, 57:1, 63:7 and 91:4, in Matthew 23:37 and in Luke 13:34.

[4] David wrote this song for Jeduthun, one of the three worship leaders at his Tabernacle, who was also known as Ethan. We will talk more about Jeduthun when we look at his own Psalm 89.

[5] Although the title of Psalm 62 does not tell us when David wrote it, verses 3–4 suggest strongly that it was when Absalom's co-conspirators took advantage of David's sickness to try to topple him from his throne.

[6] There is a play on words here in Hebrew, since the phrase *"Surely the lowborn are but a breath"* can also be translated *"Surely the sons of Adam are but Abel."* Abel was the first human being to taste death.

[7] He says this in 62:1 and 5. These two facts made God his *Rock*, his *Salvation* and his *Fortress* in 62:2 and 6.

That's why we can also keep singing when times are hard. There is no better context in which to get to know God and to find rest for our souls in him.[8]

I love looking at the stars from my back garden in London. There aren't too many of them, but those few balls of fire many light years away are enough to capture my attention. Earlier this month, however, I went on holiday to the countryside in the south of France and, away from the bright lights of London, I could see a whole host of amazing new stars which I never see at home. Psalm 62 teaches us to value the times in our lives when the night seems darkest.[9] They are the times when we see God's character shining brightest, when we can gain an even greater passion for his name.

In Psalm 63, David's troubles strip away everything until all he is left with is *a passion for God's friendship*. The English proverb claims that absence makes the heart grow fonder, and when Absalom's rebellion forced David to flee from the Tabernacle he discovered that it's true.[10] He hid in the scorching desert of Judah, *"in a dry and parched land where there is no water"*, but he confesses that his true thirst was to know deeper friendship with the Lord (63:1).[11] As he faces up to the fact that he may die, he confesses that he values the Lord's love more than his life (63:3).[12] He struggles with hunger as a desert outlaw but insists that if only he can enjoy God's friendship, *"I*

---

[8] This requires discipline on our part. David's soul only found rest in God (62:1–2) because he commanded it to do so (62:5–6) by meditating on these two great facts.

[9] Job understood this and talks in Job 35:10 about *"God my Maker, who gives songs in the night"*.

[10] Although David also hid from Saul in the desert of Judah, 63:11 makes it clear that he wrote this psalm during his second period on the run after he became king (2 Samuel 15:23–28).

[11] David refers literally in 63:1 to *getting up early to seek* the Lord and to his *flesh* desiring the Lord. One of our biggest challenges in developing friendship with the Lord is simply getting out of bed a little earlier. If you are an evening person, David challenges you to make the most of your late nights instead in 63:6.

[12] Far worse than David's sin with Bathsheba is our own sin of breaking the command of Deuteronomy 6:5 and Matthew 22:36–37.

will be fully satisfied as with the richest of foods" (63:5). As he lies awake in bed, he uses the same Hebrew word which is used for husbands and wives becoming one with each other to suggest that God's friendship is even better than the intimacy he enjoys with his royal wives (63:6–8).[13] He enjoyed fellowship with the Lord while he lived in luxury in the palace, but when all those luxuries were stripped away he discovered an even deeper passion for God's friendship.

In Psalm 64, David's troubles strip everything away until all he is left with is *a passion for God's salvation.* He is honest with God in this psalm of complaint, but he also recognizes his trial as an opportunity to rely on God. As a king in a palace he could rely on many things, but his hardships stripped away the wrapping paper around his heart and revealed a greater faith in God's salvation than had been there before.

That's why Charles Spurgeon encourages us to sing like David when times are hard, because there is no greater blessing than that of being stripped by God:

> *Any blessing that comes as the result of the Spirit's work in your soul is a true blessing; though it humbles you, though it strips you... Riches may not do it. There may be a golden wall between you and God. Health will not do it: even the strength and marrow of your bones may keep you at a distance from your God. But anything that draws you nearer to him is a true blessing... My faith shakes off the disguise, snatches the covering from the blessing, and counts it all joy in various trials for the sake of Jesus and for the reward that he has promised. "Oh, that we may be blessed!"*[14]

---

[13] The Hebrew word *dābaq* in 63:8 means *to cleave* or *to stick like glue*, and it is used to describe the intimate union of a husband and wife in Genesis 2:24 and 1 Kings 11:2.

[14] This comes from Charles Spurgeon's sermon at the Metropolitan Tabernacle in London on 11th June 1871.

Summer Precedes Winter
(65:1–68:35)

Where morning dawns, where evening fades, you call forth songs of joy.

(Psalm 65:8)

I spend most of my summers in London plus a couple of weeks in the small farming community where my wife's family live. The difference is enormous. Summer in London is all about stopping work and resting, relaxing and enjoying a few weeks of sunshine. Summer in the farming community is all about busy activity in order to get fences and barns ready for winter. That's why it shouldn't surprise us that we find four psalms in Book II which praise God during the good times as part of our lesson in how to sing when times are hard. They were placed here deliberately in order to teach us how to make the most of summer days to prepare our souls for winter days to come.

We can tell that Psalms 65–68 belong together by the way that all four of them are marked in their titles not only as *psalms* but also as *songs*. Two were written by David and two are anonymous, but all four of them are marked for congregational singing. They are a reminder that thinking that we can learn to sing in the tough times when the tough times arrive is as foolish as a farmer who sunbathes all summer and only starts repairing his barns once the winter storms are upon him. Don Carson points out that

> *One of the major causes of devastating grief and confusion among Christians is that our expectations are false. We*

do not give the subject of evil and suffering the thought it deserves until we ourselves are confronted with tragedy. If by that point our beliefs – not well thought out but deeply ingrained – are largely out of step with the God who has disclosed himself in the Bible and supremely in Jesus, then the pain from the personal tragedy may be multiplied many times over.[1]

These psalms were placed here to help us make the most of our soul's summer in order to prepare for its winter.

Psalm 65 is a song of happy praise, but don't let that stop you from noticing how similar it is to a farmer preparing for winter. David wrote it for the worshippers at his Tabernacle on Mount Zion (65:1) and for those who would throng to the courtyards of Solomon's Temple in days to come (65:4).[2] He wanted them to prepare one another for times of hardship by singing about God's faithfulness in times of crisis before they got there, reminding themselves that he answers prayer (65:1–2), forgives sin (65:3), performs miracles (65:5–8) and provides (65:9–13). *"Happy are those you choose and bring near to live in your courts,"* he reminds us, because *"We are filled with the good things of your house."*[3] Unless church leaders teach Christians to sing songs about God's all-sufficiency and power during the good times, they will never make it through the bad times.

Psalm 66 is another song of exuberant praise, but it also prepares worshippers for the wintertime to come. It tells them to worship the Lord for what he has done in the past (66:1–4), and reminds them that the Lord parted the Red Sea and the River

128

---

[1] D.A. Carson in *How Long, O Lord?: Reflections on Suffering and Evil* (1990).

[2] This psalm seems to progress in its three stanzas from the Exodus to the Red Sea to Israel's entry into the Promised Land. In that case, 65:2 and 5 reminds us that he saved Israel in order to save all nations.

[3] 65:4 uses the same Hebrew construction as is used in 1:1 to say *"How happy is the one…"* The great hymn writer Isaac Watts used this verse to argue that *"Nearness to God is the foundation of a creature's happiness."*

Jordan (66:5-7).[4] It calls people from every nation to worship alongside Israel because the Lord refined his People through the crucible of suffering in Egypt and brought them out of slavery into the Promised Land (66:8-12).[5] It tells them to bring their own thanks to God for the many ways he has delivered them in times of trouble (66:13-15), and it stirs them to testify to one another about what God has done for them (66:16-20).[6] Songs like this build our faith for fresh interventions from God whenever winter returns to our lives.

Psalm 67 is the shortest of the four psalms, but it reminds us that God cares more about our being blessed than we do. Verse 1 is a summary of the priestly blessing which the Lord told Aaron and his sons to use in Numbers 6:22-27, and it is followed by a *selāh* or *instrumental solo* which enables worshippers to meditate on the words of that great blessing. When this musical interlude ends, we are encouraged to celebrate the fact that God will surely bless us because this is how he demonstrates his character to the unbelieving nations. Nothing can keep us singing during the winter of our souls as much as a deep understanding that God's eternal plan to save the nations involves him turning our wintertime into glorious spring and summer.[7]

Psalm 68 is the longest of the four songs because David prepares us for days to come by giving us a lengthy overview of Israel's history. The first verse deliberately echoes Numbers 10:33-36 because this psalm recalls the journey which the Ark

[4] 66:6 speaks literally in Hebrew about God drying up the *sea* and allowing them to cross a *river* on foot. This verse is therefore referring to Joshua 3-4 as well as to Exodus 14-15.

[5] Compare 66:10 with 1 Kings 8:51 and Isaiah 48:10. Although this is Israel's history, the psalm deliberately includes the Gentiles in its call to worship in 66:1, 4, 5, 8 and 16.

[6] 66:18 warns us to deal with sin in our hearts today if we want our prayers to be answered in times of trouble tomorrow. This warning is repeated in Proverbs 15:29, Isaiah 1:15, John 9:31, James 5:16 and 1 Peter 3:7.

[7] This theme is repeated in Genesis 12:2-3, Esther 8:17, Zechariah 8:23 and Acts 9:42.

of the Covenant made from Mount Sinai to Mount Zion. The Lord revealed his name to Moses as *Yahweh* at the burning bush on Mount Sinai and then used him to turn a lonely group of slaves into a free nation (68:4–6).[8] He provided water for them in the desert (68:7–10), and he needed to speak only one word in order to drive out the Canaanite kings[9] who were living in the Promised Land (68:11–14).[10] The Lord enabled David to capture Mount Zion and to build a new Tabernacle for his Ark there (68:15–18), and he enabled him to subdue Israel's enemies all the way from the fertile Mount Bashan on Israel's eastern border down to the Mediterranean Sea (68:19–23). David therefore tells worshippers to celebrate the fact that the Ark has now come to rest in the Tabernacle (68:24–27) and to pray for God's blessing in the present as in the past (68:28–31), so that they can continue to worship him as he deserves (68:32–35).

The fact that Paul quotes from Psalm 68:18 and applies it to the life of Jesus in Ephesians 4:8 should remind us that we have an even better song to sing than these four psalms from the Tabernacle on Mount Zion. It should remind us that we have New Testament as well as Old Testament songs to sing in our own summertime. Let's not be foolish and forget that winter always follows summer. Let's sing songs such as these during the good times in order to prepare ourselves to have faith in God's purposes and his promises when the bitter winds of winter blow on our lives.

---

[8] 68:4 is the first time Psalms uses the name *Yah* as a poetic abbreviation for *Yahweh*. It is used twice in Exodus, 47 times in Psalms, 4 times in Isaiah, once in Song of Songs, and nowhere else in the Bible.

[9] Since Paul treats 68:18 as a prophecy about Jesus' ascension to heaven in Ephesians 4:8, Handel's *Messiah* treats 68:11 as a prophecy about the Gospel going to the nations after Pentecost. Just as the Israelite women sang about their army's victory, Jesus the Bridegroom entrusts this task to the Church his Bride.

[10] *Zalmon* was a mountain near Shechem. Since its name means *Shady*, David seems to be contrasting its black appearance with the whiteness of snow. God can turn our dark nights into glorious dawn with just a word.

Seven Dark Days
(69:1–71:24)

I declare your power to the next generation, your
mighty acts to all who are to come.

(Psalm 71:18)

Being told what to do is one thing, but it's no substitute for watching other people do it and copying them. I didn't learn how to play the guitar by reading a book but by watching others, and it's the same with worshipping God when times are hard. That's why I'm so grateful that these three psalms point to seven dark days in Scripture and show us how other people have used the Psalms so that we can follow their example.[1]

The first dark day was when Jesus was betrayed and arrested. He found it so hurtful that Judas would betray him and that those he had created would kill him that he told his disciples, *"My soul is overwhelmed with sorrow to the point of death."*[2] How did he strengthen himself to bear the pain of such betrayal? He turned to Psalm 69:4 and reassured his disciples in John 15:25 that this was simply the fulfilment of David's prophecy about the Messiah: *"They hated me without reason."*[3]

The second dark day was when the early Christians were

---

[1] In quoting from 69:9 in Romans 15, Paul specifically tells us that it was written to teach and encourage us.

[2] Matthew 26:38.

[3] Note that Jesus treats this compilation of Psalms as part of *the Law*, his shorthand phrase for the complete Old Testament. The prophecy in 69:4 is also given in 35:19.

falsely accused of blaspheming God's Temple, as we read in Acts 6:13–14 and 21:28. John was one of them and he tells us in John 2:17 that they drew comfort from the words of Psalm 69:9. If Jesus himself was accused of dishonouring the Temple while fulfilling David's prophecy that *"Zeal for your house will consume me"*, then they could expect be too. Paul also drew strength from Psalm 69:9 and quoted it in Romans 15:3 to argue that we should not be surprised that *"The insults of those who insult you have fallen on me."* David loved the Tabernacle yet was exiled from Mount Zion. Jesus loved the Temple yet was crucified by its priests. So it should therefore not surprise us when those we thought were brothers hate us too.

The third dark day was when Jesus was crucified. When Jesus cried out in John 19:28 that *"I am thirsty,"* John tells us that he did this *"so that Scripture would be fulfilled"*. It fulfilled Psalm 69:3 – *"I am worn out calling for help; my throat is parched"* – and Psalm 69:21 – *"They put gall in my food and gave me vinegar for my thirst."* Even as the soldiers laughed that their cruel mixture of wine and vinegar would make Jesus even thirstier, he drew encouragement from this psalm that every single one of the Old Testament prophecies about him was being fulfilled.[4]

The fourth dark day was when Peter and the other apostles tried to come to terms with what their friend Judas Iscariot had done to Jesus. We read in Acts 1:15–26 that Peter rallied the remaining 120 believers after Jesus' ascension and turned to Psalm 69:25, saying, *"Brothers and sisters, the Scripture had to be fulfilled in which the Holy Spirit spoke long ago through David concerning Judas... For it is written in the Book of Psalms: 'May his place be deserted; let there be no one to dwell in it.'"*[5] How did

---

[4] Handel's *Messiah* treats 69:20 as Jesus' words from the cross too. Although this entire psalm makes sense in the mouth of David when on the run from Absalom, we also need to read it with New Testament eyes.

[5] Peter must have understood that Ahithophel's betrayal of David in Psalm 69 was an Old Testament picture of Judas betraying Jesus. We can also see this by comparing 2 Samuel 17:23 with Matthew 27:1–5.

Peter encourage the tiny remnant of Christians in the aftermath of one of the apostles being unmasked as a traitor? How did he teach them to face forwards and to find a replacement leader instead of wallowing in their leadership disappointment? He did exactly the same thing which we need to do in the same situation. He turned to the Psalms and strengthened their faith that God is Lord of what appears to go wrong as well as Lord of what appears to go right.

The fifth dark day is tackled by Paul when he writes to the Romans in 57 AD. He lays hold of one of the biggest questions which was being asked in his generation all across the Roman Empire: why had so few Jews recognized Jesus as their Messiah? It was such a painful question for the former Pharisee Paul that he confesses in Romans 9:2–3 that *"I have great sorrow and unceasing anguish in my heart. For I could wish that I myself were cursed and cut off from Christ for the sake of my people, those of my own race, the people of Israel."* Yet rather than languish in his pain and sorrow, he goes to find his answers in the book of Psalms. He quotes from Psalm 69:22–23 in Romans 11:9–10 to encourage his readers that, since God had predicted the hardheartedness of the Jews in 69:22–29, he had also predicted their ultimate revival and salvation in days to come in 69:30–36.

The sixth dark day belonged to David himself, since this seems by far the best explanation for the highly unusual Psalm 70. If you have been reading closely, you will notice that it is nothing more than a slightly revised repeat of Psalm 40:13–17. The worship leaders who compiled the book of Psalms appear to have included it as an example of how David used his own psalms so that we can do the same. They mark it as a *reminder psalm* because David used a few verses from a psalm he had written previously in order to remind the Lord of his fresh plight.[6] They want us to learn to do the same as David. They

---

[6] Most English translators assume that God does not need reminding and therefore mistranslate the Hebrew word used in the titles of Psalms 38 and 70 as *a petition*. However, the main reason this psalm is included in the collection

want us to draw encouragement from these songs in our darkest hours, like Jesus, Peter and Paul.[7]

The seventh dark day also belonged to David just before he died. Psalm 71 is technically anonymous, but its style is so similar to David's and it fits so well with what we know happened in David's final years that he probably wrote it when his son Adonijah tried to seize the throne just before David died in 1 Kings 1. This would also fit well with the fact that the psalm which follows it is the first in the collection which was written by Solomon, David's rightful successor as king.[8] David reminds the Lord that he has been faithful to him in the springtime of his youth (71:5–6) and in the summertime of his adult reign (71:15–17),[9] and he prays that therefore the Lord must not abandon him in the wintertime of his old age (71:9 and 18). We are invited to watch David, still praying after all those years, in order to learn how to do the same.[10]

Three psalms. Seven dark days. Seven examples of how those who follow the Lord have always used the book of Psalms to keep them singing when times are hard. Let's follow their example and use these 150 songs in the same way. When the night is darkest, the book of Psalms lights up the way for us to journey on.

---

is precisely because God wants us to remind him of prayers we have already prayed.

[7] Note the balance of 70:1 and 5. David sings and rejoices in the Lord during his trials, but he also begs repeatedly for his trials to be over very soon. Rejoicing *in* trials is different from rejoicing *over* trials!

[8] Psalm 71:18 focuses on David's desire to hand his throne over well to the next generation. Psalm 72 focuses on the splendour of Solomon's reign as a result. There is nothing random about the order of the Psalms.

[9] David was the greatest worshipper in the Old Testament, but he tells us in 71:15–17 that even his long life of worship has not exhausted him of reasons to praise the Lord. Neither will ours.

[10] As with Psalm 70, David appears to have taken 31:1–3 and reworked his earlier words to form 71:1–3.

When the King Arrives
(72:1–20)

*Endow the king with your justice, O God, the royal
son with your righteousness.*

(Psalm 72:1)

Book II of Psalms ends like any good story. The hero finally
arrives on stage and changes everything. This is the first psalm
so far which was written by Solomon (the other one is Psalm
127), and the editors of Psalms have kept it back for this moment
for a reason.[1] They want to end Book II with one last reason
for us to sing when times are hard. They want to show us what
will happen when the King arrives.

To understand Psalm 72 it helps to know a little Hebrew
grammar. It's important to grasp that Hebrew "imperfect
tenses" talk about something which *is* or *will be*, while Hebrew
"jussives" express a prayer that something *might be* a certain
way. Since imperfect and jussive verbs look identical in most
cases, Solomon wrote this psalm with deliberate ambiguity.[2]
The original NIV translation treats the verbs as imperfect tenses,
telling us for example in 72:11 that *"All kings **will** bow down to
him and all nations **will** serve him."* The revised NIV translation
which was published in 2011 takes the opposite view and treats
the verbs as jussives, praying *"**May** all kings bow down to him*

135

---

[1] The Hebrew title could technically mean that the psalm was written *for*
Solomon, but elsewhere it means the psalms *of* David. 1 Kings 4:32 tells us
Solomon was in fact a prolific songwriter.

[2] We can tell that the verbs are imperfect in 72:2 and 11 and jussives in 72:11
and 15, but the other verbs are unclear.

and **may** all nations serve him." It isn't a question of which one of them is right. The whole point is that the meaning is deliberately ambiguous.

If we read the verbs as jussives, the final editors of Psalms are showing us that Solomon's reign might have been the answer to Israel's anguished prayers. Since many of the hardships in Book II were caused by sin, injustice, civil war and foreign invasion during the reigns of Saul and David, they want to show us that these prayers really made a difference. None of the songs we sing when times are hard is ever forgotten by God. Solomon's name meant *Peaceful One* and his reign was to be a golden age of peace and prosperity for God's People.

Solomon told the Israelites to pray that he would rule with justice and righteousness (72:1–2). He told them to pray that his reign would be peaceful and prosperous (72:3–7), and that foreign rulers would come to Jerusalem bearing tribute instead of bearing arms (72:8–11).[3] He told them to pray that his reign would be marked by care for the poor and needy (72:12–14), that it would be long and successful (72:15–17a) and that it would fulfil God's promise to Abraham in Genesis 12:2–3 that Israel would be blessed and become a blessing to the nations (72:17b). They were to pray this psalm as a series of jussives which asked the Lord that his reign *might be* the answer to the prayers which fill Book II. Solomon told them to end their prayer with celebration that the Lord could turn their *might-bes* into *will-bes* (72:18–19).

On one level Solomon was right: his reign was just as the Israelites prayed. We read in 1 Kings 10 that a foreign visitor to Jerusalem exclaimed that *"Because of the Lord's eternal love for Israel, he has made you king to maintain justice and righteousness."* We read that foreign rulers brought so many tributes to his palace that *"Nothing was made of silver, because*

---

[3] The *River* was the Euphrates, *Tarshish* was in Spain, and *Sheba* and *Seba* were modern-day Yemen and Sudan. These were the eastern, western and southernmost limits of Hebrew world geography.

silver was considered of little value in Solomon's days... The king made silver as common in Jerusalem as stones." We even read that some of the foreign visitors left the Temple as worshippers of the God of Israel.

But on another level Solomon was wrong: we read in 1 Kings 11 that he was a very human king who couldn't go the distance. Midway through his reign he started worshipping idols and Israel started suffering from Edomite and Aramean raiding parties before tumbling into a civil war which tore apart their kingdom. Solomon was not to be the ultimate answer to the painful prayers which we find throughout Book II. A better King was yet to come.

If Solomon was a partial answer to the prayers prayed in Book II, Jesus was the complete and better answer.[4] The jussive prayers turn into future prophecies as we read that Jesus *will be* the righteous judge (72:1–2), who *will* crush the great oppressor Satan to save the souls of anyone who cries out under the burden of their sin (72:3–4). His reign *will* endure forever (72:5–7), which is why Isaac Watts based his hymn "Jesus shall reign, where'er the sun does its successive journeys run" on 72:5 and 17. His Kingdom *will* stretch *"from sea to sea"* and *"to the ends of the earth"* (72:8–11). He *will* save us from death (72:12–14), and there *will* be no end to his Kingdom rule (72:15–17a). He *will* save people from every nation and people group, uniting them together to sing the words of 72:18–20 as a doxology, or as final verses of praise. Whereas Israel prayed that Solomon *might be* and hoped that he *would be*, Jesus tells us that his Kingdom *has come* and that we can now experience it by praying *"Let your kingdom come."*[5] Read this way, Psalm 72 isn't just the last psalm in Book II. It is also the book's conclusion.

---

[4] Jesus made this link between Solomon's failure and his own perfection when he told the Jews that *"one greater than Solomon is here"* (Matthew 12:42; Luke 11:31).

[5] Verse 15b reminds us that we get to extend the Kingdom through our prayers (Matthew 6:10).

In the story *The Lion, the Witch and the Wardrobe*, the beavers recall an ancient prophecy about what will happen when the lion Aslan appears to put an end to their suffering under Narnia's endless winter. *"Wrong will be right, when Aslan comes in sight; At the sound of his roar, sorrows will be no more; When he bares his teeth, winter meets its death; And when he shakes his mane, we shall have spring again."*[6] C. S. Lewis tells us that when the children heard the words of the song, *"that strange feeling – like the first signs of spring, like good news – had come over them"*, and that's what the editors of Psalms want us to feel as we reach the end of Book II and understand that it is a description of King Jesus. Although Solomon's psalm ends in 72:19 and 72:20 is strictly just an editorial marker before Book III,[7] they want us to treat 72:18–19 as a doxology which ends the whole of Book II and not merely this psalm. Whatever desperate prayers we have sung in the dark of night and dead of winter, they want us to praise God that our prayers will be answered just as soon as the King arrives.

The Israelites sang this song with jussive verbs which dreamed of what might happen when their Messiah finally came. We get to sing it as a glorious statement of our new reality in light of the fact that King Jesus has indeed come.

So let's sing. Let's sing. Let's sing when times are hard. Let's sing because everything has changed for us with the arrival of the King.

---

[6] C. S. Lewis in *The Lion, the Witch and the Wardrobe* (1950).

[7] This is obvious from the fact that Psalm 72 is not a prayer of David at all! The editors of Psalms are preparing us for the fact that Book III consists mainly of psalms by Asaph, Ethan and the Sons of Korah.

Book III – Psalms 73–89:

Sing Out How You Really Feel

Why Does God Allow Suffering? (73:1–28)

*When I tried to understand all this, it troubled me
deeply till I entered the sanctuary of God; then I
understood their final destiny.*

(Psalm 73:16–17)

You may think that you hate hypocrisy and playacting, but God
wants you to know that he hates it even more. He can't stand
it when people pour out empty religious words which don't
reflect what they are truly feeling on the inside. Prayer is a two-
way conversation in which we express our deepest feelings to
the Lord and take time to listen to his reply. That's why Book
III of Psalms tells us to sing honestly about how we are really
feeling. It tells us that God hates us lying. Even when we do it in
church on Sunday.

Those who have understood Psalms best throughout
Church history have always been surprised at how raw and
honest the psalmists are. John Calvin described Psalms as *"an
anatomy of all the parts of the soul; for there is not an emotion of
which anyone can be conscious that is not here represented as in
a mirror."*[1] Athanasius observed that

> *Elsewhere in the Bible you read only that the Law
> commands this or that to be done, you listen to the
> Prophets to learn about the Saviour's coming, or you
> turn to the historical books to learn the doings of the*

---

[1] Calvin wrote this in about 1556 in the preface to his *Commentary on the
Book of Psalms*.

kings and holy men; but in the Psalter, besides all these
things, you learn about yourself. You find depicted in it
all the movements of your soul, all its changes, its ups
and downs, its failures and recoveries.[2]

Only one of the seventeen psalms that make up Book III
was written by David. All of the others were written by the
worship leaders he appointed. It's as if the editors of Psalms
grouped these seventeen songs together in order to show us
how ordinary men and women should express their ordinary
feelings to the Lord.

But expressing our feelings to the Lord is not enough. The
psalmists want to help us to be changed even as we pray. John
Calvin continues by observing that *"Genuine and earnest prayer*
proceeds first from a sense of our need, then from faith in the
promises of God. It is by studying these inspired compositions
that people will be best awakened to a sense of their maladies
and, at the same time, instructed how to find remedies for their
cure." Athanasius adds that *"Whatever your need or trouble,*
from this same book you can select a form of words to fit it, so 141
that you do not merely hear and then pass on, but learn the way
to remedy your ill." Let's therefore learn from these seventeen
songs which were written by Asaph, Ethan and the Sons of
Korah.[3] Let's sing to God about how we really feel and let him
change us as we do so.

Asaph wrote the eleven psalms which form the first two-
thirds of Book III.[4] He starts with one of the biggest questions

---

[2] Athanasius wrote this in about 370 AD in his *Letter to Marcellinus on the Meaning of the Psalms*.

[3] Asaph wrote Psalms 73–83, the Sons of Korah wrote Psalms 84–85 and 87–88, David wrote Psalm 86 and Ethan wrote Psalm 89. Since these worship leaders were all Levites, Book III is known as "the Levite Psalter".

[4] Asaph was the main worship leader at David's Tabernacle, while Ethan and the Sons of Korah led worship at Moses' Tabernacle (1 Chronicles 16:37–42). Once the Temple was built, their three worship choirs came together. Asaph wrote Psalm 50 and Psalms 73–83.

which can trouble our hearts: Psalm 73 deals with the question, *Why doesn't God stop all the suffering in the world?* He states the general principle in 73:1 that God is good and just, but then launches into thirteen verses of complaint about how he feels when he looks at the suffering all around him. Even though he is one of the main worship leaders at the Temple, he confesses that he almost lost his faith when he saw the wicked prospering (73:2–3) and supposing that God doesn't see the wicked things they do (73:4–12). He confesses that he almost threw in the towel on his faith once and for all (73:13–14).[5] What is even more shocking than Asaph's direct language is that the Lord seems rather pleased with his honesty in prayer. He calls Asaph a prophet in Matthew 13:35 and looks back fondly in Nehemiah 12:46 to the days when Asaph prayed prayers which were music to his ears!

Unless Asaph had been this honest, he would not have received an answer. The fourth-century theologian Ambrose described psalms like this one as *"A gymnasium which is open for all souls to use, where the different psalms are like different exercises set out before him. In that gymnasium, in that stadium of virtue, he can choose the exercises that will train him best to win the victor's crown."*[6] The first half of Asaph's prayer is like a workout for his soul, and he reaps the benefit of his exercise in the second half of his prayer. He tells us that when he went into the Temple to meet with God, he started to grasp why he does not always appear to judge the wicked.[7] He caught a big vision of God which made him realize how blinkered he had

---

[5] Asaph is deceived, since God *does* judge the wicked in this life, but that is not the point. This psalm teaches us to express the way we feel, even when our feelings are wrong.

[6] Ambrose was Archbishop of Milan and wrote this in about 385 AD in his *Commentary on the Psalms*.

[7] Asaph refers literally in 73:17 to *the sanctuaries of God*. If he wrote during David's reign, he means both Tabernacles, but if he wrote during Solomon's reign, it refers to the different parts of the Temple. Either way, this verse reminds us that we need fellowship with other Christians when we are feeling down.

been (73:15–17).[8] God will surely judge the wicked swiftly and suddenly (73:18–20),[9] and Asaph felt as stupid as a donkey not to have seen this all along (73:21–22). He worships the Lord for the fact that ill-earned riches will not last, but that the righteous have the Lord as their portion, both in this life and for evermore (73:23–28).[10] Like Job, Asaph discovers that when he shares his feelings honestly in prayer he receives an answer through a fresh revelation of the Lord which changes everything.

The big question which confronts us in Psalm 73 and the rest of Book III is *Will we pray this way ourselves?* Will we be as bold and honest as Asaph in prayer, or will we fall for the lie that God wants sweet platitudes which masquerade as prayer? When did you last speak to God with the same frank emotion as Asaph in this psalm? Unless you unburden your heart in prayer, you must not be surprised if your prayer life feels repetitive and lifeless. But if you pour out your heart like Asaph, you will discover that emptying your heart enables God to fill it with fresh faith and a fresh desire to worship him. When we express who we really are in prayer, the Lord responds by revealing to us who he really is.

If you are a church leader or a worship leader, God wants to speak to you urgently through Book III. When was the last time you helped your congregation to express their deepest, darkest and most unspoken emotions to God? Let's not short-change those we lead with upbeat songs and well-crafted sermons

[8] Note Asaph's wisdom in 73:15. As Israel's worship leader, he knows better than to harm those he leads by blurting out his feelings. He does not mark this psalm for congregational singing because leaders need to pray honestly in private so they can share with those they lead what God has said in reply (73:21–28).

[9] It was this knowledge which helped David in Psalm 37:37–38, Job in Job 27:8 and Solomon in Ecclesiastes 8:12–13, when they prayed their own honest prayers about the injustice in the world.

[10] The Lord had promised in Numbers 18:21–24 and Deuteronomy 10:9 and 18:1–2 to be the Levites' portion instead of giving them land. Asaph is a Levite and he invites us to treat the Lord as our portion too.

while forgetting that their real need is to be taught to pray.[11] Let's teach them the message of Book III of Psalms. Let's teach them to sing about the way they really feel.

---

[11] This is even true of non-Christians. 73:17 reminds us that this kind of praying can achieve more breakthrough in their searching than a brilliant lecture in apologetics.

Crisis Prayers (74:1–23)

O God, why have you rejected us forever?

(Psalm 74:1)

If you were shocked by the honesty of Asaph's prayer in Psalm 73, then hold onto your seat for Psalm 74. If anything, Asaph gets more honest and more shocking as he expresses his feelings about God's judgment on Jerusalem.

Psalm 74 appears to describe the Babylonians destroying Jerusalem and its Temple in 586 BC. Since it describes Mount Zion as the place *"where you dwelt"* and speaks of Israel's enemies burning the Temple to the ground, most readers assume that Asaph can't actually have written it. They wonder if perhaps it was written by the leaders of his worship choir long after he died.[1] Yet the final editors of Psalms insist that Asaph wrote it, and they place it among his other songs for a reason.[2] In 2 Chronicles 29:30 we are told that Asaph was a *seer* of visions and Matthew 13:35 tells us that he was a *prophet*. The Lord appears to have granted him a vision of what would happen to Jerusalem in days to come, and Asaph expresses back to the Lord how that vision makes him feel. He marks his prayer as a *maskīl* because he wants to teach the Israelites how to pray when the events of his vision finally come to pass. He also wants to teach us how to pray whenever we feel that God's People are in crisis.

Just like the previous psalm, Asaph begins Psalm 74 with

---

[1] We can tell that his worship choir still existed many years later from Ezra 2:41 and 3:10–11.

[2] These titles existed in the earliest Hebrew manuscripts. We can tell that the psalmists wrote many of them from the way that Asaph uses the title of Psalm 77 to dedicate it to his friend Ethan.

several very frank verses about how he is feeling (74:1–11). He reminds the Lord in 74:1 that the Israelites are his *sheep* and that he therefore needs to be the Shepherd which he promised he would be in Psalm 23. He accuses the Lord of rejecting them (which Romans 11:1 tells us categorically isn't true), and he worries that the Lord has rejected them forever (despite the fact that he vowed not to do so in Deuteronomy 30:1–6). It doesn't matter that Asaph is wrong-headed. That's simply not the point. He is modelling how we should pray when we are overcome by the disaster which has befallen God's People.

Asaph launches into a detailed lament in 74:2–11.[3] He reminds God of his history with Israel (74:2) and of the arrogance and sinfulness with which the enemy soldiers destroyed the Temple (74:3–8).[4] He accuses God of depriving Israel of miracles and of prophets (74:9),[5] pointing out that the Lord's reputation has been dragged through the gutter because of what has happened to his People (74:10). He ends by accusing God of having his hands in his pockets when he should be rising up to destroy the wicked and to save his People (74:11). If you have never prayed this way, you need to learn from Asaph's *maskīl*. This kind of honesty may sound forceful, but it is music to God's ears.

As with the previous psalm, the halfway mark proves to be a turning point. We learned in 62:8 that *pouring out our hearts*

---

[3] Book II taught us how to sing when times are hard, and one of its features was that it used the general name *Elōhīm* instead of the more intimate name *Yahweh*. Asaph continues this up until Psalm 83, at which point the psalmists revert to using *Yahweh* as their primary name for God.

[4] Solomon had been too devout to allow chisels to be used on site during the building of the Temple (1 Kings 6:7), yet the Babylonians dared to use *axes* and *sledgehammers* to destroy it. They then probably raised up banners of their idols before going out to destroy the Lord's other shrines throughout the rest of Judah too.

[5] This wasn't true, since Jeremiah and Ezekiel both prophesied before and during the exile. Asaph is teaching us to express how we feel to the Lord, even if some of what we feel is wrong.

to God is a key part of coming through to a place where we can *trust in him at all times*, and Asaph discovers that this is true. As he sings out his deepest frustrations and confused questions, he pricks his own conscience that he has lost sight of God's character. Of course the God of Israel hasn't got his hands in his pockets, he realizes in 74:12. *"God is my King from long ago,"* he confesses. *"He brings salvation on the earth."*

Asaph showed us in the previous psalm that telling God how we really feel can change our perspective. The same thing happens here, as he becomes confident in the second half of Psalm 74 that he can trust the Lord. If God brought Israel out of Egypt and across the Red Sea, he will also bring back Judah from Babylon and across the River Euphrates (74:13–14).[6] If God prospered Israel in the wilderness by bringing forth water from a rock, he will also prosper Judah during their exile (74:15a).[7] If God dried up the River Jordan and kept the sun in the sky to help Joshua defeat the Canaanites within the boundaries of the Promised Land, he will also resettle the survivors of the exile back in the Promised Land (74:15b-17).[8] The key word in the first half of this psalm was *why?*, but the key word in each of these five verses is *you*. When we are honest with God it makes room for him to refocus our vision and to transform our hearts even as we pray.

Asaph is now able to end his prayer in a way which is guaranteed to get an answer (74:18–23). He still asks the Lord to remember the enemy's arrogance and still tells him that he feels as if he has forgotten his afflicted People; he still pleads with him not to forget his covenant with Israel and to get up off

---

[6] The *Leviathan* was a sea monster but Asaph uses it as a metaphor for Egypt. Isaiah 52:11–12 and Ezra 1:4 pick up on Asaph's idea that the return from Babylon will be a "second exodus" for Israel.

[7] Exodus 17:1–7 and Numbers 20:1–11. Since 74:14 tells us literally that *the people of the desert* ate what was left of shattered Egypt, this may also be a reference back to Exodus 12:36.

[8] This appears to be a reference to Joshua 3:15–17 and 10:12–14.

his throne to fulfil his purposes; he still asks him not to ignore the noisy clamour of those who have destroyed his Temple;[9] but this time his perspective has completely changed. His desperate confusion has given way to faith that God will answer his anguished prayers. He no longer sees the Babylonians as strategic geniuses who have thwarted the will of God, but as *"fools"* who have bitten off more than they can chew by defying the Lord.[10] He is no longer worried that God has his hands in his pockets. He is convinced that the Lord will hear his prayer and will get up off his throne to fight.[11]

We need to pray these kind of honest prayers today. In my country, England, over 80 per cent of people attended church in 1945, but that number has haemorrhaged down to only 6 per cent in 2005.[12] The number of people in their twenties attending church dropped by 55 per cent in the twenty years from 1985 to 2005, so that now only three in every hundred twenty-somethings attend church.[13] Frankly, the situation for the People of God in my country is as terrible as the one which Asaph saw in his vision. We need to cry out our honest prayers to God, because when we do so Asaph promises us that God will respond to our honesty with answered prayer.

---

[9] There is a deliberate parallel between 74:18 and 74:2, between 74:18 and 74:10–11, between 74:19–20 and 74:1–2, and between 74:20–23 and 74:4–9. Asaph makes similar points but with a different perspective.

[10] The Lord would humiliate King Nebuchadnezzar in Daniel 4:28–33 before handing Babylon over to the Persians in 539 BC, but it also appears that he transformed the hearts of Nebuchadnezzar and many of the Babylonians (Daniel 4:34–37). God answers our heartfelt prayers far more than we can ever imagine.

[11] Asaph described the Israelites as *sheep* in 74:1 and he describes them as a *turtle dove* in 74:19. He may be thinking of David's promise that Israel is God's *dove* in 68:13, and trusting him to care for his fragile People.

[12] This data comes from the English Church Census in 2005.

[13] From a UK Evangelical Alliance survey entitled *The 18–30 Mission: The Missing Generation?* (2009).

Get Ready (75:1–77:20)

I remembered my songs in the night.

(Psalm 77:6)

Captain John Franklin thought he had prepared for his expedition to the North Pole in 1845. He and his crew took more provisions with them on board their two ships than any other Arctic explorers, either before or since. But when the frozen remains of his dead party were discovered, it became evident just how superficial his preparations had been. He had taken silver cutlery, crystal glasses, china plates and a library of over 1,000 books. He had taken all the trappings of an English gentleman but he hadn't taken Arctic clothes. His superficial preparations had looked impressive but had proved fatal. We can't expect anything different ourselves if we prepare ourselves for spiritual wintertime with superficial prayers.

Asaph is very positive in Psalms 75 and 76. These are songs which he wrote during the good times before he experienced the harsh temperatures of spiritual wintertime. But don't miss the honesty as he praises God while things are going well. It would make all the difference to his life when things suddenly started to go wrong.

Psalm 75 is set to the same tune which David used for the three songs which he wrote under intense pressure in Psalms 57–59. That's very important because it means that these upbeat words were set to a sombre tune which warned that troubled times were just around the corner (think of "The Imperial March" in *Star Wars*). It explains why Asaph does not fill these ten short verses with superficial thank-yous and empty praise. He doesn't just thank God for his name in theory, but that his name is *near* (75:1). He doesn't just talk about God's judgment but quotes the Lord's promise that he will judge *at the appointed time* (75:2–5).[1] He doesn't wait until his world starts shaking before he reminds himself that the Lord is the one who holds its pillars firm. He prepares himself for Arctic temperatures while it is still summertime.

Asaph worships the Lord for being sovereign over every promotion and demotion (75:6–8).[2] This is perhaps the clearest statement in the whole of the Bible that *"No one... can exalt themselves... He brings one down, he exalts another."* Asaph doesn't wait for the sting of being passed up for promotion before he prepares his heart to react in a godly fashion. He writes a song of deep and frank emotion which ends by praising God that he alone lifts up and casts down, and he promises to *"declare this forever"* (75:9–10).

He continues in the same vein in Psalm 76. This is another song which was sung during the good times, and this time Asaph focuses on God's power to defend Jerusalem. There is nothing superficial about his worship as he prepares himself for dangers yet to come.[3] Whereas he began the previous psalm by saying that the Lord's name is near, he begins Psalm 76 by saying that the Lord's name is *great in Israel* (76:1–3). He reminds himself that the invisible God is seen through his People as they gather to worship him in the Tabernacle on Mount Zion.[4] It would be

---

[1] Since many of our trials are caused by God's delays, we need to praise God in the good times that he is the God who always acts *"at just the right time"* (John 7:6; Romans 5:6; Galatians 4:4).

[2] *Horns* represented *strength* in a community which was used to farming bulls and goats. Ethan uses a similar metaphor in 89:17, and so do 148:14 and Zechariah 1:21.

[3] The title in the Greek Septuagint says that this proved an important psalm for Israel when Assyria besieged Jerusalem. English translations do not include this because it was not in Asaph's original title.

[4] Asaph talks about the Tabernacle rather than Temple in 76:2, which explains why this is the only Old Testament reference to *Salem* outside Genesis 14:18.

safer to attack a lion's lair than to besiege the mountain where God dwells.[5] Asaph reminds himself that God's enemies are defeated *there* – at the Tabernacle where his people worship.[6] Asaph praises the Lord during the good times that he answers prayer in order to prepare himself for tougher times to come.

Asaph now bursts into seven verses that recall God's victories in the past, but he majors on his feelings about those victories rather than on the historical detail (76:4–10). It doesn't matter which precise victories he has in mind; what matters is that he sings that God is glorified by judging the wicked and that no one can stand before the Lord when he is angry (76:10).[7] He ends his song by urging Israel to obey the Lord and by turning to the pagan nations and warning them to fear him too (76:11–12). There doesn't appear to have been any threat of foreign invasion when Asaph wrote this, but he sings about the Lord's great power in battle during peacetime to prepare himself for times to come.[8]

Sure enough, tough times arrive in Psalm 77. If Asaph had acted like Captain Franklin and sung superficial songs during the good times, he would never have survived. He expresses his frank bewilderment that God does not appear to be answering his anguished prayers (77:1–9). His language suggests that the crisis was personal rather than national, but the fact that he dedicates the psalm to his friend Ethan reminds us that such

---

That was the name for Jerusalem when Melchizedek was king, so Asaph is linking David to the priest-king Melchizedek (see Psalm 110).

[5] The Hebrew word translated *dwelling place* means literally a lion's *den*, and it is used this way in six out of its eight other uses in the Old Testament. We are meant to understand that the Tabernacle is God's mighty lair.

[6] Jesus also taught that victories are made in the place of prayer and only worked out subsequently on the battlefield (Mark 9:29 and John 11:41).

[7] The Hebrew of 76:10 could mean either that God's wrath glorifies him by causing the survivors to fear him, or that human wrath glorifies him when he turns people's angry schemes to his own advantage.

[8] Note that Asaph worships the Lord for living both in Zion (76:2) and in heaven (76:8). We need this double view of both God's nearness and his greatness to sustain us through the tough times.

personal crises are common to us all.[9] Asaph is as honest as he was back in 74:1 that he feels as if the Lord has rejected him forever and as if the Lord might have forgotten his covenant love towards him (77:7–9).[10] The key which unlocks these verses can be found in 77:6, where Asaph says: *"I remembered my songs in the night."* He is not referring to songs he sings in the night, like Job 35:10 or Psalm 42:8, but to the fact that in the night-time of his soul he remembers the songs he used to sing. Asaph is telling us that he would have frozen to death in his soul's winter had he not sung out how he really felt in summertime.

Unlike the superficial Captain Franklin, Asaph is well prepared for his ordeal when it arrives. He tells us that he *remembers* and that he *meditates* on days gone by (77:10–12), and this proves the turning point in his prayers. He remembers that the Lord is still the God of Psalms 75–76, the God who redeemed Israel from Egypt (77:13–15),[11] parted the Red Sea (77:16–19) and led them to the Promised Land (77:20).[12] Neither he nor Ethan need therefore flounder in their present crises because they have stored up more than enough faith in their hearts to weather out this icy storm.

Captain Franklin wrote a last message home on 28th May 1847. It simply read, *"All well."* Two weeks later, on 11th June, he died among the frozen trappings of an English gentleman. Don't be like him and waste your summer days mouthing superficial worship to the Lord. Express your deepest feelings during the good times and your words of worship will sustain you when Arctic winds begin to howl.

---

[9] We will read Ethan's own psalm in Psalm 89. His nickname *Jeduthun* meant literally *The Praise Man*, and David also dedicated Psalms 39 and 62 to him.

[10] The word for *unfailing love* in 77:8 is *ḥēsēd*, a word used 127 times in Psalms to describe the Lord's love towards his covenant People.

[11] When Asaph prays in 77:14 that *"You are the God who performs miracles,"* he is reminding himself that such things are simply part of God's character. Miracles are simply what God loves to do.

[12] Asaph is struggling to see God at work in his life, so he reminds himself in 77:19 that God's footsteps were not seen when he parted the Red Sea either.

God-Centred Prayers
(78:1–80:19)

I will utter hidden things, things from of old – things we have heard and known, things our ancestors have told us.

(Psalm 78:2–3)

Eugene Peterson writes:

Our culture presents us with forms of prayer that are mostly self-expression – pouring ourselves out before God or lifting our gratitude to God as we feel the need and have the occasion. Such prayer is dominated by a sense of self. But prayer, mature prayer, is dominated by a sense of God. Prayer rescues us from a preoccupation with ourselves and pulls us into adoration of and pilgrimage to God... Fundamentally, prayer is our response to the God who speaks to us. God's word is always first. He gets the first word in, always. We answer.[1]

I find that observation very helpful. It helps us to grasp that singing to God about how we feel does not simply mean expressing what is in our hearts. As Asaph shows us in Psalm 78, our hearts can become lifeless and bereft of spiritual emotion unless we feed them on God. The worship which sustains us through the tough times does not begin with our own emotion. It feeds on the character of God and, after it has eaten, it finds

---

[1] Eugene Peterson in *Under the Predictable Plant* (1992).

that it is full of deep feelings to speak back to the one who initiates all true prayer.

Psalm 78 is so significant that Jesus quotes from it twice, referring to 78:2 in Matthew 13:35 and to 78:24–25 in John 6:31. Asaph wrote it as a *maskīl*, or *teaching psalm*, and he begins it by reminding us that he is a teacher and a prophet (78:1–8).[2] This is the second longest psalm in the whole collection because Asaph wants to give us a detailed reminder of what the Lord did in the lives of believers long before we were ever born.[3] The reason we often feel subdued in our worship is that we have become too focused on ourselves. Asaph wants to stir our emotions by reminding us that God's grace is far, far bigger than our own little lives.[4]

Asaph reminds us in 78:9–16 that the Lord performed miracles to liberate the Israelites from their slavery in the Promised Land. He guided them through the Red Sea and led them with a pillar of cloud and fire in the desert, providing them with water from the rocks along the way. He also reminds us that, despite such miracles, the Israelites refused to trust the Lord enough to invade the Promised Land under Moses.[5] He reminds us in 78:17–31 that God continued to perform miracles during their forty years in the desert, providing manna and quail for them, and that they still remained rebellious and unbelieving. He does not mention their idolatry with the Golden Calf because the essence of their sin was far more basic: *"They did not believe*

---

[2] The Hebrew word which Asaph uses for his teaching is *tōrāh*, the word normally used for Moses' Law. He wants us to see his words as a Holy Spirit-inspired commentary on the Old Testament so far.

[3] Although the reference to God *shepherding* Israel in 78:52 and 70–72 links forward to 79:13 and 80:1, it also links back to 74:1 and 77:20. This psalm is a detailed survey of the miracles which Asaph spoke about in 77:13–20.

[4] Note the balance of 78:4 and 5. We must meditate on both the works of God's *Spirit* and the detail of his *Word*.

[5] *Ephraim* is a poetic name for Israel. *Zoan* was one of the great royal cities of Egypt.

in God or trust in his deliverance."[6] Every time he forgave them, they quickly forgot and flattered him with false and superficial worship which simply led to yet more sin (78:32–39).[7]

Much of the time, our half-heartedness in worship stems from a knowledge that we haven't followed the Lord as we should. We fool ourselves that God sees this low-level sense of guilt as humility and is somehow pleased with our lacklustre praise. That's why Asaph makes it clear that the Israelites did not receive the Promised Land because they were virtuous (78:40–55). The Lord drove out the Canaanites before them in spite of their sin and forgetfulness of all that he had done for them.[8] Self-centred worship never leads to lasting joy because our spiritual performance is so variable. God-centred worship keeps us joyful because his spiritual performance stays the same. Asaph reminds us that, even in 1 Samuel 4, when idolatrous Israel provoked the Lord to destroy Moses' Tabernacle at Shiloh and allow the Philistines to capture the Ark of the Covenant (78:56–64), he still remembered his love for Israel and raised up David to rebuild a new Tabernacle on Mount Zion (78:65–72).[9] Asaph's history lesson is unashamedly God-centred, and it gives our sluggish hearts plenty of reasons to worship the Lord.[10]

---

[6] Note the balance in 78:32 and 37. Israel ignored the miracles of God's *Spirit* and the content of his *Word*.

[7] 78:39 tells us God does not save people because they are impressive, but because he takes pity on them.

[8] The key word is *remember* in 78:35 and 42. Israel's sin was caused by failure to remember, which is why Asaph warns us in 78:1–8 that much depends upon our singing worship songs which stop us from forgetting.

[9] 78:54 tells us literally that *"He brought them to the border of his holy place, to **this mountain** which he had bought with his right hand."* The crescendo of the psalm sees David becoming king and bringing the Ark back to his new Tabernacle on Mount Zion. Asaph is not saying in 78:67–68 that God has completely rejected the northern tribes of Israel, but that he has chosen Mount Zion in Judah instead of Shiloh in Ephraim.

[10] 78:72 emphasizes that David had both giftedness (*skilful hands*) and character (*integrity of heart*). God-centred worship helps us to develop character to match our gifting.

We see why this matters in Psalms 79 and 80, two psalms which link closely to Psalm 78 through their references to God as the Shepherd-King of Israel. Both are songs of anguish, and both appear to have been written when Asaph received prophetic visions of what would happen in days to come.[11] Psalm 79 forms a deliberate contrast with the final verses of the previous psalm, where the Lord shepherded Israel as his inheritance through David, since it tells us that the nations have invaded God's inheritance, defiled the Temple and reduced David's city to rubble. God has done to Jerusalem what he did to Shiloh because the Israelites have acted like their ancestors and rebelled against the Lord. If Asaph had been used to singing self-centred worship songs, he would have been unprepared in his moment of despair. Because he knew God's history with Israel, however, he could simply remind the Lord that the Israelites were still his *"sheep"* and that it was time to forgive and restore them again as he had done *"from generation to generation"*.[12]

Psalm 80 is very similar. Asaph doesn't pray this time about the future ruin of Jerusalem, but about the future ruin of the northern kingdom of Israel. He sings to the tune of *"The Lilies of the Covenant"* and reminds the Lord that he has covenanted to be the Shepherd-King of all twelve tribes of Israel.[13] Even though he rules from the Tabernacle on Mount Zion, he must also shine forth to restore the fortunes of the three key northern tribes of Ephraim, Benjamin and Manasseh.[14] Asaph draws strength

---

[11] Like Psalm 74, Asaph's visions were so accurate that some readers assume he cannot really have written Psalms 77–78. But the final editors of Psalms insist in the titles that he did.

[12] Asaph's prayer in 79:12 was answered. The Persians sacked Babylon forty-seven years after it sacked Jerusalem, and they immediately let the Jewish survivors return to Jerusalem to rebuild their ruined Temple.

[13] Note Asaph's intensifying plea to *God* (80:3), to *God Almighty* (80:7) and to the *Lord God Almighty* (80:19).

[14] The Lord dwelt between the cherubim on the lid of the Ark of the Covenant on Mount Zion (Numbers 7:89), but Asaph points out that this was simply the throne on which he ruled for the sake of all Israel.

from his God-centred worship and reminds the Lord that he planted Israel as his *vine* in days gone by, and must therefore rebuild the walls of his ruined vineyard.[15]

So let's worship the Lord in a way which is focused more on him than it is on ourselves. As we speak to our own hearts about his character, his purposes, his promises and his faithfulness to previous generations, we will find our worship takes on a much deeper sense of awe and emotion. We will find that our hearts have been strengthened while we worship. We will find that our God-centred worship has prepared us for what lies ahead.

---

[15] The prophets pick up on Asaph's picture of Israel being the Lord's *vine*, and so does Jesus when he describes himself as *"the true vine"* in John 15:1 – that is, *the true Israel*. He is also the true *Man at Your Right Hand* and the true *Son of Man* in 80:17.

Lessons from a Barbecue
(81:1–83:18)

> *Sound the ram's horn... on the day of our Feast; this is a decree for Israel, an ordinance of the God of Jacob.*
>
> (Psalm 81:3–4)

I have learned a lot of lessons from a barbecue. I have learned that even if a burger is charred on the outside it may still be raw on the inside. I have learned that adding extra kerosene after lighting the coals will probably cost you your eyebrows. Most of all, I have learned that blocks of charcoal burn very brightly close together but stop burning very quickly when they are scattered on their own. Asaph doesn't say anything about burgers or kerosene, but he does say a lot about burning brightest when we are together. He didn't need a barbecue to understand that human hearts grow cold to God quickly whenever we try to follow him on our own.

Asaph wrote Psalm 81 for the Israelites to use at their festivals in Jerusalem. He reminds us in 81:3–4 that the feasts which gathered Israel together at the Temple were not just a good human idea. The Lord decreed them as an ordinance because he knew that his People, left alone, soon grow weary in their worship.[1] Even Martin Luther, one of the great hymn writers of the sixteenth century confessed that he found it hard to praise God for a sustained period on his own: *"At home in my own house there is no warmth or vigour in me, but in the*

---

[1] See Numbers 10:10; 28:11; 2 Kings 4:23.

church, when the multitude is gathered together, a fire is kindled in my heart and it breaks its way through."[2] That's why Asaph fills 81:1–5 with words which remind the worshippers at the Temple that they belong to a community: *Jacob*, *Israel* and *Joseph*. It's why he fills 81:6–16 with words which remind them that they have a common history together: they once carried *burdens* and *baskets* as slaves in *Egypt*,[3] and they enjoyed God's provision together from the *rock* at *Meribah*.[4]

We live in a busy world where it is easy to despise the Sunday and midweek gatherings of God's People. Committing to be at church every Sunday, and to share our lives with a small group of a dozen believers, like Jesus did, doesn't sit well with our self-gratifying age. That's why we need to hear what Asaph says we gain by committing ourselves to these New Covenant equivalents of the Jewish gatherings at the Temple.[5]

He reminds us in 81:1–2 that nothing stirs us to worship as much as taking our place in a community of noisy worshippers. The worshippers address one another, rather than the Lord, in the opening verses of this psalm, and they mention at least four different instruments because each one of us has something different to bring to our worship gatherings.[6]

Asaph tells us intriguingly at the end of 81:5 that *"I heard an unknown voice say"* the whole of 81:6–16. Some readers assume he is talking about the Israelites not knowing the

---

[2] Quoted by Robert G. Rayburn in O Come, Let Us Worship (1980).

[3] 81:6 looks forward to Matthew 11:30. One of the reasons we often worship the Lord half-heartedly is that we forget the Gospel is a glorious promise that we do not have to work like slaves to please the Lord.

[4] Exodus 17:1–7 tells us that Israel put the Lord to the test by refusing to trust him at Meribah, but 78:7 says that the Lord was actually testing them! Even now, he promises us sweet provision if we trust in him.

[5] If the Septuagint is right that *"according to gittith"* in the titles of Psalms 8, 81 and 84 means *to sing at the winepresses*, then the *Feast* in 81:3 is the autumn Feast of Tabernacles. We have a better festival in Christ.

[6] Paul says something similar in 1 Corinthians 14:26. When we neglect communal worship we are not the only ones who miss out. We also rob other believers of what we have to bring.

language of Egypt, but this can't be the case because we know that they were forced to learn the language of their masters.[7] We need to understand this verse in the context of 1 Chronicles 25:1, where David *"set apart some of the sons of Asaph, Heman and Jeduthun for the ministry of prophesying, accompanied by harps, lyres and cymbals"*. Asaph appears to be telling us that he heard somebody prophesying these verses at a gathering at the Temple and that he records them here to remind us of yet another benefit of our gathering together. I find it easy to forget God's promises when I am on my own, but when I join with other Christians and hear them prophesy I find my heart renewed and filled with fresh reasons to praise. The prophet tells the worshippers twice that *"if only"* they would act a certain way, they would experience God's greater blessing.[8] We will receive similar encouragement when we worship the Lord with anointed Christian brothers and sisters instead of on our own.

Psalm 82 continues to underline the importance of our gathering to worship God together. Asaph tells the worshippers in 82:1 that *"God presides in the great assembly"* of his People, then he deliberately shocks them by referring three times to the Israelites as *"gods"*. It's so shocking that most translators assume that *"gods"* refers to the arrogant rulers of the earth, but that doesn't make sense in 82:1 and 6, and it doesn't concur with Jesus' New Testament commentary on this psalm. Jesus quotes this verse in John 10:34–35 and says that Scripture *"called them 'gods'* **to whom the word of God came** – *and Scripture cannot be set aside"*.[9] Shocking as it seems, Asaph must to be referring to what 2 Peter 1:4 describes as our being invited to *"participate*

---

[7] 114:1 tells us that Egyptian was foreign to the Israelites but not that it was unintelligible to them.

[8] *"If only… but… so I gave them over to their stubborn hearts"* appears to be the Old Testament background to verses such as Acts 7:42; Romans 1:24, 26 and 28 and 2 Thessalonians 2:10–12.

[9] I appreciate that many commentators maintain that *"gods"* is a sarcastic dig at the blasphemous boasts of pagan rulers. I am simply pointing out that this view is at odds with Jesus' argument in John 10:32–36.

in the divine nature". We are not gods – Asaph makes that very clear by emphasizing that we are sinful (82:2–4), ignorant (82:5) and mortal (82:6–7) – but we have nevertheless been invited to sit on God's throne and to be united with his divine Son. If we are united together in God, we have no excuse for not uniting ourselves together on earth in worship. To reject fellowship with the Church is to reject fellowship with God himself.[10]

This leads into Psalm 83, another song which Asaph seems to have written after receiving a prophetic vision of things to come. He speaks in very general terms – in fact, these nations would never unite together in a single attack upon Israel – so he appears to have seen a general vision of God judging rebellious Israel through wave after wave of foreign invasion.[11] He reminds the Lord in 83:1–8 that anyone who comes *"against your people"* has forged *"an alliance against you"*, and he points out that the battle is between *"Lot's descendants"* and the children of Abraham's grandson Israel.[12] Asaph's faith is rooted in the fact that he is part of God's People, not simply an individual follower of God.[13] He trusts the Lord in 83:9–16 because he is part of the same People whom God delivered from the Midianites under Gideon and from the Canaanite general Sisera under Barak and Deborah.[14]

Asaph therefore ends these three psalms – the last of his

---

[10] In Matthew 25:40 and 45 and in Acts 22:7–8, Jesus treats our actions towards the Church as actions towards him.

[11] Hezekiah's men wiped out the Amalekites (1 Chronicles 4:41–43), but Asaph's vision need not have been of the Assyrian invasion in the days of Hezekiah. He only mentions Assyria as a me-too invader in 83:8.

[12] Moab and Ammon were descended from Lot but the other nations were not (Genesis 19:36–38). Asaph is more interested in expressing how he feels about his vision than he is in which exact nations are involved.

[13] He refers to the Israelites literally as God's *treasured ones* in 83:3. His faith is based on a sense of community which makes the Israelites heirs to the promises of Exodus 19:5–6 and Deuteronomy 7:6.

[14] *Oreb*, *Zeeb*, *Zebah* and *Zalmunna* were the Midianite commanders and kings killed by Gideon in Judges 7–8. *Endor* was a town near the battlefield of Megiddo where Barak defeated Sisera in Judges 4–5.

twelve psalms in the collection – by reminding the Lord that his name is bound up in the name of his People (83:17–18). The nations long to erase the memory of God's People (83:4), but the Lord will stop them doing so in order to reveal his own name through his People (83:18).[15]

So whatever other lessons you may have learned from a barbecue, don't forget that this is the most important one. If you want to stay on fire for God and full of desire to praise him, love your local church as much as Asaph loved the congregation of Israel. God doesn't simply love you as an individual. He loves you as part of his chosen People.

[15] Psalms 42–83 distinctively tend to use the name *Elōhīm* or *God* instead of *Yahweh* or *the Lord*. It is fitting that this final verse praises God that his name is *Yahweh*. From now on Psalms refers freely to *Yahweh* once more.

Fathers and Sons (84:1–12)

*I would rather be a doorkeeper in the house of my
God than dwell in the tents of the wicked.*

(Psalm 84:10)

Sons aren't always like their fathers. For the Sons of Korah, that
was very good news. If you want to understand the first of these
four psalms by the Sons of Korah, you need to know a little bit
about the tragedy which went before.[1]

Korah was one of the leading Levites appointed by Moses
to serve at the Tabernacle in the desert. He looked like a devoted
worshipper, but he never learned to sing to God about how
he really felt. If he had, he would have confessed that he was
consumed with jealousy towards Aaron. He was just as much a
Levite as Aaron, so why hadn't the Lord chosen him to be high
priest of Israel? Instead of singing about his frustrations as
frankly as Asaph, he tried to deny his jealous thoughts until one
day they finally destroyed him.

In Numbers 16, we read that Korah launched a rebellion
against Moses and Aaron: *"The whole community is holy, every
one of them, and the Lord is with them. Why then do you set
yourselves above the Lord's assembly?"* It sounded egalitarian
but it disguised Korah's lust to become the high priest who
entered into the Lord's presence instead of Aaron.[2] The Lord
had warned in Numbers 3:38 that anyone who tried to enter his
presence uninvited would be put to death and, sure enough, the

---

[1] We have already seen that the Sons of Korah wrote Psalms 42–49 as well
as 84–85 and 87–88.

[2] Moses recognizes in Numbers 16:10–11 that Korah is not seeking his role
but that of the high priest Aaron.

glory of the Lord provoked an earthquake which killed Korah and all of his children. All of his children, that is, except for one who became ancestor to these psalm-writing Sons of Korah.[3]

God's grace is truly amazing.[4] Levi had three sons – Gershon, Kohath and Merari – but, while Asaph led the Gershonite choir and Heman led the Merarite choir, the choir of Kohathite singers led by Ethan became commonly known as *the Sons of Korah*. The descendants of the man who tried to barge his way into the presence of the Lord were actually appointed as gatekeepers for the Temple in 1 Chronicles 9:19. So when the Sons of Korah sing in 84:10 that *"I would rather be a doorkeeper in the house of my God than dwell in the tents of the wicked,"* they are saying something very profound. They are sons who are saying that they are not like their rebellious father.

Let's read Psalm 84 with this in mind. They begin by telling the Lord that they love his Temple so much that they envy the birds which have built their nests in its courtyards and therefore manage to stay there even when the gatekeepers have to go home to sleep (84:1–4).[5] Whereas they longed from afar in Psalm 42 to go back to the Tabernacle or Temple, their frustration in this later psalm is that they ever have to leave it.[6] They don't repress their feelings like their ancestor Korah, but tell God frankly that they want nothing more than the opportunity to remain always in his presence. They use the same phrase which

---

[3] Numbers 26:11. They wrote 12 psalms – as many as Asaph and more than anyone else except for David.

[4] This is particularly true in view of the fact that Jude 11 uses Korah as a picture of any false teacher today.

[5] The Hebrew word they use in 84:1 can mean either that the courtyards are *lovely* or *much beloved*. If you lead a church, cultivate God's presence in your worship. Then people will travel from afar to join you.

[6] Whereas Psalm 42 might refer to either the Tabernacle or the Temple, there are several clues that Psalm 84 refers to the Temple. For a start, God's dwelling place has courtyards (84:2, 10) and is dominated by an altar (84:3). Also, the Sons of Korah refer literally to God's *tabernacles* in 84:1 because the Temple combined and replaced both Moses' and David's tents.

David used to begin the book of Psalms when they exclaim that anyone is *blessed* who can dwell in the Temple or even make a short pilgrimage there (84:4–7).[7]

By singing about how they really feel, they escape the trap which snared their father Korah. Even as they sing about how much they long to enter the forbidden Holy Place and offer incense on its golden altar,[8] they realize that God has anointed Solomon as king (84:8–9),[9] and that he has been incredibly gracious even to have appointed them as his gatekeepers. They tell the Lord that even being in his courtyards is a thousand times better than being anywhere else, and that they would rather stand obediently in his doorways than recline in luxury in the tents of the disobedient. They are happy for God's high priest to remain the high priest. They are content to be mere doorkeepers because God's presence is so wonderful that getting close is close enough.

Now let me tell you something surprising. God doesn't want you to sing this psalm. In fact, God is tired of Christians who content themselves with nothing more than standing in his courtyards. We are not the Sons of Korah. We are the sons and daughters of the Sons of Korah! God wants us to be as different from them as they were from their own father.

When Jesus died on the cross, Matthew 27:51 tells us that *"the curtain of the temple was torn in two from top to bottom"*. The great veil which separated gatekeepers in the courtyard from God's presence in the Most Holy Place was torn apart as a sign that Jesus has enabled us all to become *"priests to serve his*

---

[7] We know of no such place as the *Valley of Baca* anywhere in Israel. Since it means the *Valley of Weeping*, the Sons of Korah may simply be saying that the thought of God's presence offsets all the tears on our journey.

[8] In 84:3–4 they want to enter the *house* and they refer literally to *"your altars"* – in other words, the golden altar of incense in the Holy Place as well as the bronze altar of blood sacrifice in the courtyard.

[9] The Hebrew word *māgēn* normally means *shield*, but it means *king* here, just like in 47:9, 89:18 and Hosea 4:18.

God and Father" (Revelation 1:6). This is explained further in Hebrews 10:19–25, which urges us:

> *Since we have confidence to enter the Most Holy Place by the blood of Jesus, by a new and living way opened for us through the curtain, that is, his body… let us draw near to God with a sincere heart and with the full assurance that faith brings, having our hearts sprinkled to cleanse us from a guilty conscience and having our bodies washed with pure water.*

What this New Testament commentary is telling us is that what wicked Korah tried to seize is freely ours to enjoy through the death and resurrection of Jesus. It is telling us that what the Sons of Korah were right not to try to grasp is something we would be equally wrong not to lay hold of ourselves. It is telling us that we can be filled with the Holy Spirit and dwell every minute of the day and night with the Lord, as the Sons of Korah longed to do. So take a moment to reflect on how astounding this Gospel message truly is. We mustn't sing Psalm 84 in the same way as our fathers did.

We must sing a better song about what is ours to enjoy. The Sons of Korah blessed those who made a short pilgrimage to the Temple, so we must sing about the better pilgrim lifestyle which is ours. The Sons of Korah prized one day in the courtyards of the Temple more than a thousand days elsewhere, so we must not be too busy to spend large chunks of time enjoying the presence of the one who dwelt in the Most Holy Place in Jerusalem.

The Sons of Korah weren't like their father. By God's grace, we aren't like them either. Let's sing about our better covenant and let's enjoy the intimate presence of the Lord which they could only celebrate from afar.

Heman and His Friends
(85:1–88:18)

You have taken from me friend and neighbour –
darkness is my closest friend.

(Psalm 88:18)

Most of us have got a friend who is ridiculously emotional. They laugh too loudly at jokes. They cry too easily at movies. They get easily excited and just as easily depressed. They blurt out their feelings when they ought to think before they speak. Perhaps the worship leaders who compiled Psalms were concerned that we might think that Asaph is the same. Perhaps that's why they didn't let him write the whole of this book which tells us to sing about how we really feel. The final third of Book III was written by Heman and his friends – other people who did exactly the same. These psalms remind us that the message of Book III is for all of us. God wants each one of us to sing about how we really feel.

Heman was the greatest of the Sons of Korah. He not only led their worship choir, but 1 Chronicles 6:31–48 tells us he was the main worship leader at the Temple, overseeing Asaph and Ethan as his deputies. He wrote Psalm 88 himself and he trained the other Sons of Korah to write Psalms 85 and 87. Their songs are as emotional as Asaph's because, no matter who we are, that kind of praying is always music to God's ears.

Like Asaph, the Sons of Korah remind themselves of God's faithfulness towards Israel in the past in 85:1-3.[1] They put

---

[1] The Hebrew phrase used in 85:1 can mean either *"to restore fortunes"* or *"to bring back from exile"* (as in 14:7, 53:6, 126:1 and 126:4). We do not know the date of this psalm but nothing necessarily forces a late dating.

a *selāh*, or *instrumental solo*, towards the end of these verses in order to meditate on this fully before they launch into their complaint. Having done so, they question the Lord, just like Asaph, in 85:4–7, asking whether he is going to be angry with Israel *"forever"* and *"through all generations"*. They pour out their hearts and then stop to listen to what the Lord says in reply in 85:8–9.[2] This frank kind of praying was clearly not unique to Asaph, and it proves very fruitful for the Sons of Korah. They end by praising the Lord in 85:10–13 that he has heard their prayer.[3]

Psalm 86 sticks out like a sore thumb in Book III. This book is known as "the Levite Psalter" because all of its songs were written by the Levite worship leaders Asaph and Ethan and Heman and the Sons of Korah. There is really only one satisfying explanation why a stray psalm of David has made its incongruous way into Book III. It is one of David's most despairingly honest psalms, which aims to show us that another of Heman's friends – none other than his mentor as a worship leader – also prayed the brutally honest kind of prayers which are music to God's ears.

David does not try to get the Lord's attention in 86:1–7 by pretending he is doing better than he really is. Instead, he frankly confesses that he is *poor* and *needy* and *in distress*, and he tells the Lord literally in 86:4 that *"I lift up my soul to you."* He knows that his only hope lies in confessing to the Lord how he really feels, and he finds that when he pours out his feelings he makes room for fresh faith to come. He is able to worship the Lord in 86:8–10 that no one is like the God of Israel and that even the nations who oppose him will one day bow before the Lord. He is able to ask the Lord in 86:11–13 to sift his emotions and teach him how to worship with *"an undivided heart"*. David's life

---

[2] Our times of worship need to make room for the Lord to speak. When the Sons of Korah listen to God they are encouraged in 85:9 that God is more eager for revival than we are because he wants to be glorified.

[3] Note that each of the four stanzas of this psalm uses the name *Yahweh*. The so-called "elohistic psalms" are well and truly over.

is still under threat in 86:14–17, but his perspective has been completely changed in the course of his simple prayer.[4] It's quite a turnaround, but it's what happens to anyone who learns to sing to the Lord about how they really feel.[5]

Psalm 87 takes us back to the Sons of Korah, and it is the only one of these four psalms which was written during good times. It reminds us that we need to express our happiness as honestly as our pain, because it celebrates all that is going well in Jerusalem.[6] These gatekeepers celebrate that *"the Lord loves the gates of Zion"* and that pagans from all over the earth are hearing about the city's reputation and coming through its gates to be saved. These new converts include Israel's great enemies – Egyptians, Babylonians and Philistines[7] – along with the wealthy merchants of Tyre and black Africans from the far-away land of Cush. The Sons of Korah can't contain their excitement that people are coming from every nation to be counted as spiritual citizens of Jerusalem and to drink its living water. If you are part of the Church, the true Mount Zion,[8] you must not be less excited that the Gospel is saving people from far-flung nations which were unknown to the Sons of Korah.

Finally, we come to a song which was written by Heman himself.[9] He wrote it as a *maskīl*, or *psalm of instruction*, and he set it to a tune called "The Suffering of Affliction", which was

---

[4] We tend to think of our prayers changing God. It is truer to say that this kind of praying changes us.

[5] In the Hebrew, 86:17 can mean either *"grant me a sign of your goodness"* or *"turn me into a sign of your goodness"*.

[6] It was probably written during Solomon's reign or later because 87:1 refers literally to *"the holy mountains"*, which seems to include Mount Moriah, the site of the Temple, alongside Mount Zion.

[7] *Rahab* was a poetic name for Egypt (Isaiah 30:7; 51:9–10). Although it looks the same in English as the woman who was saved from Jericho by Joshua, it is actually spelt differently in Hebrew.

[8] Hebrews 12:22–23.

[9] *Ezrahite* describes Heman's role rather than his parentage, since Ethan is also called an Ezrahite in the title of the next psalm. 1 Chronicles 6:33–38 tells us Heman was descended from Korah through Samuel the judge.

a very appropriate tune for the words which follow. Heman was one of the wisest men of his generation (1 Kings 4:31) and a distinguished prophet (1 Chronicles 25:5), so we have much to learn from this chance to hear him pouring out the feelings of his troubled heart before the Lord. He tells the Lord that he feels as though he is about to die (88:1–5) because he is convinced God has rejected him and left him to drown in deep, dark waters (88:6–18). He even starts to fear that he will go to hell,[10] and it is strangely encouraging that that he ends his song on a note of despair. He doesn't really doubt his salvation – he is clear about that in 88:1 – but he shows us that it isn't unchristian to cry out to the Lord about our doubts in times of trouble. If one of the wisest prophets and songwriters of the Old Testament could be this honest with God, we can be reassured that God doesn't want any of his followers to pretend. He wants us to sing out how we really feel.

Perhaps that's why the last verse which was written by Heman and the other Sons of Korah is a cry of deep and honest pain. The worship leader Tim Hughes reminds us that

> There has to be a place for expressing pain in our churches. We need a bigger picture of what worship is. Questioning God doesn't mean we are disobeying Him. Expressing doubt doesn't mean we are lacking faith... Expressing anger and pain to God is a beautiful and intimate act... In our everyday lives, the people that we are most likely to share our deepest fears and hurts with are those we love and trust the most. True intimacy can be experienced when we choose to share honestly and vulnerably.[11]

---

[10] He not only uses the Hebrew word *she'ōl* in 88:3, which can mean *hell*, but also uses the word *abaddōn* in 88:11, which nearly always means *hell* or *place of eternal destruction*.

[11] Tim Hughes in *Holding Nothing Back: Embracing the Mystery of God* (2007).

One-Hit Wonder (89:1–52)

Lord, where is your former great love, which in your faithfulness you swore to David?

(Psalm 89:49)

Ethan was a rather impressive worship leader. Next to Asaph and Heman, he led the third worship choir at the Tabernacle and Temple. He lived up to his name, which meant *Faithful* or *Steadfast* or *Reliable*, but his friends also appear to have given him the nickname Jeduthun to describe his character even further.[1] It means *The Praise Man* and it is likely that David and Asaph dedicated Psalms 39, 62 and 77 to him because they knew that only he would truly lead the people in singing them the way they should be sung. We are told in 1 Kings 4:31 that he was one of the wisest men of his generation, and in 1 Chronicles 25:3 and 2 Chronicles 35:15 that he was so gifted in singing prophetic songs that King David appointed him as the royal seer. Ethan was so impressive that it is somewhat surprising that only one of his songs made it into the book of Psalms. Asaph and the Sons of Korah contributed twelve songs each, but Ethan was a psalmist one-hit wonder.

Some readers would even like to deny him the one hit he had. They point out that Ethan served under David and Solomon, whereas this psalm laments the failure of David's dynasty.[2] They forget that Ethan was a prophet and just as capable of

---

[1] Most commentators agree on this, since Scripture refers to *"Asaph, Heman and Jeduthun"* and *"Asaph, Heman and Ethan"*, but never to *"Jeduthun and Ethan"* (1 Chronicles 15:17–19; 25:1–6; 2 Chronicles 5:12; 35:15).

[2] *Ezrahite* in the title refers to his role rather than his parentage. Heman is also called this in the previous title.

seeing visions of the future and writing psalms in response as Asaph was in Psalms 77, 79, 80 and 83. Regardless of our objections, the editors of psalms insist in the title that this song was indeed written by Ethan. Here we can read the single psalm of Ethan the one-hit wonder.

When we read Psalm 89, we are struck by just how wonderful his one hit truly was. It is the third longest psalm and one of the very best constructed. It is marked as a *maskīl*, or *psalm of instruction*, because we need to learn how to express our deepest feelings to God in a way which gets an answer.

Ethan's introduction in 89:1–4 celebrates God's *faithfulness* and *covenant love*. These aren't just abstract concepts to Ethan. They consume his soul, and he uses each of these two Hebrew words seven times in this psalm as the bedrock of his prayer. He expands on why he praises God for his *faithfulness* and *covenant love* in 89:5–18.[3]

Ethan's introduction also celebrates the covenant which the Lord made with David in 2 Samuel 7. He expands on why the Davidic covenant means so much to him in 89:19–37, getting excited that the Lord spoke to David as a young man and promised to raise him up to be his messianic king and firstborn son over his People.[4] Ethan rejoices in the fact that God has promised not to reject David's dynasty even if his children prove to be sinful and rebellious, instead of being like their father. He expresses his delight that the Lord has promised that the sun and moon will stop shining before he forsakes David's dynasty. All of this keeps Ethan singing for thirty-seven verses, which is longer than most of the other psalms. He makes us think he is about to close the psalm with a final verse of worship – but he has a big surprise in store.

---

[3] As we saw in Psalm 87, *Rahab* means Egypt. *Tabor* and *Hermon* were the highest mountains in Israel.

[4] The Hebrew says literally that the Lord gave this vision to his *holy one*, not *holy ones*. Ethan is stressing David's devotion to the Lord, just as he stresses that David was God's trusty *servant* in 89:3, 20, 39 and 50.

Verse 38 is the equivalent of a learner driver trying to change gear without using the clutch. No, it's worse than that. It's the equivalent of the learner driver trying to change into reverse without using the clutch while travelling down the motorway at high speed. Ethan shocks us so much with his sudden change of tone that we can almost hear the screeching engine and smell the burning rubber. But he didn't pull this manoeuvre primarily for our sake. He is showing us how to pray in a way that gets an answer.

One of the greatest pieces of oratory in English literature is the speech which Mark Antony makes over Julius Caesar's dead body in William Shakespeare's play. Mark Antony never attacks Brutus for assassinating Caesar, but while he describes Caesar's noble character he keeps repeating that *"Brutus is an honourable man."* Eventually, the glaring contrast between his two messages proves too much for the Romans to bear, and they start shouting, *"We will burn the house of Brutus!"*[5] Ethan makes a similar contrast here in order to stir the Lord to answer his prayer.

He points out in 89:38–45 that it looks as though the Lord has been unfaithful to his covenant with David. He has rejected him, thrown his crown into the dust and let foreign armies freely plunder his cities. He has kicked his throne into the mud and has given him defeat and shame in spite of having promised him victory and honour. Ethan is as skilful as Mark Antony as he tells God how he feels about the prophetic vision he has seen of Israel's future. He does not actually accuse the Lord of wrongdoing, but he expresses his contrasting feelings with such passion that he cannot be ignored.

Ethan is just like his friends Asaph and Heman as he pours out the misery of his heart in 89:46–51. He asks why God is hiding and points out that he can no longer see the *faithfulness*

---

[5] William Shakespeare wrote these lines in about 1599 in *Julius Caesar* (Act 3, Scene 2).

and *covenant love* which made him celebrate so noisily in the first two-thirds of this psalm. *"I bear in my heart the taunts of all the nations,"* he complains, but he doesn't make the mistake of thinking that singing about how we feel means simply blurting out our feelings. He arranges his prayer with all the skill of William Shakespeare and Mark Antony. He only needs to make six verses of requests because he has built up to this moment with the forty-five verses which went before.

Ethan's prayer ends with the Hebrew word *messiah*, since 89:52 appears to be the final doxology which ends the whole of Book III. That final word reminds us what was achieved through this one-hit wonder. Even though the northern kingdom of Israel saw nine different dynasties come and go, God preserved David's dynasty as the only house which ever ruled over the southern kingdom of Judah.

But more than that, the Lord answered Ethan's prayer centuries later by sending Israel a far better Messiah. Jesus of Nazareth would be heir to David's throne, the true Holy One (89:19), the true Servant (89:20), the true firstborn Son of God (89:26–27) and the true King of kings whose rule will last forever (89:29).[6]

Ethan reminds us that it is not how much or how long we pray that matters. It's how much we express what God has placed in our hearts and how much we make a compelling case for the Lord to do all that he has made us want him to do. That's what Ethan shows us through this great psalm of crunching contrasts and anguished pleas. We will see our own prayers answered too if we learn a lesson from Ethan the one-hit wonder.

---

[6] John 12:34 tells us that the Jews knew Ethan's prayer was partly about God's Messiah who was yet to come.

Book IV – Psalms 90–106:

Sing About God's Plan

The Living Faith of the Dead
(90:1–91:16)

*Lord, you have been our dwelling place throughout
all generations.*

(Psalm 90:1)

The idea of worshipping God didn't start with our generation. I know that's pretty obvious, but it's surprisingly easy to forget. I've lost track of the church services I have attended where none of the songs date back more than twenty years, where no one makes any reference to the Church's worship throughout the centuries and where the entire focus of the worship experience is on *God and me today*. Even in ancient Israel, worshippers had a tendency to forget that they were simply one generation in God's purposes. That's why Book IV teaches us that we need to sing about God's plan.

If you like traditional services and dislike contemporary worship, this may be music to your ears. But be careful. It's equally possible that what you have in mind isn't music to God's ears at all. Tradition at its best means that we celebrate the living faith of the dead, but tradition at its worst quickly creates a dead faith among the living. Book IV of Psalms doesn't tell us to prize tradition over innovation. It simply points out that we are part of a long chain of worshippers and that, the more we understand our place in God's story, the more pleasing to God our worship will become. The German writer Goethe once quipped that *"He who cannot draw on three thousand years is living hand to mouth."* These seventeen psalms can be referred to as "the Exodus Psalter" because they take us back into history to teach us how to worship.

Tim Keller helps us to strike the right balance:

> *When we ignore historic tradition, we break our solidarity with Christians of the past. Part of the richness of our identity as Christians is that we are saved into a historic people. An unwillingness to consult tradition is not in keeping with either Christian humility or Christian community. Nor is it a thoughtful response to the postmodern rootlessness that now leads so many to seek connection to ancient ways and peoples... Worship that is not rooted in historic tradition will often lack the distance to critique and avoid the excesses and distorted sinful elements of the surrounding, present culture... We forge worship best when we consult the Bible, the cultural context of our community, and the historic tradition of our church.*[1]

Book IV begins with the oldest song in the book of Psalms. We are told in the title of Psalm 90 that Moses wrote it, the only title to say this, so Goethe would be pleased: this song is almost 3,500 years old. The worshippers at the Temple might think that God's plan was all about his dwelling place on Mount Zion, but Moses starts with a reminder that the Lord has *"been our dwelling place throughout all generations"*. He existed before Mount Zion or any other mountain was ever made, because he exists *"from everlasting to everlasting"* (90:1–2). A thousand years is like a day or a short watch of the night to him so, no matter how important we think our own generation is, it will come and go as quickly as grass in a sun-scorched land (90:3–6). A person who dies at seventy is lucky and a person who sees their eightieth birthday is even luckier, so we need to pray, *"Teach us to number*

---

[1] Timothy Keller argues this in his short paper entitled "Evangelistic Worship" (2001), included in *Worship by the Book* by D. A. Carson.

our days, that we may gain a heart of wisdom" (90:7–12).[2] We need to make the most of the few days we have, passing on the baton to our children, and trusting in the Lord to establish the work of our hands as we make our contribution to history as a whole (90:13–17).

We can tell from Exodus 15 and Deuteronomy 32 that Moses was a very gifted songwriter. You might be wondering why the editors of Psalms chose this song out of Moses' entire back collection. It helps to remember that Moses led a dying generation who knew that their disobedience meant that they were destined to die in the desert. He therefore became expert in teaching them to look back to God's promises to the patriarchs and forwards to the things which God would do through their children once they were gone.[3] He was the perfect psalmist to teach us the lesson of Book IV, and this was the perfect song through which to do it. The kind of worship which is music to God's ears isn't me-centred or even my-generation-centred. It sings about his bigger plan for the human race as a whole.

Many readers believe that Moses also wrote the anonymous Psalm 91, one of the most beautiful celebrations of God's protection in the entire Bible. They point out that 91:5–8 describes what happened to the Israelites during the Ten Plagues which fell on Egypt,[4] and that the Hebrew word for *the serpent* in 91:13 is the same word which the Hebrews used to describe the cobra-goddess whose image the pharaohs wore prominently on their crown.[5] If this is true, it makes this psalm

---

[2] Moses himself lived to the age of 120, so a lifespan of 70–80 years is neither a promise nor a threat. This has simply been the maximum age that most healthy people could ever hope to reach throughout history.

[3] This is probably why Moses talks about the agony of years wasting away under God's judgment. The thirty-nine years spent in the desert because of Israel's refusal to enter the Promised Land must have felt like a very long time.

[4] 91:5–8 parallels Exodus 8:22–23; 9:3–7, 26; 10:23 and 12:13.

[5] This same Hebrew word *tānnīn* is used to describe the snakes in Pharaoh's palace in Exodus 7:9–12 and it is also used to describe Pharaoh and his officials in Psalm 74:13.

3,500 years old too. When we are in danger and afraid, it helps us to know that God has been protecting his People ever since the dawn of time.

Psalm 91:1–8 promises that God will protect us against four threats: from terror at night, from arrows by day, from pestilence in the darkness and from plague at midday. It gives us four names through which he protects us: the Most High, the Almighty, the Lord and my God. It tells us four things that God is to us: the shelter we can dwell in, the shadow we can rest in, the refuge we can count on and the fortress we can trust. Four plus four plus four. People have always found God faithful whenever they have relied on him throughout the generations.

Psalm 91:9–16 promises that the Lord will protect us against four opponents: from the lion, the cobra, the great lion and the serpent. This does not mean that believers have never been harmed by such animals, but it means that God has proved himself faithful in these ways throughout all generations.[6] We need to do four things to lay hold of him as our own protector: make his name our refuge, express our love for him, acknowledge his name and call on him to answer.

If we learn from Moses' humility in Psalm 90 and see our own generation as a brief flash in history, and if we take time to study God's faithfulness throughout the ages in Psalm 91, we will be able to worship him with the deeper and more seasoned kind of faith which pleases God. We will sing to him as part of his multigenerational People, and it will be music to his ears.

---

[6] When Satan quotes from 91:11–12 in Matthew 4:6 and Luke 4:10–11, Jesus warns him not to misapply God's general promises and therefore put him to the test. Satan was too scared to carry on and quote 91:13!

Timeless (92:1–94:23)

Your throne was established long ago; you are from all eternity.

(Psalm 93:2)

If you look closely at the titles of the psalms in Book IV, you will notice something very peculiar. Psalms 90, 101 and 103 were written by Moses and David, but the other fourteen psalms are entirely anonymous. Now that's very interesting. The authorship of the eight anonymous psalms in Books I to III is fairly easy to guess, but these fourteen psalms are genuinely anonymous – in fact, the title of Psalm 102 is deliberately evasive over who exactly its writer was. We can't even be sure when these songs were written.[1] It is as if the editors of Psalms wanted to keep them faceless and timeless in order to emphasize that these are the kind of songs which God's People have always sung at every moment in their many-thousand-year-old history.

Psalm 92 keeps itself very generic when its title simply tells us that it was written for use on any Sabbath day. It is an ideal song for the editors of Psalms to use here to remind us that present-day worshippers are only brief participators in a divine plan which spans the ages. Our lives of worship are dominated by the cycles of *morning* and *night* (92:1–3), but God warns that we are as foolish as the animals if we only ever think in terms of this daily cycle. Our generation is one of a great many in God's

---

[1] The Greek Septuagint states the author of 9 of these 14 psalms but, whereas the Hebrew titles are as old as Psalms itself, the Septuagint is notoriously wild in some of the speculations in its titles.

plan, and it will pass away as quickly as the grass (92:4–7).[2] Verses 4 and 5 place the emphasis where it belongs: on what the Lord is thinking and doing in our particular generation.

The psalm pivots on its contrasting central verse. 92:8 exclaims, *"But you, Lord are forever exalted."* Unlike us, he reigns forever, and the quality of our worship depends on how much we grasp this distinction. We are just passing through this world, but he is eternal. A.W. Tozer contends that *"The Church has surrendered her once lofty concept of God and has substituted for it one so low, so ignoble, as to be utterly unworthy of thinking, worshipping men... If we would bring back spiritual power to our lives, we must begin to think of God more nearly as He is."*[3] A great place for us to start doing so is here in these three psalms.

When we see God as he really is, we worry less and trust him more. When we grasp that we are part of a single generation in his fully mapped-out plan for the whole of human history, we are stirred to devote our lives to his eternal purposes. How can we not, when he cuts the wicked off in the prime of life (92:9–11) yet prospers the righteous even into old age (92:12–15)? The Danish philosopher Søren Kierkegaard complained that *"Life can only be understood backwards; but it must be lived forwards,"* yet these psalms tell us we can understand life's meaning up front from start to finish if we study God's plan in the Scriptures. David did so and Acts 13:36 tells us that *"When David had served God's purpose in his own generation, he fell asleep."* Let's live in such a way that our lives can bear that epitaph as well.

Psalm 93 continues the same theme. It wrenches our eyes away from the trivia of our own daily lives to see the Lord who has reigned from eternity and who will continue to reign throughout eternity. It models the kind of worship that is music to God's ears, rejoicing that *"Your throne was established long*

---

[2] The comparison between time-bound humans and brute beasts in 92:6 links to 73:22 and 94:8. The comparison between human lives and the grass of the field in 92:7 links to 90:5–6 and 103:15–16.

[3] A.W. Tozer in *The Knowledge of the Holy* (1961).

ago; you are from all eternity." The Lord stands firm against the high tides and low tides of the world's turbulent history because he is sovereign and holy *"for endless days"*. That's why it's probably deliberate that this psalm is anonymous. It is trying to tell us that these things were true for Adam and for Noah and for Moses and for David and for Solomon and for Asaph and for Ezra – and that they are also just as true for us today. Don't move on from this psalm until you have begun to fathom something of the gulf which exists between our mortal nature and God's eternal nature. Wayne Grudem observes that,

> *Only God exists by virtue of his very nature... He was never created and never came into being. He always was... God's being is also something totally unique. It is not just that God **does not** need the creation for anything; God **could not** need the creation for anything... The difference between God's being and ours is more than the difference between the sun and a candle, more than the difference between the ocean and a raindrop, more than the difference between the arctic ice cap and a snowflake, more than the difference between the universe and the room we are sitting in: God's being is **qualitatively different**. No limitation or imperfection in creation should be projected on to our thought of God. He is the Creator; all else is creaturely. All else can pass away in an instant; he **necessarily exists** forever.*[4]

Psalm 94 therefore models how we are to pray in view of this. It asks the Lord to take vengeance on the wicked (94:1–3) because Israel is full of oppressors who ignore God's eternal purposes for his People (94:4–7). They boast that the Lord is deaf and blind towards their evil deeds because they have forgotten the Lord's history of disciplining nations in his anger. They are so

---

[4] Wayne Grudem in *Systematic Theology: An Introduction to Biblical Doctrine* (1999).

self-centred that they forget that their Creator made the human race for a reason, and that he laughs at all their futile human plans (94:8–11).[5] They forget that the Israelites are *God's People* and that he has made a commitment to protect them as *his inheritance* (94:12–15). They consider Abraham to be ancient history and forget that the Lord remembers walking with Abraham and making his covenant with him far better than they remember their own conversations over breakfast that morning. The psalmist therefore ends by asking the Lord to protect him with his *covenant love* which endures forever like a rock, and to judge the irreverent boasting of his oppressors (94:16–23).

So let's not be like the brute animals and try to worship the Lord as if our little lives were everything. Let's be God-focused and not us-focused when we praise him. Let's be more consumed with his eternal purposes than we are with the detail of our own lives. Let's be conscious as we sing to him that we are a tiny part of a great People which he is gathering out of every generation.

Because when we sing this way, the psalmists encourage us, it is music to God's ears.

---

[5] Paul quotes from 94:11 in 1 Corinthians 3:20 in order to warn us not to live according to *"the wisdom of this world"*.

David Was Never King (95:1–99:9)

> For the Lord is the great God, the great King above
> all gods.
>
> (Psalm 95:3)

"*L'État, c'est moi,*" declared King Louis XIV of France. "*I am the State.*"[1] At least he was honest in his arrogance, but the same sense of self-importance is commonly concealed by the way that many of us live our lives. Our parliaments and offices and neighbourhoods are full of individuals who swagger with a sense of messianic self-importance. Louis XIV has a great many heirs today. Most people live and act as if the world revolves around themselves.

If anybody had a right to feel this way, it was David. Our messianic pretensions are unjustified, but the Lord had actually anointed David as his messiah. He had raised him up to be king of Israel and had inspired him to build the Tabernacle on Mount Zion and to teach the Israelites how to worship the Lord. If anyone might have felt that he had a lead role in God's plan, it was David. But he didn't. In fact, these six psalms go out of their way to tell us, shockingly, that David was never even King.

The New Testament reveals in Hebrews 4:7 that the anonymous Psalm 95 was written by David. It says much about his humility that he was willing in 95:3 to let his subjects

---

[1] He is reputed to have said this in a clash with the French parliament. Years later, sobered by his own evident mortality on his deathbed, he confessed: "*I am departing but the State will always remain.*"

worship the Lord as *"the great King above all gods"*.[2] The Persian King Darius executed anyone who insisted on worshipping their God instead of him. The Roman emperors killed Christians for daring to suggest that Jesus was a greater Lord than Caesar.[3] So don't miss the significance of David's statement in these psalms that the Lord is King and he is not. It shows his grasp of his own position within God's plan throughout world history. The Lord had always been the King of Israel, with a capital "K", and David was only king, with a small "k", for a brief moment in time.

Psalm 95:1–7a proclaims that the Lord is the eternal King. He is the one who made the seas and the dry land and the mighty mountains, and he is the one who is the Maker of us all. Despite the celebrations in 78:70–72 that the shepherd-boy David had become the shepherd-king of Israel, David insists in 95:3 and 7a that the Israelites are the Lord's flock and that he is their true King and Shepherd. David looked back to the past and remembered that the Lord had spoken through Moses 450 years earlier in Exodus 15:18 and declared literally that *"The Lord rules as King forever and ever."* He remembered the Lord's anger against the Israelites when they asked for a human king and how he said in 1 Samuel 8:7, *"They have rejected me as their King."* He also looked forward to the future and remembered that Jacob had prophesied in Genesis 49:8–10 that a man from the tribe of Judah would only wield the royal sceptre *"until he to whom it belongs shall come and the obedience of the nations shall be his"*. David remembered that the Lord had not permitted him to build a Temple in Jerusalem because not all of his plan was going to be accomplished in David's generation.

As if to underline this, David returns in 95:7b–11 to Book IV's focus on the Exodus. He began by telling the Israelites to worship God as *the Lord* and *the Rock of our Salvation* – two names

---

[2] He also tells them to do this in 5:2 and 145:1.

[3] Daniel 6. This was the main grounds for the execution of Christians in the Roman Empire.

by which God revealed himself to Moses in the desert[4] – and he expands on this second name in the second half of the psalm, reminding us that the Lord provided water for the Israelites when they were dying of thirst in the desert at Massah and Meribah.[5] They were a generation who forgot the past and as a result forfeited their future. David warns us not to be like them, but to follow the Lord wholeheartedly as our eternal King.[6]

We can tell that David wrote most of the anonymous Psalm 96 because it is a revised version of part of his song in 1 Chronicles 16:7–36.[7] Since he entrusted that song to Asaph, it appears that his worship leaders revised the psalm for the opening of the Temple – changing the call to *"come before him"* into a specific call to *"come into his courtyards"* at the new Temple. Yet again, in 96:10 David tells the worshippers to proclaim that *"the Lord rules as King".*[8] This psalm reminds us that God's plan is far bigger than the establishment of a tabernacle or a temple or a church; he wants to spread the sound of his worship to every single nation and people group on the earth.[9] Me-centred worship always shrinks God down to our own size, but God-centred worship always stirs us to become part of God's great mission to save the world.[10]

186

---

[4] Exodus 3:14–15; Deuteronomy 32:15.

[5] *Massah* means *Testing* and *Meribah* means *Quarrelling*. See Exodus 17:1–7.

[6] Hebrews 3:7–11 quotes the second half of Psalm 95 in its entirety and spends a whole chapter explaining what it means for us today. This should remind us how vital it is that we learn to sing about God's plan.

[7] 1 Chronicles 16:8–22 became the first third of Psalm 105, 16:23–33 became the whole of Psalm 96, and 16:34–36 became three key verses in the much larger Psalm 106.

[8] It is not clear in English, but the Hebrew verb *to reign* is linked to the word for *King*. The Hebrew verb is a perfect tense so perhaps this is best translated, *"The Lord has proclaimed himself King"* (also 93:1, 97:1 and 99:1).

[9] David talks about nations in 96:3 but drills down further to the tribes within nations in 96:7.

[10] Psalm 96 points towards the Great Commission in Matthew 28:18–20. 96:2 reminds us that we have been commissioned to share the Gospel with unsaved people *"day after day"*.

Psalm 97 begins with this same proclamation that *"the Lord rules as King"*. It tells us that no obstacle can stand before the extension of his Kingdom and that *"all peoples"*, even those on *"distant shores"*, will discard their idols and worship him. There is perhaps a hint in 97:10 that those who side with his Kingdom will be persecuted, but it is surrounded by promises that his Kingdom is the only place where we will find true joy. Psalm 98 continues this theme of worshipping *"the Lord, the King"* (98:6) and proclaiming his salvation to the nations. It is very similar to Psalm 96 and continues this chorus that David was only ever king with a small "k".[11] He only played a small role in the much greater reign of the eternal King.

Psalm 99 ends this series of five songs with the same proclamation that *"the Lord rules as King"* from his throne room on Mount Zion (99:1–3). *"The King is mighty"* and the earth is merely the footstool to his throne (99:4–5),[12] so people from every nation must worship him as the King who ruled in the time of Moses and Aaron and Samuel, who all led the rebellious Israelites as viceroys for the King.[13]

Louis XIV was not the State. David was not the King. And however important we may think we are, these verses remind us that we are simply small-part players in a bigger drama starring God the King. Let's therefore bow down and worship him as the eternal King of kings, and let's get back onto our feet to work as his loyal subjects, spreading the news to every nation that his Kingdom has come.

---

[11] This illustrates perfectly the call in 96:1 and 98:1 to *"sing to the Lord a new song"*. Psalm 96 was a new song based on 1 Chronicles 16:23–33, and Psalm 98 was a new song based on Psalm 96.

[12] 2 Chronicles 9:18 reminds us that ancient thrones often had inbuilt footstools. See also Matthew 5:34–35.

[13] Psalm 99 is very skilfully written. It uses the name *Yahweh* seven times and each of its three sections ends with a statement he is *holy* (99:3, 5, 9). This fits alongside Isaiah 6:3 which tells us that the Lord is holy, holy, holy.

The Right Entrance
(100:1–101:8)

Enter his gates with thanksgiving and his courts with praise.

(Psalm 100:4)

The people who owned my house eighty years ago had a live-in butler and maid. There is still a rear entrance for the servants to use and a back staircase so they didn't have to mingle with their masters in the hall. Nowadays, the back door and staircase are just a helpful way for our lodger to have some privacy, but when they were built they meant something more. The servants who lived in the small accommodation upstairs were not to enter the house in the same way as their social superiors who lived in the main home.

Many Christians use the servant's entrance whenever they come to the Lord in prayer. They have misunderstood the previous five psalms and think that the King is honoured by his People sneaking in through the back door. You can recognize these tell-tale symptoms in your own life if you tend to begin your prayers with a long confession of sin, or if you spend the first ten minutes of worship at church feeling like you don't deserve to be at church at all. God loves it when we are humble enough to confess our sin to him, but that isn't how he wants us to enter his presence. He tells us in Psalm 100:4 that we are to *"Enter his gates with thanksgiving and his courts with praise."*[1]

Imagine you are staying the night as a guest in my home. I

---

[1] We are not told that David's Tabernacle had any *courtyards*, so this psalm appears to have been written after Solomon built the Temple and its courts.

tend to get up early and go into my study, and my children tend to run in to find me when they get out of bed. Now imagine that you hear my three-year-old daughter tiptoeing into my room and saying: *"I'm so sorry, Daddy. I was so naughty yesterday that I don't deserve to be in your study. Please forgive me. Please forgive me. I'm just here to offer to polish your shoes."* You would immediately think that there was something very wrong with me as a father! What kind of father expects his children to snivel their way into his presence? What kind of ogre must he be to make his children grovel and fawn that way? Can you see that if we browbeat ourselves as we enter God's presence, we actually dishonour him? Psalms 100 and 101 teach us how to enter the presence of the King. These two songs are our instruction in royal protocol.

The title of Psalm 100 tells us it was written *"for giving grateful praise"*. It teaches us to use the front door and not the back door when we come into God's presence because he is glorified, not by our self-doubt, but by our belief in what he has done for us through the Gospel. It tells us we should enter God's presence with *shouts for joy*, with *worship*, with *gladness* and with *joyful songs* (100:1–2). We should enter with confidence that he isn't just the God who made us, but also the God who redeemed us. He is the King who chose us to be his People and the Shepherd who calls us to be his flock (100:3). Unless we grasp this, we haven't really understood our King at all. John Stott reminds us that *"Far above us in his greatness, he is yet close to us in his goodness."*[2] Our King is glorified when we enter his presence with joyful confidence because we remember that he is good.

Every king or queen has a royal protocol for how people should enter their presence. The kings of Persia forbade anyone on pain of death from coming without an invitation. One fifteenth-century Romanian ruler was so incensed when a

---

[2] John Stott in *The Canticles and Selected Psalms* (1966).

group of Turkish envoys refused to take off their turbans in his presence that he ordered his guards to nail their turbans to their heads.[3] With the Lord, the royal protocol is altogether friendlier. He tells us to step through the front door because of the Gospel and to come as his sons and daughters instead of servants. Jesus explains in Matthew 22:1–14 that none of us deserves to enter God's presence at all. Both the *"good and bad"* need to put on the gift of his clothes of righteousness and then enter his presence joyfully to praise him for his unmerited grace and mercy. Jesus ends his parable by putting the spotlight on a man who tried to sneak into God's wedding feast through the back door. The guest probably thought that he was being humble, but his lack of faith in the Gospel meant that he was thrown outside.

Jesus provides further commentary on 100:4–5 in what has become known as the Lord's Prayer. He repeats the message of this psalm when he tells us in Matthew 6:9–13 to enter God's presence through the front door with the words, *"Our Father"*. He tells us to begin our prayers by celebrating the wonders of God's name and to move into praying that his Kingdom rule may be established throughout the earth. He tells us to bring our everyday needs before our loving Father, and *only then* does he tell us it is time to confess our sins. There is a time for confession, and it's a very important time, but it isn't the place where we begin. We need to enter God's gates with *thanksgiving* and his courts with *praise* and further *thanks*. We need to praise him for his *goodness* and his *loving kindness* and his *faithfulness* towards us. Only after we have praised him for who we are in Christ, regardless of our own character, are we ready to confess how far short of Christ's character we have fallen on our own.

David wrote Psalm 101 and it comes next in order to complete our instruction in royal protocol. It is a song of self-consecration and it makes two deliberate connections between

---

[3] Esther 4:11. Admittedly, the Romanian example was very extreme! The ruler was Vlad the Impaler.

"my house" and the house of the Lord in the previous psalm (101:2 and 7). David says that those who are welcomed into the Lord's house through the front door cannot respond to such grace without getting very radical with sin.[4] His status through the Gospel makes him want to change the state of his own life (101:1–3a), the state of his circle of friends (101:3b-7) and the state of anyone else he can influence for good (101:8).[5] Those who sneak in through the back door may continue to harbour sin in their lives, but those who use the front door are changed for good.

Jesus tells us that the Prodigal Son tried to enter his father's presence with the confession, *"I have sinned against heaven and against you. I am no longer worthy to be called your son; make me like one of your hired servants."* Psalms 100–101 teach us why the father interrupted him and would not let him finish. Praise God for his royal protocol: *"Bring the best robe and put it on him. Put a ring on his finger and sandals on his feet. Bring the fattened calf and kill it. Let's have a feast and celebrate!"*[6]

---

[4] See Hebrews 12:14. Imputed holiness makes us long for greater imparted holiness.

[5] David did not live up to this psalm fully. It was only truly fulfilled in David's greater Son, Jesus.

[6] Luke 15:11–32.

God's Plan Has Not Failed (102:1–28)

For the Lord will rebuild Zion and appear in his glory.
(Psalm 102:16)

One of the big traditions of an British summer is the Last Night of the Proms. If you're not British, let me explain. It is the final evening of eight weeks of classical concerts and it ends with people singing the old songs of the British Empire together. They sing, *"Rule, Britannia! Britannia, rule the waves,"* and *"Land of Hope and Glory... God who made thee mighty, make thee mightier yet."* I like to watch it on television, and my eight-year-old son asked me which countries are actually in the British Empire. I told him the truth: Gibraltar, the Falkland Islands and a few tiny islands in the Caribbean. After seeing so much fuss being made on television, he was more than a little disappointed!

It's good to sing about God's eternal plan, but if we're not careful a lot of our singing can be as empty as the Last Night of the Proms. We sing loudly about God's plan to save people from every nation, but we only need the insight of a eight-year-old to spot that there is a gulf between what we sing about and what we actually see. Psalm 102 reminds us this is so, and seeks to teach what it really means to sing about God's plan today.

Psalm 102 has a very long title but it doesn't actually tell us who wrote it. This is undoubtedly intentional so as to emphasize that the frustrations of this psalm are common to anyone who sings about God's Kingdom in any generation. It is the *"prayer of an afflicted person who has grown weak and pours out a lament before the Lord"*. The affliction is personal in 102:1–11, but it becomes very clear in 102:12–22 that this is simply part of a bigger, national affliction.[1] The distress and tears and loss of appetite and sleeplessness and sense of loneliness are all caused by intense grief about what has happened to God's People. The Lord sits on his throne as King in every generation (102:12), yet Mount Zion is often turned to rubble (102:16) and his People are often defeated by the unbelievers they were sent to save (102:20). For all our hearty singing, God's plan often looks as if it has failed.

It is important that we grasp this, because God doesn't want self-deluded singing from us, as if we were guests at the Last Night of the Proms. He wants us to face up to this dilemma, which is why I love the final six verses of this psalm, where the writer effectively asks the Lord not to take him off the pitch at half-time (102:24). He says he knows that the final whistle hasn't blown yet and he is excited about all that the Lord must be about to do in the second half of the game. *"Your years go on through all generations,"* he sings. God created the world at its outset (102:25) and he will still be King when the world wears out and gets thrown away (102:26–27).[2] The writer is completely confident that God's plan which looks so moribund in his own lifetime will go on to succeed in future generations in a blaze of victorious glory (102:28).

God wants you to sing about his plan with this mature perspective. Celebrating the Lord's great purposes, while ignoring the reality of the Church's current position in the world, isn't faith. It's living in a dream world. The bigger our perspective of God's purposes, the more we can trust him when the Church looks very weak in our own place and time.

193

---

[1] It is counted as one of the seven "penitential psalms" (along with 6, 32, 38, 51, 130 and 143) because the writer is crying out for God to restore the nation of Israel in spite of its sin.

[2] Hebrews 1:10–12 quotes 102:25–27 and applies it directly to Jesus. Of course the psalmist does not actually mean that the Lord will throw this world away. He will re-create it at the end of time (Matthew 19:28).

We don't know when Psalm 102 was written because crises like this one were common throughout Israel's history. It looked as though God had finished with Israel when the Egyptians started murdering their baby boys in order to commit genocide within a couple of generations. No one could have known that God was raising up Moses to lead a mighty revival among his People. It looked as though God had finished with Israel when they chose a human king and reaped disaster under Saul through a Philistine invasion. Nobody could have known that in an unremarkable field near Bethlehem the Lord had already found a great deliverer in David. It looked as though God had finished with the Jews when they rebelled against the Lord and saw their land annexed by the Romans. Nobody could have known that a virgin in Nazareth had just conceived a child through the Holy Spirit. Jesus was about to run onto the pitch. Don't ever judge the outcome of a big game by the half-time score.

It looked as though God had finished with Europe at the start of the sixteenth century, when the clergy were sinful and corrupt, and when the best minds were so much more obsessed with scientific discovery than with knowing God that Thomas à Kempis was forced to warn them: *"A humble countryman who serves God is more pleasing to Him than a conceited intellectual who knows the course of the stars, but neglects his own soul."*[3] Yet it was at that precise moment, when the night seemed darkest, that a German monk named Martin Luther nailed ninety-five Christian statements to a church door and the greatest European revival of modern times began.

It looked as though God had finished with Europe again when the English writer Thomas Woolston predicted in 1710 that Christianity would be extinct within two centuries. Little did he know that in few years' time George Whitefield and John Wesley would be used by God to launch a revival which reached the farthest nations of the globe. When the French thinker

---

[3] Thomas à Kempis wrote this in *The Imitation of Christ* (c.1427).

Voltaire predicted towards the end of the eighteenth century that Christianity would be extinct within fifty years, he had no idea that the nineteenth and twentieth centuries would see more converts to Christ than the previous eighteen centuries combined. Philip Jenkins observes that

> *We are currently living through one of the transforming moments in the history of religion worldwide. Over the past five centuries or so, the story of Christianity has been inextricably bound up with that of Europe and European-derived civilizations overseas, above all in North America... Over the past century, however, the centre of gravity in the Christian world has shifted inexorably southward, to Africa, Asia, and Latin America... Sometime in the 1960's another historic landmark occurred, when Christians first outnumbered Muslims in Africa.*[4]

So let's not sing about God's plan like people at the Last Night of the Proms, pretending that God's Kingdom is triumphing when it is not. Let's tell God how we feel when the Church looks weak, like the afflicted person who wrote Psalm 102, and let's end our prayers in the same way as the final six verses of the psalm. Let's see all that the Lord is doing in every nation of the world, in spite of all the setbacks. Then we can truly celebrate, with eyes wide open, the unstoppable fulfilment of God's plan.

---

[4] Philip Jenkins in *The Next Christendom* (2002).

Green and Blue Planet
(103:1–104:35)

He set the earth on its foundations; it can never be moved.

(Psalm 104:5)

The British philosopher Bertrand Russell famously argued that

Man is the product of causes that had no prevision of the end they were achieving; that his origin, his growth, his hopes and fears, his loves and his beliefs, are but the outcome of accidental collocations of atoms; that no fire, no heroism, no intensity of thought and feeling, can preserve individual life beyond the grave; that all the labours of the ages, all the devotion, all the inspiration, all the noonday brightness of human genius, are destined to extinction in the vast death of the solar system, and that the whole temple of Man's achievement must inevitably be buried beneath the debris of a universe in ruins.[1]

If you find the prevailing Western worldview today a bit depressing, it's hardly surprising. People actually believed him.

The message of Psalms 103–104, however, is that Bertrand Russell was entirely wrong. The Earth may just be one small planet in our solar system, just one of 200 billion planets in the Milky Way, and one of trillions in all the galaxies, but these two psalms tell us that there is nothing random or inconsequential about our green and blue planet. These songs

---

[1] Bertrand Russell in *A Free Man's Worship* (1903).

tell us that God's plan infuses the spinning rock which we call home with meaning.

David wrote Psalm 103 to help us sing about God's dealings with humankind. We must not lose a sense of wonder that, across the vast gulf of space, God made our planet the theatre in which his eternal purposes would be outplayed. He has not come to live on any other planet and he has never taken the form of a plant or animal. He made humankind uniquely in his image and chose to relate to us quite differently from any other life form there may be in the many galaxies. God's great plan involves human beings like you and me. That's the irony of Bertrand Russell's statement and of the pessimism which pervades our culture. While human beings attempt to erase the fingerprints of their Maker, he has invested their lives with profound meaning.

David warns us in 103:1–6 not to forget all that God has done for fragile human beings. This is so easy to do that he talks to himself in 103:1–2 because worship does not always come naturally to his lazy soul.[2] The Lord *forgives* us, he *heals* us, he *redeems* us, he makes us the object of his *covenant love* and *compassion*, he *satisfies* us with all we need, he *refreshes* us, and he blesses us with his *righteousness* and *justice*.[3] Your life is of great cosmic importance because the Creator God has chosen to make you the object of his affections.[4]

David illustrates this in 103:7–12 by cataloguing this grace in action towards Moses and the Israelites, one of the great themes of Book IV of Psalms.[5] He quotes from God's words in

197

[2] If you often find it difficult to worship, you should find this encouraging. Even the psalmists had to discipline themselves and stir their souls to worship. See 42:5, 11; 43:5; 57:8; 103:22; 104:1, 35; 146:1.

[3] Linguistically, 103:6 is actually part of the stanza 103:6–19, but both 103:6 and 103:19 serve as bookends which bridge the main part of the psalm to its introduction and conclusion.

[4] Psalm 8 makes a similar argument to Psalms 103–104. See also Psalm 19:1–6.

[5] We can see specific links between the list of benefits in 103:1–6 and what God did for Israel at the Exodus.

Exodus 34:6 when he revealed his character to Moses, telling us that the Lord's very nature is to be compassionate and gracious and patient and loving towards us (103:8). He did not destroy the Israelites when they worshipped the Golden Calf and refused to enter the Promised Land, because his love towards his People is as great as the universe itself (103:11). He forgave them and removed their sins as far-away from them as they could imagine (103:12).[6] Our sins can no more come back to haunt us than a person can hope to throw a tennis ball from Greenland and hit New Zealand.

David broadens out this lesson from the Exodus in 103:13–18 to include humankind in general. He points out that the Lord made us out of dust in Genesis 2:7, and that our mortal lives are like the grass or flowers which quickly bloom and just as quickly die and are forgotten.[7] Without God in the equation, Bertrand Russell is right: our fragile lives mean nothing. But with God in the equation, everything changes. He loves us *"from everlasting to everlasting"*. He gives our lives eternal meaning because he made us to play a crucial role in his master plan. David therefore concludes his song with references to God's *throne* and *kingdom* and *rule* and *dominion* (103:19–22). Our life on this green and blue planet really matters because we are loved by the eternal King.

Psalm 104 is anonymous, but it is so similar in its opening and closing verses to the previous psalm that it was either written by David or by someone who deliberately made it a counterpart to Psalm 103. Here the spotlight turns onto our green and blue planet itself, as the psalmist praises the Lord for displaying his glory through the world he has made. Instead of

---

[6] David emphasizes the completeness of our forgiveness in 103:10–12 by using three different Hebrew words for *sin* (*hēt'*), *iniquity* (*'āwōn*) and *transgression* (*pesha'*).

[7] Verses 15 and 16 link back to the start of Book IV in 90:5–6 and 92:7. Jesus looks back to these verses in Matthew 6:30, and so do James 1:10–11 and 1 Peter 1:24.

Bertrand Russell's *"accidental collocations of atoms"*, the song praises God for the splendour and majesty of his creation. The light of the sun is his clothing, the expanse of the heavens is his tent, the clouds are his chariot, the winds are his messengers and the lightning bolts are his servants (104:1–4).[8]

Having therefore celebrated in the opening four verses days one and two of creation, the psalmist continues by praising the Lord for creating dry land and for watering it with rain on day three (104:5–18).[9] He praises the Lord for creating the sun and moon on day four (104:19–23), the fish on day five (104:24–26) and the animals on day six (104:27–30). What the psalmist fails to mention, and it's so startling that it must be on purpose, is human beings, who were also created on day six. It's as if he wants to underline the message of the previous psalm, that there is something quite different between the animals and the hairless bipeds whom the Lord has chosen to be his friends. We don't receive a mention until the conclusion of the psalm, where we are encouraged to sing praise to the Lord for all that creation teaches us about the goodness of his eternal plan (104:31–35).[10]

199

"Not enough evidence, God, not enough evidence," Bertrand Russell retorted when asked what he would say to God if he died and found that his Maker demanded a reason for his lack of faith in him.[11] These two psalms were written to warn us not to be so blind. Everything about our green and blue planet points towards its Creator. When we consider what God has done for us on this spinning piece of rock in the vast universe, it fuels our hearts to worship him and to celebrate God's plan.

---

[8] Hebrews 1:7 quotes 104:4 from the Greek Septuagint and assumes that by *messengers* it means *angels*.

[9] The clouds were God's *upstairs bedrooms* in 104:3, so he waters the earth from his *upstairs bedrooms* in 104:13.

[10] Verse 34 can either mean *"May my meditation on him be sweet"* or *"My meditation on him is sweet."* There is deliberate ambiguity here in Hebrew between a "jussive" and an "imperfect", as we saw in Psalm 72.

[11] Richard Dawkins shares this quote gleefully in *The God Delusion* (2006).

They soon forgot what he had done and did not wait
for his plan to unfold.

(Psalm 106:13)

I once got embroiled in an argument between some Greeks and Macedonians over which of their countries was the homeland of Alexander the Great. The Greeks pointed out that he was a Greek-speaker, while the Macedonians countered that his full name is King Alexander III of Macedon. It struck me as surprising that this question was so important to them, even though one of their nations was almost bankrupt and most people could not identify the other on a map of Europe. But that's how it is with famous ancestors and family history. We all know that where we have come from makes an enormous difference to where we are going.

That's the basic premise behind Psalms 105–106. They are the last songs in Book IV, and they bring its message to a crescendo. They show us why we must not move on until we have learned to sing about God's plan. Both songs begin and end with the word *Hallelujah*, or *Praise the Lord!* (a copying error in the Hebrew text means that the word which should start Psalm 105 is sometimes placed at the end of the previous psalm[1]), and they are a matching pair of songs which teach us about our family history. The first song charts Israel's history

---

[1] This is backed up both by the Greek Septuagint text and by the way that many other psalms also begin and end with the word *Hallelujah*. See Psalms 106, 113, 135 and 146–150.

from Abraham to Joshua, and the second song charts it from the Exodus to the time of the judges.[2]

The first fifteen verses of Psalm 105 are lifted almost word for word from David's song in 1 Chronicles 16:8–22 for the dedication of his Tabernacle. It therefore appears that Asaph or one his friends took those words and turned them into a far more comprehensive history lesson for God's People. After David's history of Abraham[3] and the other patriarchs (105:5–15),[4] it continues into Joseph's ministry in Egypt (105:16–22), the arrival of Jacob and his other sons, their persecution under the Egyptians,[5] the Ten Plagues and their final Exodus (105:23–38). It recalls their time in the desert following the pillar of cloud and fire, and how the Lord provided them with quail, manna and water from the rock (105:39–41) before he led them into the Promised Land (105:42–45).

Psalm 106 retells this history from a different perspective. Whereas the first of the two songs stresses God's faithfulness to Israel, this second song stresses the Israelites' unfaithfulness to God. It tells us that they didn't cross the Red Sea because of their faith but despite their lack of it (106:6–12), and that the miraculous provision of quails was God's response to their impatience which led to many of them dying of disease (106:13–15).[6]

It tells us that they rebelled against Moses and Aaron's

201

---

[2] A further link between the two songs is that Psalm 105:1–15 is taken from 1 Chronicles 16:8–22, while Psalm 106:1, 47–48 is taken from 1 Chronicles 16:34–36.

[3] The writer deliberately changes *"seed of Israel"* in 1 Chronicles 16:13 to *"seed of Abraham"* in 105:6.

[4] David was God's messiah but he deliberately emphasizes God's purposes throughout the generations by saying literally that the patriarchs were *messiahs* too (1 Chronicles 16:22 and here in 105:15).

[5] Verse 25 tells us that it was God who turned the Egyptians' hearts against the Hebrews. He is faithful in working out his plan even when his strategies look disastrous to us at the time.

[6] Numbers 11:33. Our lack of faith can prompt the Lord to answer our prayers in a way which disciplines us.

leadership,[7] that they worshipped a Golden Calf, that they would have been destroyed had it not been for Moses' intercession, and that they failed to trust the Lord enough to enter the Promised Land, which is why a whole generation of Israelites died in the desert (106:16–27).[8] It tells us that they fell for Balaam's trap, committing idolatry on the plains of Moab, and that they were only saved by the courageous action of the young priest Phinehas (106:28–33). They even provoked the normally patient Moses into sin.[9]

It tells us that they disobeyed the Lord when they finally entered the Promised Land by failing to wipe out the Canaanites and by intermarrying with them, soon worshipping their idols as the Lord had warned them that they would (106:34–39). They descended into the spiral of backsliding, judgment and short-lived repentance which marked the whole period of the judges (106:40–46). This contrast between God's faithfulness to his People and their unfaithfulness to him doesn't make pleasant reading.

A key theme in these two psalms is that of *remembering* and *forgetting*. The Lord remembers, so he is faithful (105:8, 42; 106:45). The Israelites forget, so they are not (106:7, 13, 21). That's why two of the many things we are told to do at the beginning of Psalm 105 are to *"tell of all his wonderful acts"* and *"remember the wonders he has done"*. We short-change ourselves when all our worship songs are about God's goodness in general or about our own feelings in particular. We need to learn to sing about our family history, because this helps us to remember and

---

[7] *Dathan* and *Abiram* were Reubenites who joined Korah's rebellion. The psalmist does not mention Korah, perhaps out of sensitivity towards his friends, the Sons of Korah.

[8] *Horeb* in 106:19 is Mount Sinai. *Ham* in 105:23, 27 and 106:22 is a poetic name for Egypt, which was descended from Noah's son of that name.

[9] Verses 28–31 link to Numbers 25:1–13 and verses 32–33 link to Numbers 20:1–13.

remembering helps us to obey. This is what some of the best ancient hymns have always done:

Praise, my soul, the King of heaven;
To His feet thy tribute bring;
Ransomed, healed, restored, forgiven,
Who like me His praise should sing?...
Praise Him for His grace and favour
To our fathers in distress.
Praise Him, still the same forever,
Slow to chide and swift to bless.[10]

Or if you prefer modern songs:

Looking back through history,
Your People, they have always had a song they must
*   sing,*
A song they must sing.
We are the People of God,
We'll sing your song here on the earth![11]

FAMILY HISTORY (105:1–106:48)

203

There are some good songs out there, but Psalms 105–106 suggest that they are not enough and that the ones we do have should give us more detail about our history to help us remember. Book IV of Psalms has shown us the importance of understanding that our generation is just one link in the long chain of God's eternal purposes. As we come to the doxology which ends this fourth book in 106:48,[12] let's not move on before taking some time to reflect and to sing about God's plan.

---

[10] "Praise, my soul, the King of heaven" by Henry Lyte (1793–1847) is based on Psalm 103.

[11] Extract taken from the song "All Over The World" by Matt Redman & Martin Smith. Copyright © 2005 Thankyou Music & Curious? Music.

[12] We can tell that 106:48b ends Book IV rather than Psalm 106 because 106:48a repeats the final line of David's song in 1 Chronicles 16:36.

Book V – Psalms 107–150:

Sing Your Response to God

Use Your Mouth (107:1–43)

Let the redeemed of the Lord tell their story… but all the wicked shut their mouths.

(Psalm 107:2, 42)

Lord Uxbridge was sitting on his horse next to the Duke of Wellington while the British were fighting the French at the Battle of Waterloo. Suddenly, he was hit by a round of grapeshot from one of the French cannons, practically severing his right leg below the knee. Still sitting on his horse, and with all the self-restraint of an English gentleman, he exclaimed, *"By God, sir, I've just lost my leg."* Wellington looked at him briefly and without any emotion in his voice replied: *"By God, sir, so you have."*[1]

Sometimes it strikes me that I live in a culture which isn't very good at expressing how it feels. Yet I have also noticed that we are very good at using our mouths to express how we feel on big sporting occasions. When Jonny Wilkinson scored a last-minute drop-goal to win the Rugby World Cup Final in 2003, even the most stiff-upper-lipped English gentlemen started shouting. When Didier Drogba scored a penalty with his last kick in a Chelsea shirt to win the European Champions League Final in 2012, the roar of the celebrations could be heard all across south London. So it shouldn't surprise us that the theme of Book V of Psalms is that we need to open our mouths to sing in response to God. This is known as "the Hallelujah Psalter" because it uses the word *hallelujah!*, or *praise the Lord!*,

---

[1] This exchange is recorded in the *Oxford Dictionary of National Biography* (2004).

twenty-four times.[2] It isn't just the last of the five books which make up Psalms. It also tells us how we are to respond to Psalms as a whole.

It isn't only Englishmen who don't find this very easy. It takes effort for all of us to verbalize the way we feel. The same is true in marriage, which is why any husband or wife can tell you that a commitment to communicate is one of the keys to a happy marriage. When I give my wife a birthday card, I don't just write *"I love you."* I tell her how much I love her and how she makes me feel and some of the reasons why. I can't just write: *"I still love you. Please see last year's card for full details."* If I did so, her response would take me back to Book V of Psalms!

Psalm 107 is so similar to the two final psalms in Book IV that some readers assume that it must be by the same author. We cannot know for sure because the acts of deliverance it describes were quite common throughout Israel's long and eventful history.[3] What we can know for certain is that this is the perfect introduction to Book V, with its call to sing out our response to God. It begins with a phrase which is sometimes translated, *"Let the redeemed of the Lord tell their story,"* but which is probably more accurately translated *"Let the redeemed of the Lord say so!"* This introduction is meant to form a contrast with the end of the psalm, which rejoices that *"All the wicked shut their mouths."* If we have been saved into the glorious promises we have read about in Psalms, it is time for us to say it and say it loudly. Being as understated as Lord Uxbridge or the Duke of Wellington is not a virtue. When we cheer more at sporting events on Saturday than with the People of God on Sunday, something is very wrong.

Psalm 107:2–9 reminds us that we have been saved from

---

[2] The only other place where the word *Hallelujah* is used in Scripture is four times in Revelation 19:1–6.

[3] Most of the Hebrew verbs in this psalm are "imperfect tenses". They can therefore just as easily be translated as present tenses which describe the general experience of God's People throughout history.

the four corners of the earth, and that we were saved by using our mouths. It is possible that the writer is talking about the Jewish return from exile, but it is equally possible that he is talking about the many Gentiles who came to Solomon's Temple to be saved. Either way, it is certainly talking about the global make-up of the Church today. The writer points out that we were saved by *crying out to the Lord* with our mouths, and he tells us to use those same mouths to say thank you. It's the only reasonable thing for us to do.

Psalm 107:10–16 reminds us that our unsaved lives were like a prison. We experienced spiritually what the Hebrews did as slaves in Egypt and what the Jewish exiles did in Babylon.[4] We were saved from our chains by *crying out to the Lord* with our mouths. We need to use them to give thanks to him for freeing us.

Psalm 107:17–22 reminds us that many of us have received healing through the same Gospel which brought us forgiveness and freedom. We were afflicted and some of us might have died, but everything changed when we started *crying out to the Lord*. The Lord sent out his word to heal us in response to our call for help,[5] so we ought to use those same voices to give him thanks with songs of joy for all he has done for us.

Psalm 107:23–32 speaks of the many stormy troubles we have encountered throughout our short lives.[6] We were at our wits' end until we started *crying out to the Lord*. When we did so, he calmed the storm and brought us into the safe harbour which we requested. We therefore need to use our mouths to

---

[4] The Lord promises King Cyrus of Persia something very similar to 107:16 in Isaiah 45:2. He may even have been quoting from this psalm.

[5] The New Testament wants us to grasp that Jesus fulfilled 107:20 when we read in Matthew 8:8, 16 and 32 and in Mark 7:34 that Jesus healed and drove out demons *"with a word"*.

[6] Our comfort in such storms is that 107:25 tells us God is behind them and can therefore instantly stop them.

thank him – on our own, in church on Sunday and in front of anyone else who will listen.[7]

Psalm 107:33–42 reminds us that we have known barren times.[8] There have been periods when we have sinned and reaped the penalty for forgetting God, and there have been times when we have remembered him and enjoyed his provision in answer to our prayers. This final section of the psalm is the only one which does not contain a reference to our *crying out to the Lord*. Instead it ends with a statement that the upright will always *"see and rejoice"*. Only the wicked ought to *"shut their mouths"*.[9]

The eighteenth-century revivalist John Wesley instructed his converts in how to bring God worship which was music to his ears. He came from the same country as Lord Uxbridge, yet he agreed with the writer of Psalm 107 that those who have been saved need to celebrate it with their mouths: *"Sing lustily and with a good courage. Beware of singing as if you were half dead, or half asleep; but lift up your voice with strength. Be no more afraid of your voice now, nor more ashamed of its being heard, than when you sung the songs of Satan."*[10]

If you have been redeemed through the Gospel, don't let anything stop you saying so. Use your mouth to thank the one who saved you when you cried out to him.

---

[7] The Greek Septuagint translates the Hebrew word *qāhāl* or *assembly* in 107:32 as *ekklēsia*, the Greek word which the New Testament uses for the *Church*.

[8] Isaiah may have been inspired by this psalm, since 107:33–35 is echoed in Isaiah 41:18, 42:15 and 43:19–20.

[9] The sections 105:2–9, 10–16, 17–22 and 23–32 are all identical in their penultimate line, telling us to *thank* the Lord. Verse 42 is the penultimate verse of 105:33–43, so it may parallel these other commands.

[10] John Wesley wrote these "Directions for Singing" in the preface to his *Select Hymns* (1761).

Appoint someone evil to oppose my enemy; let an accuser stand at his right hand.

(Psalm 109:6)

Psalms 108 and 109 tell us to do two things in response to God: we feel comfortable doing one of them but decidedly uncomfortable about doing the other. These two psalms could hardly be more different. One of them tells us to bless and the other one tells us to curse.

You may find Psalm 108:1–5 a bit familiar. That's because it is an almost word-for-word repeat of 57:7–11.[1] David wrote these words while hiding from Saul in a cave, but they are repeated here to remind us that our response to the message of Psalms should be to bless God. They tell us to *sing* and *make music* and use *musical instruments*. They tell us to *praise* and *sing* about the Lord in front of unbelievers so that they can discover him too. If David celebrated like this when he was in a cave (Psalm 57) or reeling from an unexpected Edomite invasion (Psalm 108), we need to learn to bless the Lord in every circumstance too.

Psalm 108:6–13 is equally familiar. It is an almost word-for-word repeat of 60:5–12. When the Edomites invaded Judah, it appears that David wrote two songs: they both ended with the same prayer, but one started with a complaint (Psalm 60) and one

---

[1] David's evident willingness to cut and paste from his own psalms is a helpful reminder that they give us a model to help our worship, not a straitjacket to restrict it.

started with praise (Psalm 108).[2] The second version appears here to remind us that we should respond to the message of Psalms by *laying hold of God's blessings*. David bases his faith for deliverance from invasion on God's love for his People (108:6), on God's promises at the Tabernacle on Mount Zion (108:7–9)[3] and on God's commitment to expose human boasting as a sham (108:10–13). The promises in Psalms make him confident that he will capture even the impregnable mountain fortresses of Edom.[4] Our proper response to Psalms has to be to lay hold of all the blessings we have been promised by the Lord.

Psalm 109 is a completely new song, and its message is very surprising. It tells us that the right response to Psalms isn't just to bless. It is also to curse. David laments that his close friend has betrayed him by returning his friendship with evil (109:1–5), and then he writes ten of the most shocking verses in Psalms (109:6–15). This "imprecatory prayer" is so full of curses that it made C. S. Lewis comment that

> *In some of the Psalms the spirit of hatred which strikes us in the face is like the heat from a furnace mouth. In others the same spirit ceases to be frightful only by becoming (to a modern mind) almost comic in its naïvety. Examples of the first can be found all over the Psalter, but perhaps the worst is in Psalm 109.*[5]

---

[2] We noted in 57:8 that when David says he will *"awaken the dawn"* in 108:2, he is not simply talking about early morning singing. He actually expects worship to change his dark situation.

[3] *Shechem, Sukkoth, Gilead, Manasseh* and *Ephraim* were all places in Israel, but *Moab, Edom* and *Philistia* were Israel's most formidable local enemies in David's day.

[4] Edom was so mountainous that its two great fortified cities, Bozrah and Sela (known to the Greeks as Petra), were well-nigh inaccessible. See Obadiah 3–4.

[5] C. S. Lewis in *Reflections on the Psalms* (1958).

Since Peter links this psalm to the actions of Judas Iscariot in Acts 1:20, David must be talking yet again about Ahithophel. So how can it be right for David to pray that Ahithophel's prayers be unanswered, his life cut short prematurely, his wife widowed, his children turned into beggars and his sins never forgotten?[6] How can this be reconciled with Jesus' prayer from the cross in Luke 23:34: *"Father, forgive them, for they do not know what they are doing"*? We need an answer to these questions if we are to respond fully to the message of the book of Psalms.[7]

Peter helps us by quoting from 109:8 in Acts 1:20, and by telling us that David spoke these words prophetically on behalf of Jesus the Messiah. This helps us to see why the New Testament is not embarrassed by the curses in the imprecatory psalms. Far from it. It quotes them in Romans 11:9–10, and in 1 Corinthians 16:22 and Galatians 1:9 it even places its own curses on anyone who rejects Jesus as Lord. Frightening as it may be, these curses describe the eternal fate of anyone who rejects Jesus' offer of friendship and betrays their Maker's kindness.[8] If we are offended that it should be this way, we have not yet understood the weight of God's holiness and glory.

Peter also warns us not to assume that these are Old Testament words meant for somebody other than ourselves. He uses them in a very New Testament context in order to tackle a real issue concerning one of his former friends. Far from criticizing David, he recognizes that those who feel true passion for God's purposes will always respond by speaking curses as well as blessing. This is what it means to pray *"Let your Kingdom come"* in a world where many people hate and reject the King.

---

[6] The Hebrew word *sātān* can mean either an *accuser* or the Accuser *Satan*, so David could even be praying in 109:6, *"Let Satan stand at his right hand."*

[7] Some people try to argue that David is simply quoting Ahithophel's curses in 109:6–15, but Peter certainly does not understand it that way. Note that David is not cursing a personal enemy but an enemy of God.

[8] Matthew 25:41. Luke 6:28 and Romans 12:14 give us a general principle, but there comes a time and a place to speak the words of 1 Corinthians 16:22.

When we see people cursing and threatening others (109:16–29) and raging against God's Messiah (109:4–5), there comes a time and place to pray for God to be swift in executing his righteous judgment. We must never pray this kind of prayer lightly, but we must never hesitate to pray it when we should.

Let me try to illustrate with a personal story. Many years ago, when I was living in Paris, I heard on the news that a group of IRA terrorists had detonated a bomb in London's docklands, killing large numbers of people. The IRA threatened that they had many more bombs and that they were planning a summer of terror. When I heard the news, I felt a sense of indignation rise up within me and was strongly reminded of the Bible verse: *"Those who live by the sword shall die by the sword."* I was with a Christian friend and asked if we could stop what we were doing and pray together that the Lord would fulfil that verse in the terrorist cell. After about half an hour, I felt my unusually heavy sense of indignation lift, so we stopped praying. The following morning I heard the news: there had been a small explosion in London and the only casualty had been the leader of the IRA cell. He had accidentally detonated one of his own bombs and been killed.

Did the prayers of two Christians in Paris really change the course of what was happening in London? Was our imprecatory praying really the means by which God brought peace where there was about to be killing? Truthfully, I don't know. But what I do know is that Psalm 109 is Scripture and that *"All Scripture is God-breathed and is useful for teaching, rebuking, correcting and training in righteousness, so that the servant of God may be thoroughly equipped for every good work."*[9] What I do know is that if we grasp the message of Psalms, we will curse as well as bless. We will pray every kind of prayer which God lays on our hearts until his Kingdom fully comes.

---

[9] 2 Timothy 3:16–17. The editors of Psalms make a similar point by stating in the title that this psalm is suitable for congregational singing.

Melchizedek (110:1–7)

The Lord has sworn and will not change his mind:
"You are a priest forever, in the order of Melchizedek."

(Psalm 110:4)

Not everybody understood what David was doing when he constructed a new Tabernacle on Mount Zion. For some of them, his religious innovation must have appeared downright illegal. Although many modern readers tend to miss this fact, it must have been the major talking point of David's day. It was so controversial that he felt he needed to explain himself in Psalm 110.

Moses' Law strictly forbade anyone from setting up a tabernacle in addition to that of Moses. It also forbade on pain of death anyone except the family of Aaron from offering blood sacrifices.[1] It particularly forbade rulers from tampering with God's deliberate separation of powers by trying to act as priests as well as kings.[2] We need to understand that when David built a second tabernacle on Mount Zion it wasn't the equivalent of planting another church just down the road. It was the equivalent of setting up a rival White House and installing a rival president of the United States of America.

Moses' Law also placed strict limits on what the priests from Aaron's family could do. The Ark of the Covenant was to be kept in an inner room within the Tabernacle, and only the high priest was permitted to enter into God's presence, and only then on a single day of the year. Instead, the priests were

---

[1] Leviticus 17:8–9; Numbers 18:7.

[2] King Uzziah was reminded of this to his cost in 2 Chronicles 26:16–21.

kept busy every day offering sacrifices on the bronze altar in the courtyard outside. When the Lord told Moses to make several items of furniture for the Tabernacle, he didn't tell him to make a chair. The priests were far too busy to sit down.

But David's Tabernacle prophesied that something far better was coming. He wore the robes and ephod of a high priest on the day of its dedication and he personally offered all of the blood sacrifices that first day.[3] Having done so, he forbade blood sacrifices from being offered there again, because he had offered a once-for-all sacrifice which meant that any commoner, both Israelite and Gentile, could now step inside. They must have been shocked to find that the Ark of the Covenant was not hidden away, but in plain view for everyone to see. David had launched the biggest spiritual revolution since the days of Moses. He explains in Psalm 110 why he did so.[4]

In one word, David's explanation is *Melchizedek*. For a slightly more detailed answer, we need to turn to Genesis 14:18–20. Melchizedek ruled as the priest-king of Salem, the ancient name for Jerusalem, on Mount Zion in the days of Abraham. Melchizedek means *King of Righteousness* and King of Salem means *King of Peace*, so David saw him as a prophetic picture of God's better King who was yet to come. That's why as a young man he took Goliath's severed head to Jerusalem to warn the Jebusites that he was coming to take their city. It's why the first three acts of his reign were to capture Jerusalem, to build a Tabernacle on Mount Zion and to bring the Ark of the Covenant up to its new home. It's also why he acted as a priest-king on the day he dedicated the Tabernacle, in order to proclaim that a new Melchizedek was on the way. But don't

---

[3] 1 Samuel 17:54; 1 Chronicles 15:27; 16:2. David appears to have written this psalm to prepare Solomon for his coronation, and Solomon also acted like Melchizedek in 1 Kings 3:15 and 9:25.

[4] Acts 2:29–36 tells us that David was explicitly aware of what he was prophesying here.

take my word for it. It's one of the biggest themes of the New Testament book of Hebrews.

Psalm 110:1 and 4 are quoted four times in Hebrews and four more times in the rest of the New Testament.[5] That makes this the most quoted psalm in the New Testament, and it tells us that the message of this psalm is absolutely vital. It tells us that the ancient king Melchizedek was a living, breathing prophecy about God's coming Messiah. If David's Tabernacle marked a radical spiritual revolution, it was meant to. It explained what Jesus the Messiah was about to do.

David begins the psalm by telling us in 110:1 what *"The Lord says to my Lord"*. The priests and kings of Israel were limited in their powers because they were only humans. Jesus would be different as the new Priest-King of Israel, because he would be God.[6] Unlike the priests at Moses' Tabernacle, he would be told to *"Sit down,"* because his blood sacrifice would save God's People from their sins once and for all. Abraham was able to eat bread and wine from Melchizedek's table, but God's People would be able to eat a communion meal which spoke of God's finished work of salvation through the Messiah's body and his blood.

David tells us in 110:4 that God the Father would tell Jesus the Messiah, *"You are a priest forever, in the order of Melchizedek."* Genesis never tells us who Melchizedek's parents were or how he died which means, for us at least, that he was without beginning and without end. Jesus will be our Great High Priest forever because he truly has no beginning or end.[7] He is the eternal King of Righteousness, so he is able to achieve what the

---

[5] Matthew 22:44; Mark 12:36; Luke 20:42–43; Acts 2:34–35; Hebrews 1:13; 5:6; 7:17, 21. Several other indirect references make Psalm 110:1 the most quoted Old Testament verse in the New Testament.

[6] Ancient kings referred to subduing nations as *making them their footstool*. See Joshua 10:24 and 1 Kings 5:3.

[7] Hebrews 7:1–4. The key verses about Melchizedek as Jesus are in Hebrews 5–10.

high priest Aaron never could. He can usher us into the presence of God forever, which is why the Ark was on full view in David's Tabernacle. Jesus sits at the right hand of God and he ushers us in to sit with him at God's right hand too.[8]

That's why the rest of Psalm 110 tells us how we should respond to Jesus, the one foreshadowed by Melchizedek, because he is a better priest with a better covenant through a better blood sacrifice, so what David prophesied through his new Tabernacle has been fulfilled and the message of Mount Zion is spreading throughout the earth (110:2). We need to give him our complete devotion and pour out our lives in the service of his Kingdom rule (110:3). His rule will never lose its energy (110:7), and he will see the complete fulfilment of God the Father's master plan (110:5–6).

So don't miss the fact that David's Tabernacle was a spiritual revolution which demanded an explanation in Psalm 110. As those who have seen this psalm fulfilled in Jesus Christ and who can read more about the meaning of this psalm in the book of Hebrews, let's not forget to worship the Lord for what David saw. Let's worship God that the days of Moses' Tabernacle are over. The days foreshadowed by David's Tabernacle on Mount Zion and by the priest-king Melchizedek have finally begun.

---

[8] Jesus has ascended to sit at the right hand of the Father (Mark 16:19; Ephesians 1:20–22; Hebrews 8:1–2; 1 Peter 3:22), and now he ushers us to sit with him at the right hand of the Father too (Ephesians 2:6).

Why Melchizedek Matters
(111:1–112:10)

Great are the works of the Lord; they are pondered by all who delight in them.

(Psalm 111:2)

Not everybody gets as excited as David when they read about Melchizedek. Some people think that the king of Salem is ancient history. They can't understand why David treats the message that Jesus is the true Melchizedek as such exciting news. That's why Psalms 111 and 112 follow straight on from Psalm 110. The editors of Psalms wanted to spell out for us why Melchizedek matters.

Psalms 111 and 112 are identical twins. This is obvious in English – they both begin with *Hallelujah!*, or *Praise the Lord!*, and they both have exactly the same structure (a one-verse introduction, two four-verse stanzas and a one-verse conclusion) – but it is even more obvious in Hebrew. Each of these ten-verse psalms contains twenty-two lines of poetry which begin with successive letters of the Hebrew alphabet.[1] They are both acrostic poems which were written with exquisite precision in order to celebrate all that is ours through the Gospel we read about in Psalm 110.

In the first stanza of the poem, Psalm 111:2–5, the focus is on *God's works*. We are told in 111:2 to ponder the things he has done, and in 111:3–4 that his deeds are glorious, majestic and unforgettable. We are reminded in 111:3–4 that his works

---

[1] Verses 1–8 of both psalms contain two lines each. Verses 9–10 contain three lines each.

reveal his *righteousness, grace* and *compassion*. God should have treated us the way King Solomon treated the rebel Joab, but instead he has treated us the way King Solomon treated his beloved mother. We read in 1 Kings 2:19 that *"the king stood up to meet her, bowed down to her and sat down on his throne. He had a throne brought for the king's mother, and she sat down at his right hand."* That's a picture of what has happened to us through Jesus' sacrifice.

When Paul wrote to the Ephesians, he got as excited about this as the psalmists. He celebrated the fact that God the Father

> *raised Christ from the dead and seated him at his right hand in the heavenly realms, far above all rule and authority, power and dominion, and every name that is invoked, not only in the present age but also in the one to come... And God raised us up with Christ and seated us with him in the heavenly realms in Christ Jesus, in order that in the coming ages he might show the incomparable riches of his grace, expressed in his kindness to us in Christ Jesus.*[2]

If this doesn't get you excited, then it really should.

In the second stanza of the poem, Psalm 111:6–9, the focus is on *God's covenant*. Because the Lord is faithful and upright and holy and awesome, he did exactly what he promised Abraham and Moses. There was something preposterous about God's pledge that he would turn the childless Abraham into the father of many nations, and turn the has-been Moses into the deliverer of Israel. But that's exactly what he did when he redeemed the children of Abraham from slavery in Egypt, made a covenant with them at Sinai and dispossessed seven nations in order to give them the Promised Land. It was equally preposterous for the Lord to pledge that he would enable sinful human beings

---

[2] Ephesians 1:20–21; 2:6–7.

like you and me to sit at his right hand, but he has done so. The message about Jesus being the true Melchizedek isn't ancient history. It's the most exciting news in town.

The last verse of Psalm 111 and the first verse of Psalm 112 link the two acrostic poems together. Don't miss the similarity between these two verses and the wisdom writings of Job and Solomon. Psalm 111:10 echoes Job 28:28 and Proverbs 1:7 and 9:10, while 112:1 echoes Proverbs 10:27 and 28:14.[3] Psalms is wisdom literature throughout, but never more so than here. If you want to know God's blessing, read what follows slowly.

In the third stanza, Psalm 112:2–5, the focus is on *God's blessing*. Far too many Christians are like the older brother in the Parable of the Lost Son, who needs to be reminded by his father that *"Everything I have is yours"* (Luke 15:31). We can be so careful about not abusing these verses by teaching a prosperity doctrine of health and wealth that we forget we can also abuse these verses by ignoring them! Nobody who knows the book of Psalms could ever argue that a believer's life will be trouble-free on earth, but we mustn't forget that it promises us great riches in heaven.[4] Paul tells the Ephesians that

> *I pray that the eyes of your heart may be enlightened in order that you may know the hope to which he has called you, the riches of his glorious inheritance in his holy people... This grace was given me: to preach to the Gentiles the boundless riches of Christ... Now to him who is able to do immeasurably more than all we ask or imagine, according to his power that is at work within us, to him be glory in the church.*[5]

---

[3] This celebration of the blessedness of following God's Word will soon be the theme of the greatest acrostic poem of them all: Psalm 119.

[4] We sometimes place more caveats on these promises than Paul, who quotes them in 2 Corinthians 9:9–11 in order to promise us that if we give generously, the Lord will entrust us with even more to give away.

[5] Ephesians 1:18; 3:8, 20–21.

In the fourth stanza, Psalm 112:6–9, the focus is on *forever*. We have not only been granted forgiveness and a seat at God's right hand as heirs to his Kingdom, but we also need *"have no fear"* because this status *"will never be shaken"*.[6] While the wicked long for things they can never have and then perish in 112:10, those who have been saved by the true Melchizedek can feast on his bread and wine forever. Abraham responded to Melchizedek's bread and wine by giving him a tenth of all he had in Genesis 14:18–20. Paul quotes from 112:9 in 2 Corinthians 9:9 to remind us that those who eat the true Melchizedek's bread and wine always give much more. We give away what others cling onto out of fear, because we know that the grace of God is ours both now and forever.[7]

This brings us back to the very beginning of these two acrostic poems. The writer wants us to sing *"in the council of the upright and in the assembly"* about why Melchizedek matters. He wants to remind those who already love the Lord that this is the Gospel which saved them, and he wants us to sing it to the wider congregation of churchgoers who have little passion for the Lord.[8] The massive vault of heavenly riches is ours, now and forever, because we sit in Christ at God's right hand.

Now that's worth singing about.

---

[6] Note the link between 111:4 and 112:6. Because the Lord's wonders are remembered forever, he promises that those who have been saved through the wondrous Gospel will also be remembered forever.

[7] Note the deliberate link between 111:4 and 112:4. Because we sit at the right hand of the Lord who is gracious and compassionate, we also become gracious and compassionate towards others.

[8] The Hebrew word 'ēdāh, or *assembly*, normally refers to Israel rather than to the unbelieving world.

The Egyptian Hallel (113:1–118:29)

I will lift up the cup of salvation and call on the name of the Lord.

(Psalm 116:13)

Most Christians don't even notice it. They barely register the throwaway detail in Matthew 26:30 and Mark 14:26. They get so absorbed in the narrative of what happened to Jesus and his disciples at the Last Supper that they miss the statement that *"When they had sung a hymn, they went out to the Mount of Olives."*

The significance of that statement lies in the hymn which Jesus and his disciples sang. Although neither Matthew nor Mark is specific, they expect us to know that Jews always sang the same thing after they drank a cup of wine together at the end of the Passover meal. They still sing what is known as "the Egyptian Hallel" today, 2,000 years later. It consists of Psalms 113–118 sung together as a single hymn.[1]

Psalms 113–114 were normally sung at the start of the Passover meal. Psalm 113 rejoices that the Lord is enthroned far above Pharaoh and the foreign rulers of the world, and it deliberately echoes Moses' question in Exodus 15:11 after leading the Israelites across the Red Sea: *"Who is like the Lord our God?"*[2] This link back to the Exodus becomes even more

---

[1] *Hallel* is simply the Hebrew word for *Praise* – as in *Hallelujah*.

[2] Mary may have been thinking about Psalm 113 when she sang that the Lord exalts the poor and needy in Luke 1:46–55. After all, the promise in 113:9 had just been fulfilled in the life of her relative Elizabeth.

explicit in Psalm 114, which celebrates leaving Egypt, crossing the Red Sea, drinking water from the rock, and crossing the River Jordan. So don't miss the significance of Jesus singing these two psalms before he ate the Passover meal with his disciples. He celebrated the fact that his imminent death and resurrection were about to work an even better Exodus for all mankind,[3] then he stooped low in death to save the needy as the psalmist promised in 113:6–9.[4]

Psalms 115–118 were normally sung at the end of the Passover meal. Although Aaron had once built a golden calf for the Israelites to worship, Psalm 115 calls the priests the *"house of Aaron"* and tells them to lead Israel's celebration that the Living God is nothing like the lifeless idols of the nations.[5] The psalm cries out to the Lord to renew his Exodus work again because the pagan nations assume he has given up on Israel.[6] Whereas the Israelites sang this song after the Passover meal and called on the Lord to act,[7] Jesus sang it before he got up to become the answer to their prayers.[8]

Psalm 116 takes the Exodus story and makes it personal. It is anonymous, like all of the six psalms which make up the

---

[3] Luke 9:31 tells us literally that Moses appeared to Jesus and *"spoke about his Exodus, which he was about to fulfil in Jerusalem"*.

[4] 113:9 is a wonderful promise for you if you are struggling to conceive. God fulfilled this verse in the life of Sarah, Rebekah, Rachel, Hannah, Samson's mother, Ruth and Elizabeth. He can fulfil it again in you.

[5] The phrase *"house of Aaron"* is not used elsewhere in the Bible except for in 118:3 and 135:19. We will note in the chapter on "The Great Hallel" that 135:15–20 strongly echoes 115:4–11.

[6] We become like what we worship. The pagans become like their dumb idols in 115:8.

[7] 115:17–18 is not telling us that we cannot worship God in heaven. Rather, it is stirring us not to let the thought of heaven tomorrow dampen our passion to see God's purposes fulfilled on the earth right now.

[8] By saying he came to *"save what was lost"* in Luke 19:10, Jesus showed us that he was keenly aware he would fulfil 115:16–18 by restoring Adam's lost authority over the earth to the human race.

Egyptian Hallel,[9] but we can tell that the writer felt as weak and helpless as the Israelites in Egypt (116:1–6). He cried out to the Lord and trusted him, speaking out his faith that the Lord would save him in spite of discouragement from others,[10] and as he did so the Lord rescued him from his personal crisis as powerfully as he had done Israel (116:7–12). Jesus must have drawn comfort just before his death and resurrection from this talk of being rescued from the anguish of the grave.[11] He must have drawn further comfort from the end of the psalm, which promises that the death of God's servants is very precious in God's eyes (116:13–16). *"I will lift up the cup of salvation and call on the name of the Lord,"* he sang as his disciples drank the cup of wine which he had given them. Our only proper response to Jesus' sacrifice must be to pour out our lives in obedient worship (116:17–18a) and in selfless service towards his Church (116:18b-19).

Psalm 117 is the shortest psalm and shortest chapter in the entire Bible.[12] It is also the middle chapter of the Bible. It is more than a simple worship song about God's faithfulness towards Israel. Paul quotes from 117:1 in Romans 15:11 and treats it as a prophecy that Jesus would be a better Passover Lamb and offer a better Exodus to *"all you nations"* and *"all you peoples"*. Some non-Israelites left Egypt with Moses in Exodus 12:38, but Psalm 117 predicts that people from every nation, tribe and language will take part in Jesus' better Exodus for all humankind.

224

---

[9] Some readers treat the similarity between 116:16 and 86:16 as proof that David wrote this psalm, but 116:19 suggests that it was written by someone who worshipped in the courtyards of Solomon's Temple.

[10] Paul quotes from 116:10 in 2 Corinthians 4:13. He quotes from the Septuagint and tells us to understand this verse to mean, *"I believed; therefore I spoke."* Faith is seen by what we say in troubled times.

[11] The Hebrew word in 116:3 is *she'ōl*, meaning *the grave* or *hell*. Jesus was not simply saved from death but from hell itself.

[12] Psalm 119, the longest psalm and longest chapter in the Bible, is only two psalms away. Size isn't everything, however. Psalm 117 is quoted in the New Testament, whereas Psalm 119 is not!

Psalm 118 is the last and best known of the six psalms which make up the Egyptian Hallel. The New Testament quotes from this psalm a record twelve times and treats it as a prophetic song about the Messiah.[13] Its first and last lines both echo the first line of Psalms 106 and 107, so the Jews probably sang the words of this psalm in Ezra 3:10–11 when they rebuilt the Temple and celebrated that *"He is good; his love towards Israel endures forever."* Verse 14 is a word-for-word quotation from Moses' song at the Red Sea in Exodus 15:2, so Jesus must have felt encouraged as he sang it that he was finishing what Moses started. He must have drawn comfort in 118:17–18 from this prophecy about his resurrection, and in 118:22–24 from this promise that the rejected Messiah would become the cornerstone of God's New Covenant Temple.[14] Even the crowds who crucified Jesus obeyed the command in 118:27 when they waved branches as Jesus entered Jerusalem on a donkey, and they sang the words of 118:25–26: *"Hosanna!"* in Hebrew or *"Please save us!"* in English.[15] As he prepared for their rejection and their cries for him to be crucified a few days later, Jesus was comforted by singing the same words which they had sung from Psalm 118.

So don't miss the significance of the statement in Matthew and Mark's gospels that Jesus and his disciples sang a hymn before they left the upper room at the end of the Last Supper. They sang these six psalms, which together form the Egyptian Hallel. They celebrated that an Exodus far greater than that of Moses was about to be fulfilled.

---

[13] Hebrews 13:6 quotes from 118:6 and applies it to us. The other 11 quotes apply this psalm to the Messiah.

[14] 1 Corinthians 3:11; Ephesians 2:20. Psalm 118:22–23 is quoted to mean this in Matthew 21:42, Mark 12:10–11, Luke 20:17, Acts 4:11 and 1 Peter 2:7.

[15] Matthew 21:9; Mark 11:9–10; Luke 13:35; 19:38; John 12:13. Jesus also quotes these verses in Matthew 23:39 to prophesy that people will also shout these words at his Second Coming.

The Longest Psalm
(119:1–176)

Oh, how I love your law! I meditate on it all day long.

(Psalm 119:97)

In the classic movie *Dead Poets Society*, Robin Williams plays an English teacher who inspires a class to express their deepest thoughts in poetry. He tells them:

> *We don't read and write poetry because it's cute. We read and write poetry because we are members of the human race. And the human race is filled with passion. And medicine, law, business, engineering – these are noble pursuits and necessary to sustain life. But poetry, beauty, romance, love – these are what we stay alive for... The powerful play goes on and you may contribute a verse. What will your verse be?*[1]

We don't know who wrote Psalm 119, but we know he deserves a place in the dead poets society.[2] Psalms contains many fine poems, but this may be the finest of them all. It is one of the best poems which has ever been written by anyone about anything, and it was written by somebody who fell in love with God's Word.

The first thing that strikes us is that Psalm 119 is very long. Its 176 verses don't merely make it the longest psalm –

---

[1] *Dead Poets Society* (Touchstone Pictures, 1989).

[2] Some people argue that David wrote Psalm 119, since it has many similarities to Psalm 19, but we simply do not know for sure.

well over twice as long as the nearest contender – but they also make it the longest chapter in the Bible itself. In fact, Psalm 119 is longer than twenty-nine of the sixty-six books in the Bible! It only took William Shakespeare fourteen lines to describe his love for a maiden in his Sonnet 18, which begins with the famous line *"Shall I compare thee to a summer's day?"*, so we ought to be challenged by the fact that it took the psalmist 176 verses to describe his love for the Word of God. Even at the end of the psalm, he finishes with a cry that he longs to gain even more understanding and sing longer.

The next thing that strikes us is that Psalm 119 was clearly constructed very intricately. The psalmist uses eight key words to describe the Scriptures (*tōrāh* or *law*,[3] *mitsōth* or *commandments*, *'imrāh* or *word*, *'ēdōth* or *testimonies*, *huqqīm* or *statutes*, *piqqudīm* or *precepts*,[4] *mishpātīm* or *judgments* and *dābār* or *word*), and virtually all of the 176 verses contain at least one of them. None of the psalm's twenty-two stanzas contain fewer than six of them, and five stanzas include all eight.[5] Robin Williams tells his students that *"Language was invented for one reason, boys – to woo women – and, in that endeavour, laziness will not do."* The psalmist was not lazy in constructing this masterpiece of ancient literature and in using it to celebrate his love for God's Word.

But neither of these is the first thing which strikes a Hebrew reader of this psalm, because Psalm 119 is an elaborate acrostic poem. It isn't just the greatest acrostic poem in the Bible; it is

---

[3] The *Torah* was strictly speaking just the first five books of the Old Testament, but the word was also used to describe the Old Testament as a whole (John 10:34; 12:34; 15:25; 1 Corinthians 14:21–22).

[4] We grasp something of the psalmist's passion for the Scriptures when we consider that the word *piqqudɪm* only occurs 24 times in the Bible, that all of them are in Psalms, and that 21 of them are in Psalm 119.

[5] The five stanzas which contain all eight words are verses 41–48, 57–64, 73–80, 81–88 and 129–136.

arguably the most intricate acrostic poem ever written.[6] Each of the psalm's twenty-two stanzas has eight lines, and the lines of each stanza all begin with the same letters of the Hebrew alphabet. Verses 1–8 all begin with the letter *aleph*, verses 9–16 all begin with the letter *beth* and so on, right down to the final letter *taw* in verses 169–176. C. S. Lewis observes that *"This poem is not, and does not pretend to be, a sudden outpouring of the heart... It is a pattern, a thing done like embroidery, stitch by stitch, through long, quiet hours, for love of the subject and for the delight in leisurely, disciplined craftsmanship."[7]* It should convince us that God's Word deserves our best attention too.

The writer warns us that how much we know and obey the Scriptures will determine how much we are able to experience God's blessing (119:1–8). He tells us that storing up God's Word in our hearts is the key to Christian maturity (119:9–16). We will be persecuted for loving God's Word in a world which seeks to silence it (119:17–24), but we will also find it strengthens us to bear up under trials (119:25–32). That's why the psalmist pleads eight times in eight verses for the Lord to help him understand the Scriptures more fully (119:33–40), and why he promises that he will not be ashamed to confess his faith in God's Word before a mocking world (119:41–48).[8]

Already we can see how the Word of God has changed the psalmist. His thinking is so at odds with his culture that he describes himself as a traveller and the Scriptures as the soundtrack which accompanies his wandering around a foreign land (119:49–56). Unlike the people among whom he lives, he pledges that he will obey God's Word swiftly (119:57–64), gladly

---

[6] The Egyptian Hallel is therefore preceded by two acrostic poems which say the wise man will listen to God's Word (Psalms 111–112), and it is succeeded by an acrostic poem which says the same (Psalm 119).

[7] C. S. Lewis in *Reflections on the Psalms* (1958).

[8] Believers will always be mocked for believing and obeying God's Word (119:51). God is looking for people who fear his Word more than their critics (119:161) and who prize it more than what it costs them (119:162).

(119:65–72), wholeheartedly (119:73–80) and consistently (119:81–88). He will see it as eternal (119:89–96), as the source of true wisdom (119:97–104)[9] and as the lamp which lights up the path ahead of him (119:105–112).[10] He promises not to be influenced by those who despise God's Word (119:113–120), and he asks God to overturn their stranglehold on his nation's culture (119:121–128). He pants for Scripture like a thirsty animal (119:129–136) and wears himself out trying to pass it on to anyone who will listen (119:137–144). He gets up early and stays up late in order to meditate on God's promises (119:145–152), convinced that understanding Scripture is the key to enjoying the fullness of God's salvation (119:153–160).[11] He ends the psalm by asking the Lord to deliver him personally (119:161–168) and to help him worship and testify about what he has discovered in God's Word (119:169–176).

Henry Venn had a passionate desire to transform his ungodly nation at the end of the eighteenth century. There was nothing unusual about his desire except for the fact that he actually succeeded. He founded the Clapham Sect, which would go on to transform nineteenth-century Britain through the Gospel under the leadership of William Wilberforce. One historian, Stephen Tomkins, even goes so far as to claim that *"the ethos of Clapham became the spirit of the age."*[12] So how did Henry Venn manage to achieve the impossible by turning his desire for culture change into national reality? He tells us in one of his letters:

---

[9] This stanza does not promote arrogant unteachability. In fact, it stresses our need for good Bible teachers.

[10] We often want the Lord to give us a long-term map, but he tends to light up our path a few steps at a time.

[11] Verse 160 probably means *"the sum of your word is truth"* rather than simply *"All your words are true."* It is therefore a reminder that verses taken out of context can be deadly. Scripture in its entirety is the truth.

[12] Stephen Tomkins in *The Clapham Sect: How Wilberforce's Circle Transformed Britain* (2010).

The 119th Psalm... This is the Psalm I have often had recourse to, when I could find no spirit of prayer in my own heart; and at length the fire has kindled, and I could pray... What has been your experience regarding this extraordinary Psalm?... Have you not found it pleasant and nourishing to your soul?[13]

So let's learn from Henry Venn to nourish our souls on the longest psalm, expressing our love for God's Word and finding that we increase it as we do so. Psalm 119 doesn't merely change its readers. It enables them to influence their nations through God's Word.

---

[13] He wrote this in a letter to Mrs Riland on 4th January 1785.

Up (120:1–124:8)

*I rejoiced with those who said to me, "Let us go to
the house of the Lord."*

(Psalm 122:1)

Not many people ever get to climb Mount Everest. Since its
peak is almost 9,000 metres above sea level, it's easy to see
why. Climbers need to wait for two weeks at Base Camp in
order to acclimatize themselves to high altitudes, and then
they stop at four separate camps for further rests along the
way. The final 1,000 metres of ascent are known as "the death
route" because conditions are so extreme that many climbers
never make it home.

Mount Zion is nowhere near as tall as Mount Everest. At
little more than 750 metres above sea level, it isn't even a tenth
as tall. Yet there was something about Mount Zion which made
the psalmists believe that nobody could tackle it safely without
similar preparation. The dangers on Mount Everest include a
lack of oxygen and the freezing cold. The danger on Mount Zion
was the holy presence of God himself. That's why Psalms 120–
134 are all marked as "songs of ascents", because they became
the fifteen songs which the Israelites sang on pilgrimages to the
Temple in Jerusalem.[1] The editors of Psalms included them as a
mini-collection within Book V to help us sing our own response
to God. We are invited to step into God's presence, and we need
to prepare ourselves for something greater than Mount Everest.

---

[1] A minority view argues that they were sung by the priests as they ascended
the fifteen steps at the Temple (Nehemiah 9:4), but I find the traditional view
much more convincing.

The Israelites begin their pilgrimage in Psalm 120 by expressing their eager desire to go to Jerusalem. They complain in 120:5 that they live in a land of Greeks and Arabs who do not understand the values of Israel's Kingdom.[2] The anonymous writer of this psalm did not necessarily know that his song would be used as a "song of ascents", but the Israelites chose it as the first of their fifteen pilgrim songs because it captured how they felt in their day-to-day lives for much of their history.[3]

The pilgrims therefore turn their eyes to Jerusalem in Psalm 121. *"I lift up my eyes to the mountains,"* they sing as they express their faith that the Lord will protect them on their journey.[4] He will not let their foot slip on the mountain roads. He will protect them from the daytime sun and from moonlit dangers.[5] He will *"watch over your coming and going both now and forevermore"*.[6] It is easy to see why the Israelites chose this psalm as their second "song of ascents", but it also has a more general application for us all. I once received some terrible news by telephone while staying at a ski resort in Austria, and the first verse of this psalm helped me to find perspective. As I looked up at the Alps, I knew that I could leave my situation in the hands of their Creator.

232

---

[2] *Meshek* was Noah's grandson via his son Japheth and ancestor to the peoples of modern-day Greece and Turkey (Genesis 10:2; Ezekiel 27:13). *Kedar* was Abraham's grandson via his son Ishmael and was ancestor to the Bedouin peoples of the Arabian desert (Genesis 25:13; Ezekiel 27:21).

[3] The name *Jerusalem* means *Foundation of Peace*, so there is a play on words in 120:6–7. Zion's values are always at odds with the ways of the sinful world.

[4] Jerusalem had five mountains: Zion, Moriah, Ophel, Bezetha and Acra. The psalmist does not place his faith in the size of the mountains but in the strength of the God who had his Temple on one of them.

[5] In 1 Kings 18:27, Elijah taunted the prophets of Baal that their idol was asleep. Our God never sleeps.

[6] Verse 8 is the fulfilment of the promise the Lord made in Deuteronomy 28:6.

Psalm 122 is the first to state its author in the title.[7] David mentions *"the house of the Lord"* in both the first and final verses, and he refers to Jerusalem by name three times in just nine verses. He tells the pilgrims to rejoice that *"Our feet are standing in your gates, Jerusalem,"* because this song sees the entrance to the city as the equivalent of Base Camp on Mount Everest.[8] David gets excited that he is within eyesight of the Tabernacle, so we should not be any less excited about the Church today. The New Testament tells us that we have a better hope than the pilgrims to the Temple because we have been invited to come *"to Mount Zion, to the city of the living God, the heavenly Jerusalem"*.[9] We must therefore long for fellowship with others in our local church (122:1), sharing our lives very closely with them (122:3) and seeing this as a matter of divine mandate rather than personal preference (122:4). We must pray for our churches to be peaceful and successful (122:6–9).[10] We have a better Mount Zion.

Getting to Base Camp means preparing in earnest, and it was the same for pilgrims once they entered Jerusalem.[11] Psalm 123 tells them to rid themselves of human pride by looking up at God's greatness (123:1), and by recognizing that we rely on him more than any slave-girl does her mistress (123:2). They must remember how much they hate seeing pride in others and approach the Lord with the humility which attracts his grace and mercy (123:3–4). Psalm 100 helps clarify that this doesn't

---

[7] David wrote Psalms 122, 124, 131 and 133. Solomon wrote Psalm 127. The other ten songs of ascents are anonymous.

[8] David refers to *thrones* in 122:5 as a way of emphasizing that the real climb is still ahead for pilgrims. Coming to David's throne was one thing but coming to the Lord's throne at his Temple was quite another.

[9] Hebrews 12:22–23; Galatians 4:25–26; Revelation 21:2.

[10] Since *Jerusalem* means *Foundation of Peace*, there is another play on words in 122:6–9.

[11] When Solomon dedicated the Temple, he pointed out eight times that the Lord's true dwelling place was not in Jerusalem but in heaven (1 Kings 8:30, 32, 34, 36, 39, 43, 45, 49). Psalm 123:1 does the same.

mean looking down at ourselves and snivelling as slaves, but looking up at the Lord with humble eyes and finding that he has saved and transformed us into sons and daughters of the King.

Psalm 124 completes these first five songs of ascents. David warns the pilgrims to be humble and to recognize that their salvation is entirely God's work, not their own (124:1–5). He tells them to be confident because God's work can never fail, and he will certainly accept them into his presence through the Gospel (124:6–8). Although our pilgrimage is spiritual rather than physical, we still need these songs of ascents. They warn us against the opposite dangers of a swaggering self-confidence and a browbeating self-pity, both of which are detestable to the Lord.

George Mallory was one of the earliest Europeans to develop an obsession with climbing Mount Everest. When reporters asked him why, he simply replied, *"Because it is there."*[12] He described *"the strange elation of seeing Everest for the first time"* and remembered that *"We saw Mount Everest not quite sharply defined on account of a slight haze in that direction; this circumstance added a touch of mystery and grandeur."*[13] He resolved to make any sacrifice, even that of his own life, for a chance to scale the mountain which lay before him. The psalmists want to stir in us a similar obsession for Mount Zion and for the presence of the Lord. They saw it through the haze of Old Testament pictures and prophecies and they sang these songs on special occasions. But we can sing these songs with far clearer revelation as we dwell in God's presence every day.

---

[12] He said this in an interview with the *New York Times* on 18th March 1923.

[13] He wrote this in *Mount Everest: The Reconnaissance, 1921*. He died three years later while trying to climb it.

Mindful of Conditions
(125:1–129:8)

May all who hate Zion be turned back in shame.

(Psalm 129:5)

When I first read about David Sharp, I didn't know whether to admire him or to pity him. The maths teacher from England had a commendable passion to climb Mount Everest, but he was totally unmindful of conditions.

On his first attempt in 2003, he tried to save money by buying cheap boots. After being forced to turn back due to frostbite, doctors amputated two of his gangrenous toes. On his second attempt in 2004, he wore cheap gloves and was forced to turn back again due to frostbitten fingers. *"I would give up more toes – or even fingers – to get to the top,"* he told a friend, but he had still not learned to be mindful of conditions. On his third attempt in 2006, he climbed solo and without a Sherpa. He failed to take a two-way radio and he tried to economize on baggage by taking insufficient oxygen for the journey. After he froze to death on the mountain slopes, a fellow climber commented that *"It almost looks like he had a death wish."* But he hadn't. He really hadn't. He had just failed to be mindful of conditions.[1]

That's why Psalm 125 reminds the pilgrims to the Temple that they need the Lord's protection if they are to experience his presence. When Aaron's two sons Nadab and Abihu tried to enter the Tabernacle on their own terms instead of God's, they

---

[1] These quotes come from a newspaper report shortly after his death in *USA Today* on 16th July 2006.

both died instantly.[2] When Christians think they can saunter into God's presence without thinking, it also spells spiritual disaster. The psalmist tells us that the crucial question is whether we have faith (125:1). If we trust in God's blood sacrifice for sin, we are as strong as Mount Zion and as safe as Jerusalem, snuggled in the safety of the city's five mountains.[3] If we fail to trust in Jesus' blood alone, we will be *banished with the evildoers* (125:5).[4] This sixth song of ascents issues us with a solemn warning. It would be safer for us to try to climb Mount Everest in just our underpants than for us to waltz into God's presence without genuine faith in the Gospel.[5]

Psalm 126 is anonymous and undated, and we do not even know whether the Hebrew phrase used in verse 1 talks about the Lord *restoring fortunes* or *bringing back captives*. It doesn't really matter whether it was written before or after the Jewish return from exile in Babylon.[6] What matters is that God restores and revives his People again and again. He delivered Samaria from an Aramean army in just one night, and he delivered Jerusalem from an Assyrian army in just one night too. He overthrew the Babylonians in just a night to send the Jews back to their homeland, and he will also transform our situations in

---

[2] Leviticus 10:1–2. They relied on man-made fire instead of fire from God's altar of blood sacrifice. Our safety before the holy God because of Jesus must never blind us to our mortal danger without him.

[3] Since *Jerusalem* means *Foundation of Peace*, there is a play on words in 125:5. Paul seems to be thinking of this verse in Galatians 6:16 when he wishes peace on the Church as *"the Israel of God"*.

[4] Verse 3 points out that if the Lord did not judge the wicked, the righteous might be tempted to copy their evil. God's judgment is a good thing. It stops us from being tempted beyond what we can bear.

[5] The only other place in the Bible which uses the same Hebrew word as 125:5 for *crooked ways* is Judges 5:6. This talks about people leaving God's highway of righteousness in order to create their own rebellious paths.

[6] Job 42:10 used the same phrase metaphorically over 1,000 years before the Jewish return from exile, and so does David in Psalms 14:7 and 53:6. Even this very psalm does so in 126:4.

an instant if we cry out to him.[7] It may seem like a dream come true that we are invited to dwell in God's presence, but we have a God who specializes in fulfilling and exceeding his People's wildest dreams.[8]

Solomon wrote Psalm 127 – only his second song in the entire collection – and it was chosen as the eighth song of ascents for a reason. The pilgrims have now arrived at the Temple courtyards and are in danger of being so impressed by the buildings in front of them them that they forget the greatness of the Lord.[9] They need to hear Solomon's warning to them that no house can be built unless the Lord is the true builder,[10] and that no city can be protected unless the Lord is its true guard (127:1–2).[11] Since most pilgrims arrived at the Temple courtyards with their families, the second half of the psalm reminds them explicitly that their children are a gift from the Lord (127:3–5). They must not be so impressed by Solomon's city and Temple that they lose focus on the Lord who helped him build them. They must worship him and trust him to help them build true faith in the hearts of their families.

This thought continues as the theme of Psalm 128, where the pilgrims spill into the Temple courtyards with

---

[7] 2 Kings 7:1–7; 19:35–36; Daniel 5:30–31. The desert lands of the Negev often experienced flash floods from sudden rains, so 126:4 is telling us that God can change our situation in a moment.

[8] Verses 5 and 6 are very encouraging if you dream of seeing large numbers of people saved through the Gospel. God promises you a great harvest if your setbacks do not make you give up (Galatians 6:9).

[9] The disciples made the mistake of being too impressed by the Temple architecture in Matthew 24:1, Mark 13:1 and Luke 21:5. Jesus firmly drew their attention away from the Temple and back onto God.

[10] These words are particularly important for church leaders who feel they are too busy to take a break from church work. Solomon warns that unless we rest and let God be God (46:10), we are labouring in vain.

[11] The Hebrew word for *beloved one* in 127:2 is very similar to Solomon's other name, Jedidiah (2 Samuel 12:25), so Solomon may be recalling how God gave him wisdom while he slept in 1 Kings 3:4–15.

their families.[12] It promises that the pilgrims' wives will be like *fruitful vines* and that their children will be like *olive shoots*.[13] Their children will be wise and fruitful, blessing their city and giving them grandchildren.[14] There is a deliberate echo between 128:1 and 1:1. Anyone who longs for the presence of God and is mindful of conditions will receive all of the blessings in the Psalms.

This links closely with Psalm 129. Whereas Psalm 128 pronounces a blessing on those who have responded to the Gospel, Psalm 129 pronounces a curse on those who have not. It rejoices that the Lord has always rescued his People from their cruel oppressors (129:1–4), and it warns that those who persist in hating Zion and in thinking that they can stroll into God's presence on the Last Day will certainly perish (129:5–8).[15]

So don't be a foolish climber and think that you can come close to the Lord without bearing in mind the state of your life and your status through the Gospel. You can only dwell in the Lord's presence if you are mindful of conditions. Because of Jesus, and Jesus alone, we can dare to keep on climbing higher.

---

[12] It is possible that the Levites sang this song to the pilgrims as they arrived in the Temple courtyards. Many modern rabbis still use Psalm 128 as a blessing for Jewish couples at their wedding ceremonies.

[13] His wife will be faithful and fruitful at home, unlike the adulteress in Proverbs 7:11. His children will gather round his table in good relationship, unlike the rebellious children in Proverbs 20:20.

[14] Once again, 128:6 is a play on words with the name *Jerusalem*, or *Foundation of Peace*.

[15] Verse 8 recalls the words which Hebrew harvesters spoke to one another in Ruth 2:4. The psalmist is praying that those who despise God's presence may be as fruitless as those who love his presence are fruitful.

Deeper and Higher
(130:1–134:3)

Out of the depths I cry to you, Lord.

(Psalm 130:1)

The final stage of scaling any mountain is always the hardest. And so it proves to be with the final five songs of ascents. As the pilgrims get ready to enter the inner courtyard of the Temple, they discover that they must go deeper before they are able to go higher.

Psalm 130 is one of the seven penitential psalms and it is often known by its Latin name *"De Profundis"*, which means "Out of the Depths". Don't be surprised that it comes at this late stage in the songs of ascents. The inner courtyard of the Temple had been deliberately constructed in a way which encouraged worshippers to confess their sin before daring to step any closer to God's presence. The inner courtyard was dominated by a massive bronze altar – always burning and always splattered with the blood of sacrificial animals.[1] Beyond this was a Sea of Cast Metal made out of bronze mirrors in which the worshippers saw their reflections and asked themselves if they were truly ready to be this close to the presence of the Lord.[2] It was this psalm which convicted John Wesley on the day of his conversion that he was a sinner and that only God could cleanse and forgive

---

[1] 2 Chronicles 4:1 tells us that the altar was a massive 9 metres wide, 9 metres deep, and 4.5 metres tall.

[2] 2 Chronicles 4:5 tells us that the Sea of Cast Metal could hold a staggering 66,000 litres of water. Exodus 38:8 and James 1:23–24 suggest that it was meant to make worshippers aware they needed cleansing.

him.[3] Psalm 130 has had that same effect on countless lives throughout the many centuries since it was written.

The psalmist felt as though he was drowning under the guilt of his sin (130:1–2), but he believed the Gospel message that God forgives and justifies the guilty (130:3–4). He trusted in the Lord, knowing that his very life depended on it (130:5–6), and he tells the pilgrims at the Temple that they must also place their faith in the Gospel if they want to go any higher (130:7–8). They must not deny their sin but nor must they despair because of it, for God himself redeems his People from all their sins.[4] Romans 1:17 explains that *"In the gospel the righteousness of God is revealed – a righteousness that is by faith from first to last."* In just eight short verses, Psalm 130 takes us from the depths of sin to the heights of God's redemption.

David was a prophet, but even he did not fully understand all the mysteries of the Gospel. That's why the next song of ascents is Psalm 131, in which David confesses that he trusts the Lord even when he does not give him all the answers.[5] He tells the pilgrims that he is like a well-fed child with its mother. He is more than satisfied with the insights God has already given him into the Gospel, and he encourages them to put their hope in the Law while they wait for God to reveal a better covenant in days to come.[6] It doesn't take long to read this psalm but it takes a lifetime to apply it. One of my close friends died yesterday after a long fight with cancer, so I have plenty of questions to ask the Lord today. David reminds us that we will always have similar

---

[3] He was converted on the evening of 24th May 1738 while listening to Luther's commentary on Romans, but God had laid the groundwork in his heart when he heard a choir sing Psalm 130 earlier that day.

[4] Verses 7 and 8 do not just promise redemption, but *full* redemption. As the pilgrims prepared to sacrifice their animals, they were reminded that these merely pointed to the true Lamb of God who was yet to come.

[5] There is a clear link between these two psalms since the first few words of 131:3 are exactly the same as the first few words of 130:7.

[6] The Hebrew phrase translated *"Put your hope in the Lord"* in 131:3 can also be translated *"Wait for the Lord."*

tough questions. We need to trust the Lord each day with what we don't know while holding onto what we do.

Psalm 132 is by far the longest song of ascents. We don't know who wrote it but we can tell a lot about it from its date and its purpose. The theme of the psalm is that David swore to build a Tabernacle for the Lord while he was still a shepherd-boy in the fields around Bethlehem, looking up at the lights of Kiriath Jearim where the Ark of the Covenant was in temporary accommodation.[7] David built the Tabernacle to become the Lord's throne room on earth, the footstool to his heavenly throne.[8] We know that it was written by the beginning of Solomon's reign because he used part of it to dedicate his new Temple (2 Chronicles 6:41–42 repeats 132:8–10). Solomon used this psalm to ask the Lord to remember his covenant with David (132:1, 10) and to dwell in the Temple as he had in the Tabernacle, making it his *"resting place forever and ever"*.[9] Subsequent pilgrims to the Temple learned to sing this psalm because they needed a deeper understanding of the background to the Temple to enable them to go higher.

Having explained God's glorious vision for his Temple, Psalm 133 celebrates Israel's unity in worship. David wrote it to celebrate the togetherness which God's People share as they worship together in Jerusalem. Aaron and his successors were anointed with oil when they became high priests,[10] but David says this once-in-a-lifetime ordination was no sweeter than the daily joy of seeing Israel worshipping in total unity

---

[7] *Ephrathah* was another name for Bethlehem and *Jaar* was another name for *Kiriath Jearim*, only eight miles away from Bethlehem. Since the Hebrew word for the Ark is masculine and *"it"* is feminine in 132:6, Israel didn't so much hear the Ark as hear God's call for them to bring it to Mount Zion.

[8] 2 Chronicles 9:18 tells us that ancient thrones often had a footstool as well as a seat. See also 1 Chronicles 28:2, Psalm 99:5 and Lamentations 2:1.

[9] The Lord more than answered their prayers in 132:17–18. He made Jesus the true Messiah, the true horn and lamp of Israel, and he sent him to die outside the walls of Jerusalem wearing a crown of thorns.

[10] Exodus 29:7; Leviticus 21:10.

through the Holy Spirit. He may even be recalling the words of Exodus 19:6 and telling the worshippers that their unity sets them apart as a nation of priests sent by God to minister to the world. Unlike Mount Hermon, to the north and four times taller than Mount Zion,[11] Jerusalem received little rain and struggled with the fact it had no river, but David says that when God's People unite together they become a human river which flows to heal the nations.[12]

Psalm 134 is the fifteenth and final song of ascents. The united pilgrims now approach the Temple building itself and sing to the priests who minister inside *"the house of the Lord"* (134:1).[13] They cannot personally enter the Holy Place to pray at its golden altar of incense so they call out to the priests to do so on their behalf (134:2). The priests shout back a blessing from the presence of the Lord within the Temple (134:3). The pilgrims have sung fifteen songs as they climbed Mount Zion to reach the Temple, so they receive a greater blessing than Sir Edmund Hillary when he became the first man to stand on the summit of Mount Everest.[14]

We will be blessed too if we cherish God's presence as much as the writers of the fifteen songs of ascents. If we long for intimacy with the Lord and commit ourselves wholeheartedly to pursuing it through the Church, we will find the blessing we are looking for. These fifteen songs have taken us deeper into the Gospel so that we can climb ever higher into the Gospel blessings which are ours in Christ.

---

[11] David refers literally to the *mountains of Zion* in 133:3. This is helpful because it shows us that when the psalmists say *Zion* they mean Mount Moriah and the other three hills of Jerusalem too.

[12] Psalms 36:8; 46:4; Ezekiel 47:1–12; John 7:37–39; Revelation 22:1–2.

[13] The reference to the priests *ministering by night* reminds us that they offered incense at twilight (Exodus 30:6–8) and were able to worship the Lord 24 hours a day (1 Chronicles 9:33).

[14] There appears to be a deliberate link between 134:3 and 121:2. The pilgrims have received the blessing they were longing for.

The Great Hallel
(135:1–136:26)

*Give thanks to the Lord, for he is good. His love
endures forever.*

(Psalm 136:1)

Reaching the top of Mount Everest can be disappointing. The
American mountaineer Jon Krakauer recalls the moment when
he reached the summit:

> *Straddling the top of the world, one foot in China and
> the other in Nepal... I understood on some dim, detached
> level that the sweep of earth beneath my feet was a
> spectacular sight. I'd been fantasizing about this moment,
> and the release of emotion that would accompany it, for
> many months. But now that I was finally here, actually
> standing on the summit of Mount Everest, I just couldn't
> summon the energy to care.[1]*

There is nothing disappointing about the summit of Mount Zion,
however. The two psalms which follow the songs of ascents are
known as "the Great Hallel" because they issue a great roar of
praise. The Jewish Talmud sees the songs of ascents as part of
the Great Hallel, but strictly speaking it is just Psalms 135 and
136 which form the summit song of Mount Zion. The Hebrew
word *Hallel* means *Praise* (as in *Hallelujah*), and the editors of
Psalms placed these songs here in order to show us the kind of

---

[1] Jon Krakauer in his book *Into Thin Air* (1997).

praise we should feel when we finally arrive in God's presence. The view from up here is amazing.

Whoever wrote the anonymous Psalm 135, they clearly intended it to follow on from the songs of ascents. Verses 1 and 2 are an adapted repetition of 134:1,[2] while verse 3 links back to 133:1,[3] and the psalm builds up in its final verse to a climax of praise that the Lord dwells in *Zion* and *Jerusalem*. We can also tell that the psalmist wrote it to form a new "Hallel" for Israel because it links back very strongly to the Egyptian Hallel in Psalms 113–118. Verses 15–20 are an adapted repetition of 115:4–11, and verses 19–21 are an adapted repetition of 118:2–4.[4] Like many of the psalms in the Egyptian Hallel, it also begins and ends with the Hebrew phrase *Hallelujah!* or *Praise the Lord!* This psalm was therefore written as a fresh song of praise for pilgrims to sing when they finally reached the summit of Mount Zion.

It tells the pilgrims to praise the Lord that he chose them out of the nations (135:1–4),[5] because he is far greater than the pagan idols (135:5–7). The Lord is not only good; he is great too. The Lord redeemed his People from slavery in Egypt (135:8–9) and drove out the Canaanites before them in order to settle them in the Promised Land (135:10–12). We should worship the Lord because this is how he always acts towards his People (135:13–14),[6] whereas pagan idols always fail those who are

---

[2] This time the call includes not just the priests in the Temple but also the Levites in the Temple courtyards.

[3] This Hebrew word for *pleasant* is only used four times in the whole of Psalms except for 133:1 and 135:3. The link between these verses, therefore, appears to be deliberate.

[4] As in 135:2, the call now includes the Levites serving in the Temple courtyards too. This is the only explicit reference to Levi in the whole of Psalms.

[5] The psalmist uses the same Hebrew word for *treasured possession* in 135:4 as the Lord uses in Exodus 19:5–6. Since any Jew who sang this psalm automatically would make this link, 135:5 may also echo Exodus 18:11.

[6] The Hebrew word *dîn* in 135:14 can mean either *to vindicate* or *to judge*. Hebrews 10:30 quotes from this verse in order to warn that the God we worship is also the one who will be our Judge.

foolish enough to worship them (135:15–18). The psalmist tells the Israelites, the priests from Aaron's family, and the Levites who served in the Temple to praise the Lord together at his throne room on Mount Zion (135:19–21).[7]

Psalm 136 is deliberately twinned with Psalm 135 as the second half of the Great Hallel. It tells the same story of Israel's redemption from Egypt and of their victory over the Canaanite kings Sihon and Og, and 136:17–22 is a clear repetition of 135:10–12. What is unusual about this psalm is that it appears to have been written to be sung antiphonally – that is, to be sung responsively. It appears that one of the Levite choirs sang the first half of these twenty-six verses and that the worshippers at the Temple sang back the second half of the verses, repeating: *"His love endures forever."* Songs like this one appear to have featured strongly in Israel's worship throughout the Old Testament.[8] Pilgrims who reached the summit of Mount Zion were told to look out across the landscape of Israel's history and sing that the Lord's *hēsēd* – his *covenant love* or *covenant mercy* – was the one constant factor in their history. It would be the constant factor in his dealings with them forever.

Once, when I was struggling with a difficult and drawn-out house sale, I took a business flight and happened to fly over the town where I lived. As I looked down on the tiny houses below me, my perspective completely changed. Of course my God was strong enough to bring my puny house sale to a speedy resolution! The writer of Psalm 136 expects the pilgrims at the Temple to find that the summit of Mount Zion changes their own perspective too. Their vantage point should remind them that the Lord's covenant love towards his People made

[7] Verses 19–21 are adapted from 115:9–11, but the psalmist changes the call to *trust* the Lord into a call to *bless* the Lord. The pilgrims needed to let their faith stir them into worship.

[8] 1 Chronicles 16:41; 2 Chronicles 5:13; 7:3–6; 20:21; Ezra 3:11.

him create the world (136:4–9),[9] redeem them from Egypt (136:10–15),[10] lead them through the desert (136:16) and drive out the Canaanites before them so that they could settle in the Promised Land (136:17–22).[11] That same great covenant love is the reason we can trust the Lord to help us when we are weak (136:23) and in trouble (136:24) and in need of his provision (136:25).[12] Words like these were more refreshing to the climbers of Mount Zion than a cylinder of oxygen.

So don't be like Jon Krakauer and fail to enjoy your view from the summit of Mount Zion. Take some time today to go back over some of the spiritual milestones in your own walk with God and to praise him for all that he has done for you. Take some time to enjoy the fresh perspective which comes from resting in God's presence. Take some time to praise him that his covenant love towards you endures forever.

---

[9] Verse 4 tells us that God performs great miracles because his love endures forever. We must not assume that he has ceased performing such miracles today, because it is unthinkable that his love should ever change.

[10] Don't miss the way that the psalmist deliberately echoes Scripture to show that these facts are indelibly true: 136:7–9 uses the same language as Genesis 1:16; 136:12 uses the same language as Deuteronomy 11:2; and 136:15 uses the same unusual word as Exodus 14:27.

[11] These verses remind us that God's covenant love involves judgment as well as forgiveness. They show us how foolish it is for us to struggle with the Bible's teaching that the God of love sends people to hell.

[12] The Persians referred to their chief idol as *"the God of Heaven"*, so the Jewish exiles adopted this as their way of describing Yahweh to the Persians (17 times in Daniel, Ezra and Nehemiah). Verse 26 might indicate that this psalm was written after the exile, while Jerusalem was still part of the Persian Empire.

Babylon (137:1–138:8)

Our tormentors demanded songs of joy; they said,
"Sing us one of the songs of Zion!"

(Psalm 137:3)

On 18th July 586 BC the Babylonians captured the city of Jerusalem. They murdered the royal princes in front of King Zedekiah and then gouged out his eyes so that his dying sons would be the last sight etched onto his memory.[1] They plundered the Temple on Mount Zion of its treasures, including the bronze altar around which the Temple pilgrims had so often sung. They torched Jerusalem and its Temple before slaughtering almost every single man, woman and child in the city. Only a tiny fraction of Jews survived to go into exile in Babylon. As they left, they caught one last glimpse of the blackened rubble which had once been their great city and its even greater Temple.

Some people find it strange that Psalm 137 should be placed here. It feels like an orphan of a psalm, sandwiched between seventeen psalms which were sung by pilgrims to the Temple and eight psalms which were written by David. In fact, there is nothing strange about its position at all, because the worship leaders who compiled Psalms were masters at using sudden contrasts for effect.[2] They deliberately placed this song straight after the Great Hallel because they want to shock us with what it meant for the Jews to go into exile in Babylon.

---

[1] Zedekiah's name meant *The Lord Is My Righteousness*. Even as he failed as king and caused the fall of David's dynasty, his name promised that a better Messianic King would arise from the ashes of Jerusalem.

[2] They placed Psalm 79 immediately after Psalm 78 to effect a similar shocking contrast.

Babylon was actually rather a nice place. Its hanging gardens were among the seven wonders of the ancient world. Psalm 137 admits this when it tells us that Babylon was built on *rivers* and full of *poplar trees*.[3] Unsurprisingly, some of the Jewish exiles fell in love with their new city and went native, deciding to call it home. They were happy to sing the songs of Zion as a bit of light entertainment for their captors. They forgot the glories of Psalms 120–136 and exchanged them for a new life in a green and pleasant land.

The writer of Psalm 137, however, refused to play along.[4] His song comes straight after the Great Hallel because it shows us how to live a godly life in a world which despises the presence of the Lord. He refuses to treat Psalms 120–136 as a bunch of ditties which might help the Babylonians to while away their Mesopotamian nights. He and his friends remember their enjoyment of God's presence on the summit of Mount Zion far too clearly to do that. They water the rivers of Babylon with their anguished tears and decorate the poplar trees of Babylon with the harps they used to play at the Temple on Mount Zion.[5] They curse themselves if ever they forget Jerusalem and the importance of experiencing God's presence.[6] We live in "Babylon" ourselves – a world where people care little for true intimacy with God – so 137:1–6 is a real challenge to our own need to remember "Zion".

Most readers get quite uncomfortable in 137:7–9. It

---

[3] Babylon was built on a network of canals fed by the great River Euphrates. Babylonia was also watered by the Tigris, the Kebar and the Ulai. See Jeremiah 51:13 and Revelation 17:1.

[4] He uses perfect tenses in 137:1–3, which imply that he has now left Babylon, so it appears that he wrote this psalm after the Persians captured Babylon in 539 BC but before they destroyed it in about 516 BC.

[5] Revelation 18:22 appears to pick up on 137:2 when it tells us that Babylonian harpists will be silenced when God judges spiritual "Babylon".

[6] 2 Chronicles 36:14–16 tells us that the Jews were exiled because they forgot the Lord and his covenant with them. They would return to Jerusalem after devout Jews refused to forget Mount Zion.

is bad enough that the Jewish exiles curse the Edomites for taking advantage of Jerusalem's misery to settle old scores,[7] but how can they be justified in blessing those who repay the Babylonians by dashing out their babies' brains on the rocks?! It is helpful to remember that the Babylonians, like most ancient armies, routinely raped young girls, stabbed pregnant women in the belly and threw babies down from city walls onto the rocks below so that they would not grow up and avenge their captured cities.[8] It helps us to grasp that the Jewish exiles are simply asking the Lord to avenge their dead loved ones by doing to their murderers what their murderers did to them. But there is another, deeper lesson for us to learn from these verses today. The Jewish exiles are showing us that we need to be radical with little sins while we live out our faith in "Babylon".

As Christians, we can often be self-indulgent when we spot the first shoots of sin sprouting in our hearts. We need to be ruthless with ourselves whenever we spot these little brats of Babylon and dash their brains out before they grow stronger and destroy us. It is easy to criticize bishops for protecting paedophile priests and allowing them to continue to abuse choirboys. It is easy to criticize the pastor who runs off with a woman in his church. But it is a whole lot harder to take the words of 137:7-9 to heart and to deal radically with every little trace of Babylon as soon as we spot it growing in our own hearts. Psalm 137 tells us that we need to remember the glories of Mount Zion in order to stop ourselves from becoming over-tolerant towards the filth of Babylon.

That's why Psalm 138 comes after Psalm 137. It is the first of eight songs by David and it comes next because it completes this teaching about how we are to live in Babylon. Without it, we might fool ourselves that being godly means rejecting the company of unbelievers altogether and turning the Church of

---

[7] Amos 1:11; Obadiah 1–21.

[8] Isaiah 13:16; Lamentations 5:11; Hosea 10:14; 13:16; Zechariah 14:2.

God into a clique of Christians. David reminds us that the more we withdraw from the ways of Babylon, the more we will want to advance into Babylon to invite people to enjoy the presence of God with us as the people of Mount Zion.

David is as eager to sing before the pagans as the previous psalmist was to remain silent before them. He longs to sing about the true God in the presence of their pagan idols[9] and to bow down towards the Tabernacle from afar (138:1–3).[10] He longs for pagan kings and unbelievers to worship the Lord as the only true God (138:4–5), and he expects the Lord to help him on each of his sorties into enemy-held Babylon (138:6–8).[11] We must never forget that the Lord transformed the hearts of King Nebuchadnezzar of Babylon, the mastermind behind the destruction of Jerusalem in 586 BC, and King Darius who ruled over Babylon for the Persians.[12] As we deal radically with sin and keep pursuing God's presence, we must expect to extend the reach of "Zion" throughout "Babylon".

In 1978 the German disco band Boney M released a single based on Psalm 137 which was entitled "By the Rivers of Babylon". It was an instant number one, selling two million copies in the United Kingdom alone, and it is still guaranteed to fill the dance floor at any party. Very few of the dancers have any idea what "Babylon" or "Zion" really mean, because they are still waiting for you and me to tell them. Let's be like the Jewish exile who wrote Psalm 137 and refuse to be polluted by the values of this God-hating world, but let's also be like David when he wrote Psalm 138. Let's explain to them why the presence of God matters and why the waters of Babylon can never satisfy.

---

[9] Asaph referred to believers (or possibly to pagan rulers) as *"gods"* in 82:1. David appears to be using the same word in 138:1 to refer to pagan idols.

[10] 1 Samuel 1:9 and 3:3 show that David is referring to his Tabernacle when he talks about *the temple* in 138:2.

[11] David uses a similar phrase in 138:8 to the one which he used in 57:2 in order to tell us literally that he knows *the Lord will fulfil his purposes for me*.

[12] Nebuchadnezzar and Darius describe their change of heart in Daniel 4:34–37 and 6:25–27.

The Song of Freedom
(139:1–24)

You have searched me, Lord, and you know me.

(Psalm 139:1)

Who am I? Who am I really? That's the question which inspires our love for movies like *The Bourne Identity* and *The Matrix*. It's the question which inspires school leavers to go travelling in order to "find themselves". It's the question which most people are still asking when God saves them and adopts them into his family. And it's the question which we find answered in Psalm 139.

As a church leader, I get to spend a lot of time talking to people about their lives. A lot of time and a lot of people: men and women, old and young, single and married, happy and sad. Every conversation is different but the root issue is usually the same. How we view ourselves and our identity is a make-or-break issue for how we live our lives. That makes Psalm 139 essential study material for all of us.[1] I have seen repeatedly that, when people truly understand this psalm, they find that it is their song of freedom.

David tells us that only the Lord truly knows who we really are (139:1–6). If you are an internal processor, he tells you God knows your thoughts from afar before you even think them. If you are an external processor, he tells you God knows what you are about to say long before the words roll off your tongue. The

---

[1] Even though the songs of ascents were written to be sung by pilgrims, this is the first psalm since Psalm 109 to be marked in its title for congregational singing. It reminds us how important this psalm is for us all.

reason so many people struggle with issues of identity is that *"such knowledge is... too lofty... to attain"*. David wants us to grasp that the Lord alone is omniscient – he alone knows everything – and that only he can reveal to us our true identity.[2]

David tells us that the Lord also knows who we are *all the time* (139:7–12). Part of our confusion about who we are stems from the fact that we act differently with our friends, with our parents, at work, at church and on our own. The American novelist Nathaniel Hawthorne reminds us that *"No man, for any considerable period, can wear one face to himself and another to the multitude, without finally getting bewildered as to which may be true."*[3] David informs us that God sees everything that happens in heaven and in hell,[4] in the dark and in the light, to the east and to the west.[5] He isn't just omniscient; he is also omnipresent. Nobody is better qualified to tell us who we really are.[6]

David takes this further and tells us that the Lord has known us *from the beginning* (139:13–18). Before our mothers even knew that they were pregnant, he was forming us as little embryos and he shaped our bodies in secret until the rest of the world finally met us when we were born.[7] *"I am fearfully and wonderfully made; your works are wonderful, I know that full well,"* David confesses as one of the great foundations of his identity in God. If you are a guy, it doesn't matter if your body

---

[2] 139:5 tells us literally that God *besieges* us and *lays his hand* on us, words which are normally used to describe an aggressor. 139:1–6 is an attack on our pride as well as an encouragement to the humble.

[3] Nathaniel Hawthorne in *The Scarlet Letter* (1850).

[4] David may simply be contrasting the sky and the ocean depths in 139:8, but in Psalms *shāmayim* and *she'ōl* normally mean *heaven* and *hell*.

[5] Verse 9 is a poetic way of saying *east* (where the day dawns) and *west* (across the Mediterranean from Israel).

[6] David's language in 139:10 is deliberately that of a father with his little child.

[7] The Hebrew word *qānāh* in 139:13 can mean *created* but it normally means *possessed*. God is saying that he possesses every embryo he creates. Abortion is therefore theft as well as murder. See also Luke 1:41–44.

doesn't look like an Olympic athlete's. If you are a girl, it doesn't matter if your body doesn't look like a supermodel's. What matters is that your body was put together by Almighty God and that he sees his fingerprints all over your beautiful body.

David hasn't finished. He knows that many of our questions about identity are not so much physical questions as emotional ones – not so much *Who am I?* as *Why am I here?* David praises the Lord that *"all the days ordained for me were written in your book before one of them came to be"*, and he worships him for the fact that he cannot second-guess what God is doing at every twist and turn.[8] One of my friends was conceived by mistake by her unmarried parents: she needs to know that this is true for her too. She needs to grasp that Jephthah's unplanned conception by a prostitute in Judges 11 was as much part of God's perfect plan as Hannah's much-prayed-for conception of Samuel in 1 Samuel 1. Another of my friends still struggles with the knowledge that her mother tried unsuccessfully to abort her: she also needs this psalm.[9] It tells her that the Lord planned her life and prevented her abortion because she has a unique part to play in his master plan.[10]

David finishes his psalm with a prayer that the Lord will purify him and make him live as the person that he was made to be (139:19–24). He renounces friendship with evildoers and asks the Lord to search his heart so that he can walk *"in the way of eternity"*.[11] When we know who we are and why we are here,

---

[8] The Hebrew word for *thought* in 139:2 and 17 is used nowhere else in the Bible except for these two verses. David is deliberately contrasting our utterly known thoughts with God's utterly unknowable thoughts.

[9] David likens the womb to *"the depths of the earth"* in 139:15 because he wants to liken life before birth to life after death. God is utterly sovereign over the timing of both our birth and our death.

[10] We could go on. It was as much part of God's plan that Leah was unattractive to Jacob as it was that Esther was attractive to King Xerxes. Whatever your own weaknesses, they are also part of God's big plan.

[11] This does not contradict the challenge of Psalm 138 to proclaim the Gospel to the world. Unbelievers are not saved because they have Christian friends,

it changes everything. It means nothing less than a glorious personal revolution when we believe that we are who the Lord says we are.

The editors of Psalms placed this song of freedom almost at the end of the collection in order to use it as part of their call for us to sing out our response to God. If you aren't a Christian, don't move on until you have surrendered to the God who made you. If you are a Christian, don't move on until you have transformed your daily thinking by accepting that you are who God says you are.

You are God's workmanship (Ephesians 2:10). You are a child of God (1 John 3:1–2). You are completely forgiven and cleansed of your past (1 John 1:9). You are loved by God the Father (John 16:27). You are a temple for his Holy Spirit (1 Corinthians 3:16). You are the light of the world (Matthew 5:14). You are heir to the riches of God's Kingdom (Romans 8:17). You are a new creation (2 Corinthians 5:17). You are Jesus' friend (John 15:15).

You are free from condemnation (Romans 8:1). You are a citizen of heaven (Philippians 3:20). You are protected from the Devil (1 John 5:18). You are seated with Christ in heaven (Ephesians 2:6). You are able to do all things through Christ who strengthens you (Philippians 4:13). You are utterly secure in God's hands (Philippians 1:6).

You are who God says you are. Believe it and praise God for it. If you are willing to find your identity in God, Psalm 139 will become your song of freedom.

---

but because they have Christian friends who are like Christ!

David's Final Struggle
(140:1–143:12)

*Set me free from my prison, that I may praise your
name. Then the righteous will gather about me
because of your goodness to me.*

(Psalm 142:7)

The book of Psalms is a very long book. It's by far the longest
book in the Bible. That's why the worship leaders who compiled
Psalms thought that you and I might need a reminder of its
message as we reach its final chapters. As we read through the
final few psalms, we need to treat them as a reminder of all that
we have learned through Psalms so far.

Psalms 140–143 remind us of the message of Book I: that
we must *sing about who God is*. David wrote Psalm 140 while he
was being hunted by a violent enemy and his instinctive response
is to focus his attention on the character of God.[1] He worships
him as *"my God"* (140:6), as the *"Sovereign Lord"* (140:7) and
as *"my strong deliverer"* (140:7). When he is attacked again, he
does the same in Psalm 141, singing that *"My eyes are fixed on
you, Sovereign Lord"* (141:8). When Saul chases him into a cave,
he focuses yet again in Psalm 142 on the character of God, telling
him that *"You are my refuge, my portion in the land of the living"*
(142:5). It may feel like a long time since you finished Book I of
Psalms, so let these songs of David remind you to sing worship
songs about who God is.

255

---

[1] Since there is no mention of David being king in Psalm 140, it was probably
written while on the run from King Saul. Since David always spoke warmly of
Saul, it is likely the violent enemy was Doeg the Edomite.

Psalms 140–143 also remind us of the message of Book II: that we must *sing when times are hard*. These songs are fairly unusual for Book V, which has tended to focus less on faith under pressure and more on God's promises, on God's Word, on God's presence and on our response to them. These four songs of anguish have been placed here in order to ensure we don't forget all that we learned in Book II about singing songs of lament which express our pain to God.

Psalm 140 has been marked in its title for congregational singing because every believer needs to learn how to worship under pressure. David sees his trial as an opportunity to praise God all the more and as a chance to gain a testimony which will stir the rest of God's People to worship with him (140:12–13). This theme continues in Psalm 141, which David appears to have written while on the run from Saul.[2] He prays for strength to bear up under his trial (141:3–4),[3] but believes that his anguished prayers are as sweet-smelling to the Lord as the incense which was burnt by the priests in Moses' Tabernacle (141:2).[4] David prays in a similar way in Psalms 142–143, worshipping the Lord despite his desperate need, his flagging spirit, his dismayed heart and his parched throat in an arid land.

Psalms 140–143 also remind us of the message of Book III: that we must *sing out how we really feel*. David uses graphic imagery in Psalms 140–141 to emphasize his sense of vulnerability. In just two short psalms, he refers to hearts,

---

[2] He appears to have written Psalm 140 when Doeg attacked him, Psalm 142 while in the cave and Psalm 143 while also in the cave (see 143:3). It is therefore likely that Psalm 141 also dates from the same period.

[3] David is not asking for more pain in 141:5. He is contrasting the positive feedback which he would have received from a righteous friend with the mean and vindictive attacks he is receiving from his enemy.

[4] See Exodus 30:7–9. David also says that worship is the ongoing sacrifice which God desires from the redeemed in 27:6 and 51:17. This is confirmed by Hebrews 13:15 and Revelation 5:8.

tongues, lips,[5] hands, feet, heads, mouths, bones and eyes. He paints a picture of his despair in the same two short psalms by talking about war, serpents, vipers, snares, cords, traps, battles, burning coals, fire, miry pits, disasters, ploughing, graves and hunting nets.[6] David uses all his best skill as a poet to express to the Lord exactly how he feels.

Psalm 142 is particularly interesting because we know from the title that David wrote it at the same time as Psalm 57. Whereas he was mainly upbeat in Psalm 57 despite the traumas of the cave, he clearly felt less positive when he penned Psalm 142. He tells God that he has a complaint to make (142:2) that *"there is no one at my right hand; no one is concerned for me. I have no refuge; no one cares for my life"* (142:4). Some readers find it shocking that David should say this to the Lord who had promised to be all those things for David. We need to note that this is a *maskīl* – the last of the thirteen songs of instruction in the book of Psalms – and that it was placed here precisely in order to remind us that the Lord wants us to tell him exactly how we feel. It is only when David has told the Lord that he feels he has no refuge that he comes through to confidence that the Lord is the refuge he is looking for (142:5). The editors of Psalms want to remind us as we near the end of their collection that it is only when we empty our troubled hearts before the Lord that we find him filling us with fresh faith.[7]

Psalm 143 is the seventh and final penitential psalm, and it is another great reminder that we must sing to the Lord about how we really feel. David confesses his sin and his desperate

---

[5] As if for emphasis, David calls for a *selāh*, or *instrumental solo*, three times at the end of 140:3, 5 and 8. The term *selāh* never occurs outside Books I, II and III except for here in Psalms 140 and 143.

[6] Paul quotes from 140:3 in Romans 3:13. Psalms is the most quoted book in the New Testament, and this is the last verse in Psalms to be quoted.

[7] As soon as David trusted the Lord to be his refuge in the cave, the Lord brought 400 soldiers to the cave as the beginning of a mighty army for David (1 Samuel 22:1–2).

need for God's intervention (143:1–6),[8] and he makes no secret of the fact he fears his soul is slipping down to hell (143:7–12). His honesty with God paves the way for him to make a bold request for God to forgive him. He tells the Lord that he expects forgiveness because of God's character (143:1), his history with Israel (143:5), his commitment to reward faith (143:8), his passion to glorify his name (143:11), his covenant love (143:8, 12) and his commitment to fulfil his purposes for David (143:12). We can train ourselves to pray in a similar fashion if we commit ourselves, like David in 143:8, to studying the Bible every morning for fresh discoveries about God's love and if we show a similar willingness to tell the Lord exactly how we feel.

We are drawing to the end of the book of Psalms, so let's learn from David and remember the lessons of Books I, II and III. Let's sing about who God is, let's sing when times are hard, and let's sing out how we really feel. David reminds us that this is what Psalms teaches us to do if we want to worship in a manner which is music to God's ears.

---

[8] In many ways Psalm 143 is the least penitential of the so-called penitential psalms. The key verses are 143:1–2, where David tells the Lord that he has sinned and is not looking for justice but mercy.

David's Final Message
(144:1–145:21)

*They tell of the glory of your kingdom and speak
of your might, so that all people may know of your
mighty acts and the glorious splendour of your
kingdom.*

(Psalm 145:11–12)

"Worship is the fuel and the goal of missions," writes John Piper, inspired by psalms like these.

> *Worship is the goal of missions because in missions we
> aim to bring the nations into the white-hot enjoyment
> of God's glory. It is the fuel of missions because we can't
> commend what we don't cherish. We can't call out, "Let
> the nations be glad!" until we say, "I rejoice in the Lord."
> Missions begins and ends in worship... [God] is preparing
> for himself a people – from all the peoples – who will be
> able to worship him with free and white-hot admiration.
> Therefore the church is bound to engage with the Lord
> of glory in his cause. It is our unspeakable privilege to
> be caught up with him in the greatest movement in
> history – the ingathering of the elect from every tribe
> and language and people and nation.*[1]

---

[1] John Piper in *Let The Nations Be Glad* (1993).

We have reached the last two songs which David wrote in Psalms.[2] He reminds us that our worship should fuel us to go out and create more worshippers like ourselves. David did not build his Tabernacle as a place for the Israelites to huddle together in selfish celebration that the Lord had chosen them and not others. He built it as the headquarters of a missionary movement which would take the Good News of Yahweh to the nations. That's why Psalms 144 and 145 continue our recap of the structure of Psalms by reminding us of the message of Book IV – that we must *sing about God's plan*.

When David dedicated his Tabernacle on Mount Zion, he wrote the psalm which we find in 1 Chronicles 16:7–36. It taught the Israelites to turn their eyes outwards to the nations of the world.[3] This song is repeated and expanded in Psalms 96 and 105–106, telling us to *"Proclaim his salvation day after day,"* and to *"Declare his glory among the nations, his marvellous deeds among all peoples."*[4] Worship and witness, praise and proclamation: David insists that they must always go hand in hand.

Unlike most of the songs in Book IV, Psalms 144 and 145 do not look backwards to focus on God's plan for his People in the past. Instead, they focus on the very real battle in which God's People are engaged in the present to fulfil God's plan by reaching the nations of the world with his message of salvation.[5] Psalm 144 is a shorter, more condensed version of Psalm 18, the song which David wrote when God gave him victory over the

---

[2] The Greek Septuagint actually includes an extra psalm of David after Psalm 150, but most scholars agree that it is a clumsy piece of work by a later Greek writer.

[3] See 1 Chronicles 16:8, 14, 23–24, 28, 30–31, 33, 35.

[4] Psalm 96:2–3. David is realistic that unbelievers may not respond to the Gospel straightaway. This is why he tells us that we will need to keep proclaiming the Gospel *"day after day"*.

[5] This message runs throughout Psalms – for example in 47:1, 57:9 and 100:1–3. Isaiah 2:2–4 predicts that Zion will truly fulfil this calling in days to come, and 1 Peter 2:9 tells us it is fulfilled through the Church.

pagan nations around Israel.[6] He rejoices that the Lord helps his People to conquer the nations (144:1–2), even though they have no great strength or skill of their own (144:3–4), and asks for help to extend Israel's influence even further over the wicked nations (144:5–8). He commits himself to a lifestyle of both worship and witness (144:9–10), and he asks for peace and success as he does so (144:11–14). He ends the psalm with the manifesto of Zion's missionary worshippers: *"Blessed are the people of whom this is true"* – meaning any people and not just Israel – *"Blessed are the people whose God is the Lord"* (144:15).

David gets even more explicit in Psalm 145.[7] This is the last acrostic poem in Psalms,[8] and it emphasizes how much care David took to spur us on into God's great mission. He confesses that the Lord is the true King of Israel (145:1–2) and pledges to fulfil his calling to be a missionary to the next generation of Israelites (145:3–7). Judges 2:7–15 reminds us that the Church is only ever one generation away from extinction, so David starts his evangelism at home rather than away. Having done so, he reminds God of his character as he revealed it to Moses in Exodus 34:6–7, and he pledges that he will preach this same message of God's grace and compassion to the nations of the world (145:8–13a). He tells us in 145:10 that the Lord is gathering a nation of *hasīdīm*, meaning *saints* or *holy ones*, and

---

[6] Psalm 18 was itself a repeat of the song in 2 Samuel 22, so this third brief repetition reminds us of the importance of this message. Psalm 144:1 comes from 18:34, 144:2 comes from 18:2, 144:6–8 comes from 18:9–16, and 144:9–10 comes from 18:43–50. The psalm also draws from 8:4, 33:12 and 39:5.

[7] Psalm 145 is the only psalm to be marked in its title as a *tehillāh*, or *song of praise*, but this is the word which was used in its plural form as the Hebrew name for the book of Psalms: *Tehillīm* or *Songs of Praise*.

[8] There are 22 letters in the Hebrew alphabet but only 21 verses here because 145:13 contains two lines. Verse 13b does not exist in most Hebrew manuscripts, but without it there is no line beginning with the letter *nun*. It may have been omitted by a Hebrew copyist since it appears in the Septuagint and Dead Sea Scrolls.

many English Bibles translate this as a *"faithful people"*.[9] David is emphasizing that "Israel" is not just an ethnic group to God. It includes *"all he has made"*, *"all your works"*, *"all people"* and *"all generations"*. It includes anyone from any nation who responds to the Gospel invitation to become part of the People of God.

This then leads into the very last verses which David wrote in Psalms. He praises the Lord for extending his mercy in a general sense to *"every living thing"* (145:13b-16), then praises him specifically for saving people who cry out to him from every nation (145:17–20). It doesn't matter if a person is a Jew or a Gentile, *"the Lord is near to all who call on him, to all who call on him in truth... but all the wicked he will destroy."* The Gospel is first and foremost the message through which Jews can be saved, but it is also the message which saves people from every nation, tribe and language.[10] Don't miss this and think that Psalms is just the song book of Israel. It is the missionary manifesto of God's marching army of worshippers as they capture hearts in every nation (145:21).

Over 1,000 years after David's Tabernacle was dismantled, a great controversy arose on the slopes of Mount Zion. A rabbi named Paul had started preaching the Gospel to the Greeks and pagans of the Roman Empire. Some Jewish Christians were furious that Paul was offering salvation to the Gentiles without circumcision and the Jewish Law. The apostle James therefore stood up at what would become known as the Council of Jerusalem in 49 AD and reminded the believers that this had always been the dream which inspired David and the other psalmists.

"After this I will return and rebuild David's fallen Tabernacle," he quoted from the prophet Amos. *"Its ruins I will rebuild, and I will restore it, that the rest of mankind may seek the Lord, even*

---

[9] The psalmists use the singular word *hāsîd* or *holy one* and the plural word *hasîdîm* or *holy ones* about 25 times throughout the book of Psalms to refer to those whom God has chosen for salvation.

[10] John 4:20–24; Romans 1:16; 2:9–10.

all the Gentiles who bear my name, says the Lord, who does these things – things known from long ago."[11]

The early Christians recommitted themselves to the vision which was preached at David's Tabernacle. They let their worship fuel their witness and became God's missionary army. They conquered the world with the Gospel in their own generation. Let's allow the book of Psalms to inspire us to do the same in our own generation too.

---

[11] Acts 15:16–18. James is quoting from Amos 9:11–12 in the Greek Septuagint because it emphasized the true message behind David's Tabernacle more explicitly than the Hebrew.

Body Language
(146:1–150:6)

*Let them praise his name with dancing and make
music to him with tambourine and harp.*

(Psalm 149:3)

I worked for several years as a professional negotiator, but before I was ready for my first big negotiation I had to learn a new language. All of my negotiations were to be in English, but my employers insisted that knowing English was not enough. Before they would entrust me with my first big negotiation, I had to become fluent in body language.

Most of us don't need a training course to tell us that a large part of what we communicate is physical and not verbal. The leading expert James Borg argues that only 7 per cent of what we actually communicate consists of our words, while 93 per cent consists of body language.[1] He argues that if somebody scratches their nose while making a statement during a negotiation, they are probably lying. If they look away and scratch their ear while you are talking, they think you are lying too. So it shouldn't surprise us that the book of Psalms ends with a reminder that our body language when we worship God is very important. Psalms 146–150 are known as the "Hallelujah Hallel" because each of these five psalms begins and ends with the Hebrew phrase *"Hallelujah!"*, which means *"Praise the Lord!"* They remind us that the message of Book V is that we need to *sing out our response to God.*

---

[1] James Borg in *Body Language: 7 Easy Lessons to Master the Silent Language* (2008).

Psalm 146 reminds us that God is looking for authentic worship which comes from deep inside us.[2] God is not fooled by our empty outward professions of devotion (146:1). The psalmist addresses his inmost self and commands it to *"Praise the Lord, my soul."* Jesus told a Samaritan woman that the Temple in Jerusalem had been superseded because *"A time is coming and has now come when the true worshippers will worship the Father in spirit and truth, for they are the kind of worshippers the Father seeks. God is spirit, and his worshippers must worship in spirit and in truth."*[3] The Lord is still *"the God of Jacob"* (146:2–5)[4] but he is also the Maker of every foreigner too (146:6–9).[5] What matters is not our race or our church membership or any other external thing. The God who was worshipped on Mount Zion is looking for worshippers who will respond to the Gospel with sincerity on the inside (146:10).

Psalm 147 reminds us that our sincere response to the Gospel will always be obvious from how we worship on the outside. Jesus taught that *"The mouth speaks what the heart is full of,"*[6] and the psalmist demonstrates this by singing, *"How good it is to sing praises to our God, how pleasant and fitting to praise him!"* The previous psalm held out the Gospel to the Gentiles but this one encourages the Israelites to *"Sing to the Lord with grateful praise; make music to our God on the harp."*[7] If your worship is often lacklustre, the psalmist warns you that

---

[2] The titles of Psalm 146–148 in the Septuagint attribute authorship to Haggai and Zechariah, but since many Septuagint titles are inaccurate and it unnecessarily splits Psalm 147 into two, this is probably unreliable.

[3] John 4:19–24. This statement about the Temple was utterly revolutionary to Jewish ears.

[4] There is a Hebrew play on words in 146:3–4. The psalmist refers to human beings literally as *"the sons of Adam"* and the word he uses for them returning to the *ground* is *'adāmāh.*

[5] These verses remind us that churches must also care passionately about helping foreigners, the fatherless, the elderly and lone parents.

[6] Matthew 12:34; Luke 6:45.

[7] Verse 2 reminds us that it is only when God's People are revived that outsiders will come to join them in their worship. The references to God

your problem isn't with your mouth but with your heart. He warns us that earthly strength can suffocate our love for God and our desire to worship him. We need to meditate on who the Lord is and on what he has done to save us. Only then will we respond to the psalmist's call to *"Extol the Lord, Jerusalem; praise your God, Zion."*

Psalm 148 stirs us to express our worship with our bodies by calling every creature in the universe to make its own right response to God. The angels and stars and planets and sea creatures and lightning bolts and mountains and trees and animals and insects and birds all have their own ways to praise the Lord. Human beings – whether young or old, male or female, weak or strong – therefore need to bring their own right response to God with the bodies he has given them.[8]

Psalm 149 takes this further, telling us to *sing a new song* (149:1).[9] These 150 songs were not given us for our mindless repetition, but as an example so that we can sing worship songs of our own.[10] They teach us to *rejoice joyfully* before the Lord (149:2),[11] to *dance*, to *lift up our hands*[12] and to *make music.* Since the tambourine and harp are musical instruments at opposite ends of the scale (149:3), this psalm tells us to explore

---

rebuilding Jerusalem, strengthening its gates and bringing back exiles may well mean that this is the psalm which was sung in Nehemiah 12:27–43.

[8] The statement in 148:14 that God has given his People a *horn* is a reference to the Messiah. Jesus would not come as an angel, fish, bird or animal, but as a mortal human being.

[9] We are also told to sing new songs in Psalms 33:3, 40:3, 96:1, 98:1 and 144:9. See also Isaiah 42:10 and Revelation 5:9 and 14:3.

[10] The word *hasidim* or *holy ones* is used in the first, middle and last verses of this psalm. Its theme is therefore that anyone who has been made holy through the Gospel should sing out their joyful response to God.

[11] Psalm 96:11–13 also stresses this when it uses four different verbs to call the world to *rejoice (sāmah)*, *shriek with joy (gîl)*, *shout with triumph ('ālaz)* and *give a ringing cry of joy (rānan)*.

[12] Psalm 28:2; 63:4; 88:9; 134:2; 141:2; 143:6. See also Exodus 9:29; Lamentations 2:19; 1 Timothy 2:8. Lamentations 3:41 suggests that this is a symbol of us lifting up our hearts towards God.

the different waters of being *quiet and meditative* and *loud and exuberant* before the Lord.[13] The psalmist wants us to become so full of worship songs that the waking hours are not enough and our praises carry on into the night (149:5),[14] spilling over into the way we live our daily lives. Then our worship will be as powerful to extend God's Kingdom as a double-edged sword in our everyday working hands (149:6).

Psalm 150 is the final song of "the Hallelujah Hallel" and also of the entire book of Psalms. It serves as the doxology, or final song of praise, to Book V and to the collection as a whole. Each of its six verses calls us to praise the Lord, and it emphasizes that our *dancing bodies* are our principal instrument of worship by placing them in the middle of eight musical instruments.[15] The Hebrew word *hallel* can mean *noisy madness* as well as *praise*, so this final psalm is noisy and excited and full of celebration. God is watching our body language very closely, so nothing less than this can be our proper response to God's mercy. Psalms is a wonderful book for us to study but our studies must excite our hearts to sing this kind of worship song which is music to God's ears.

G.K. Chesterton paid Francis of Assisi the highest compliment when he commented that *"His religion was not a thing like a theory but a thing like a love-affair."*[16] As we end the book of Psalms, don't let your response remain mere theory. Be inspired by these five final psalms to sing out your heartfelt response to God.

---

[13] This same balance is found in 95:1–2 and 6, where noisy shouting and quiet kneeling are part of the same worship song. David shows us this contrast in his own life in 2 Samuel 6:14–15 and 7:18.

[14] This is a common theme throughout Psalms. See also 42:8; 63:6; 119:55; 119:148.

[15] The Hebrew word *māhōl* means literally *twisting* or *whirling*. This is more than just foot-tapping. It is an energetic dance of joy and praise.

[16] G.K. Chesterton in *St Francis of Assisi* (1923).

Let everything that has breath praise the Lord. Praise the Lord.

(Psalm 150:6)

God loves it when we sing our worship to him. If we didn't know that before we started reading, 150 psalms have made it pretty clear. The God who tells us in Zephaniah 3:17 that he will *"rejoice over you with singing"* wants us to rejoice over him with singing too. Reading the book of Psalms together has taught us how to sing the kind of worship songs which are music to his ears.

In his classic book *The 5 Love Languages*, relationships counsellor Gary Chapman argues that love can be expressed and understood in five different ways: speaking words of affirmation, spending quality time together, buying thoughtful gifts, offering acts of service and using physical touch.[1] He argues that if a husband or wife neglects any one of those five areas, they will not communicate their love completely to their spouse. If they study their partner and learn how to speak the right love languages at the right time, they will build a happy marriage. In reading through Psalms together, we have taken the view that the best commentary on Psalms is the structure which God inspired the worship leaders at the Temple to give it. Each of the five books within Psalms teaches us a love language which makes our singing sweet music to God's ears.

The message of Book I (Psalms 1–41) was that we need

---

[1] Gary Chapman in *The 5 Love Languages: The Secret to Love that Lasts* (2010).

to *sing about who God is*. David lived in a world full of images and idols, so he taught the Israelites how to sing about the character of the true God. Idolatry may be a bit more subtle in our own day but it is no less real. We need to be constantly wary of worshipping a god of our own making, especially when we get offended by the Psalms. David deliberately shocked us by telling us to worship the Lord as the Judge and Avenger and as the Messiah who was despised and rejected by the world. Let's therefore sing about the excellencies of God's incomparable character. The eighteenth-century revivalist Jonathan Edwards reminds us that

> *God is glorified not only by His glory's being seen, but by its being rejoiced in. When those that see it delight in it, God is more glorified than if they only see it. His glory is then received by the whole soul, both by the understanding and by the heart... He that testifies his idea of God's glory [doesn't] glorify God so much as he that testifies also his approbation of it and his delight in it.* [2]

The message of Book II (Psalms 42–72) was that we need to *sing when times are hard*. One of the greatest idols which is worshipped in today's church is the false god who promises that the Christian life can be an easy ride, a bed of roses and an endless cycle of prosperity. The true God tells us up front that life will often be hard, and he promises to join us in the dust and to carry us through every crisis along life's way. Sometimes the Lord will appear distant and slow to act and even as if he has failed. Book II reminded us that nothing is sweeter music to God's ears than our songs of praise when the river banks of life squeeze us hard and we treat it as an opportunity for the river of our praise to run even faster.

The message of Book III (Psalms 73–89), was that God

---

[2] Quoted from Thomas Schafer's *The Works of Jonathan Edwards: Volume 13: The Miscellanies* (1994).

wants us to *sing out how we really feel*. In the DreamWorks animated movie *The Road to El Dorado*, a pagan worship leader teaches Native Americans how to please their false god, telling them: *"Big smile – like you mean it!"*[3] Psalms teaches us that the real God is nothing like their idol. He loves it when we tell him exactly how we feel, without any religious playacting, because it gives him room to fill our hearts with fresh faith in his character and his plans.

The message of Book IV (Psalms 90–106) was that we need to *sing about God's plan*. Only when we sing about God's history with his People in the past and about what he has promised his People in the future are we ready to live as God's People in the present. When we see ourselves as part of a People which began with Adam and Noah and Abraham and Moses, our voices become perfectly in tune with theirs. When we sing songs in the knowledge that we are part of a choir which spans the generations, those songs are music to God's ears.

The message of Book V (Psalms 107–150) was that we need to *sing out our response to God*. We learned that a proper response to God's mercy may be noisy or quiet, but that it will always be profound. We learned that body language matters and that God wants our voices and our faces and our dancing bodies to communicate the love and gratitude which consumes our soul. The Psalms make God's five love languages very clear to his would-be worshippers. As we draw to a finish, make sure that you start developing these five habits and that you start to worship as God wants you to.

David's Tabernacle stood on Mount Zion for a mere forty-five years.[4] It came and went within a generation but its work was vital because it taught God's People each of these five love languages. The Levite worship leaders at the Tabernacle – men

---

[3] *The Road to El Dorado* (DreamWorks, 2000)

[4] He erected it shortly after capturing Jerusalem in 1003 BC. Solomon took it down and put its trappings in his new Temple on the nearby Mount Moriah in 958 BC.

like Asaph, Ethan, Heman and the Sons of Korah – transferred to Solomon's new Temple their understanding of the kind of worship God is looking for. When that Temple was destroyed, Ezra taught a new generation of worshippers at a rebuilt Temple how to worship the Lord this way. When that new Temple was also destroyed, the apostles built the lessons learned at David's Tabernacle into the churches which they planted in every city.[5] They let the book of Psalms shape their theology, their understanding of God's plan, their ways of gathering together and, above all else, their worship.

So as you finish reading the book of Psalms, remember that you have not just read through an ancient song book. You have read through a collection of psalms which was compiled by worship leaders in the Temple at Jerusalem in order to spread the message of David's Tabernacle to every generation and every nation of the world. They have invited you to worship the God of Israel through five love languages which have been spoken by worshippers for over three thousand years. They have initiated you into a new lifestyle of raw and honest praise. As you finish this book, they invite you to worship in the manner which is music to God's ears.

---

[5] Acts 15:16.

TITLES IN THE **STRAIGHT TO THE HEART** SERIES:

OLD TESTAMENT

ISBN 978 0 85721 001 2

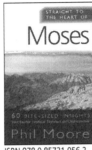

ISBN 978 0 85721 056 2

ISBN 978 0 85721 252 8

ISBN 978 0 85721 428 7

ISBN 978 0 85721 426 3

NEW TESTAMENT

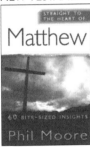

ISBN 978 1 85424 988 3

ISBN 978 0 85721 253 5

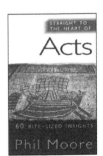

ISBN 978 1 85424 989 0

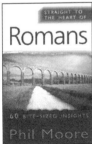

ISBN 978 0 85721 057 9

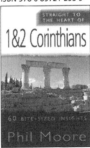

ISBN 978 0 85721 002 9

ISBN 978 1 85424 990 6

For more information please go to **www.philmoorebooks.com**
or **www.lionhudson.com**

Printed in Great Britain
by Amazon